The Beautiful Game

The Beautiful Game

A Journey Through Latin American Football

CHRIS TAYLOR

VICTOR GOLLANCZ

LONDON

First published in Great Britain 1998
by Victor Gollancz
An imprint of the Cassell Group
Wellington House, 125 Strand, London WC2R 0BB

Published in association with the Latin America Bureau

© Chris Taylor 1998

The right of Chris Taylor to be identified as author of
this work has been asserted by him in accordance with
the Copyright, Designs and Patents Act, 1988.

A catalogue record for this book is
available from the British Library.

ISBN 0 575 06507 9
[LAB paperback edition ISBN 1 899365 23 0]

Typeset by Rowland Phototypesetting Ltd,
Bury St Edmunds, Suffolk
Printed in Great Britain by
St Edmundsbury Press Ltd,
Bury St Edmunds, Suffolk

98 99   5 4 3 2 1

For my father,
Alf Taylor,
an old-fashioned inside-left.
1924–1972

Contents

Acknowledgements

THIS BOOK would have been impossible without the assistance of numerous people who have helped in a variety of ways. In addition to those mentioned in the text and the bibliography I would like to thank the following people:

First, Jim Ferguson at LAB, who originally had the idea to do a book about Latin American football and who thought of the title, and also to Sean Magee and Ian Preece at Gollancz. Second, Noll Scott, who suggested that I should write it and whose help, particularly as my idiot's guide to computers, was invaluable. My thanks are due to my old team-mates Rafael Palmier, Felipe Pinto and Murilo Vaz for showing me Brazilian football up close, and also in Brazil to Carlão Tranjan and Fernando Calazans; in Argentina, to Stephen Brown and Alejandro Prosdocimi; in Uruguay, to Jorge Aramburu and Alvaro Risso; in Colombia, to Mary Matheson, Richard Sanders, Eduardo Arias and Jeremy Lennard; in Mexico, to Phil Gunson, Andrew Paxman, Miguel Angel Ramírez and César García; in Nicaragua, to Patricio Cranshaw, Marta Cranshaw and Emiliano García. I would also like to thank Tina Leme, John Bevan, Pete Mason, Alan Oattes, Marta Zabaleta, Wyre Davies, Jane Díaz-Límaco and the Football Association library. I am also grateful for the help of my colleagues at the *Guardian*. I would particularly like to thank all the people I met in Latin America who indulged an Englishman's eccentric curiosity and went out of their way to help me in ways great and small.

Finally, I would like to thank Patricia for all her help and support and for putting up with me going on and on about football during the writing of this book.

Introduction

LATIN AMERICAN FOOTBALL, for me at least, came into existence at a precise time and place. The time is 21 June 1970, a Sunday afternoon. The place is the Aztec stadium in Mexico City, or, to be strictly accurate, the living room of our house in Whitton where, sprawled in front of the TV, I watched the grainy black-and-white images beamed from the other side of the world. It was the World Cup Final, and Brazil were playing Italy. Chelsea had won the FA Cup weeks before – a moment of unimaginable ecstasy for an 8-year-old, and many a grown man – but this was something different. Something, as George Harrison might have said, in the way they moved. The last goal was sublime. Pelé received the ball on the edge of the area and then seemed to pause for ever before rolling the ball to his right. Carlos Alberto appeared from nowhere – or at least from outside of the twenty-inch frame of the TV – to rifle the ball into the net. Eric Cantona said it was like a Rimbaud poem; if so, it must have been one with a syncopated rhythm. It all appealed to my childish sense of rightness: the best, most exciting, team in the world winning the Cup and by a proper football score (4–1). All that and Chelsea too. Frankly, football has been a bit of a disappointment ever since.

Of course, I'm not the first Englishman to be impressed by the *élan* of Latin American football. Stanley Matthews was part of the England team that took part in the 1950 World Cup in Brazil. It was the first time that England's best had seen the Latin American game up close. With the rest of the team he went to see the host nation's opening match against Mexico at the new Maracanã stadium in Rio de Janeiro. The first thing that struck him was the passion of the local fans.

11

'You've never seen scenes quite like it. Fans were climbing fences to try and get in illegally, and when the Brazilian team ran out on to the pitch hundreds of fireworks were let off. When they scored their first goal, a cannon was fired. It was our first experience of seeing fans behave with such fervour. The quality of the Brazilians' play was equally amazing. It was a fascinating spectacle. Their inside-left had a brilliant left foot and took all their free-kicks. He hit the cross-bar with one, and it was the first time we'd seen the *bent* free-kick.'[1]

Billy Wright, the England captain, was also at that game. 'We saw people bending balls, which is now part of the scene, like a banana, both ways, with the outside of the foot and the inside of the foot, skills that we'd not seen before. And that was eye-opening, the bending of the ball, the skilful use of the ball and how they could bring the ball down.'[2] Matthews was so impressed he even got the Co-op factory back in England to make him a pair of lightweight boots copied from those used by the Brazilians.

That same year Charlie Mitten became one of a handful of Englishmen to play professionally in Latin America when he signed for a Colombian team. Already an established star at the peak of his career with Manchester United, he nevertheless found a lot to learn.

'It was an entirely different type of game out there. It was a short-passing game – ten-yards passes all the time – with more activity on the run of the game inasmuch as you constantly had to hold on to the ball, pass, then move into position for the return . . . I felt my time in Bogotá improved my football: the close passing, looking for spaces, the falling-back funnel system of defence, the supreme ball control these South Americans had, bringing every part of their body into use to control the ball.'[3]

Neil Franklin, England's centre-half, also had a brief sojourn in Colombia at the same time as Mitten. Franklin discovered that the differences started long before matchday.

'The training was vastly different from the training we had been used to at home. It was much more varied and included much more ball practice, both of which are good points . . . Not only were the

South Americans fanatics about practising with a football, they also included a lot of other ball games, such as basketball. But whatever games they chose, they made sure they were games played at speed, so that you had to keep agile, your eye had to be good and your stamina had to be good.'[4]

The South Americans' exotic training practices led Franklin to observe that in England 'we place too much reliance on golf'.[5]

Along with the fans' fervour and the players' skill, English visitors were also struck by the cynical side of the South American game. Jimmy Greaves watched a match between Brazil and Argentina in São Paulo, while taking part in a tournament with England in 1964.

'Right from the first whistle Argentinian defender Messiano made it clear that his one intention was to stop Pelé from playing. He kicked him, tripped him, spat at him, wrestled him to the floor and pulled his shirt anytime he seemed likely to get past him. Finally, after about thirty minutes of this almost criminal assault, Pelé completely lost his temper. He took a running jump at Messiano and butted him full in the face.

'The Argentinian was carried off with a broken nose and, incredibly, the Swiss referee let Pelé play on!'[6]

Most striking of all, though, was the seemingly inexhaustible supply of young talent to be found playing kickabouts on wasteground and in the street. Tom Finney, of England's 1950 side, was one of the first to see what would become one of the great journalistic clichés of Latin American football: kids practising their exuberant ball skills on the beaches of Rio.

'There was hundreds, literally hundreds, of kids playing on the beach, and not with footballs. Some of them had little rubber balls, but some of them just had brown-paper parcels which were tied together with string. One youngster came along and we said, "Now, come on, let's see how often you can keep it up," and he went 100 times with this brown-paper parcel tied with string with both feet. He could keep it up 100 times. We said, "There you are, there's your answer, this is where they learn all their skills."'[7]

Football is part of the warp and weft of Latin American life, more

13

of a common language the length and breadth of the continent than Spanish or Portuguese. For two young Argentinians touring South America on a motorbike, football was a passport and a letter of introduction wherever they went. In Chile they got food, lodging and transport to Iquique, on the edge of the Atacama desert, in return for coaching a team of roadworkers before an important match. In Peru they played amongst the Inca ruins at Machu Picchu and in a lepers versus healthy game at a leper colony. In Colombia they met their legendary countryman Alfredo Di Stéfano, another wandering footballer. And in Leticia in the Colombian Amazon they killed time waiting for a plane by coaching and playing for a local side in an improvised tournament. 'During the trip we often used football to make contact with the people,' said one of the travellers, Alberto Granados. The other, a wheezy goalkeeper called Ernesto, would later be better known as Che Guevara.

Football has played a part for some of Che's political descendants. In 1980 sixteen lightly armed M-19 guerrillas seized the embassy of the Dominican Republic in Bogotá and held almost half the Colombian capital's diplomats for over a month before eventually releasing them for a $1 million ransom. Their cunning plan had been to stage a game of football outside the embassy walls and then deliberately kick the ball over into the compound. When they asked for their ball back, the gates were opened and the guerrillas rushed in.

But it cuts both ways. On 22 April 1997, Peruvian special forces burst into the Japanese ambassador's residence in Lima, freeing 71 hostages who had been held for 126 days by guerrillas of the Tupac Amaru Revolutionary Movement. All 14 captors and one hostage died in the assault. One of the main reasons for the success of the operation was that the government commandos knew that most of the guerrillas would be gathered in one place at the time. The reason? Over the weeks the young revolutionaries had got into the routine of staging a football match in the building's entrance hall every day, leaving their weapons leaning against the walls at the sidelines. The commandos set off a bomb beneath their makeshift pitch killing most of them instantly. Only days before, the leader of the hostage-takers, Néstor Cerpa, had written to his sons in exile in France dreaming of taking them to watch Peru in the 1998 World Cup. Neither he nor Peru made it.

When Ecuador went to the polls to elect a president in July 1996, the race was so close that psephologists predicted that the election could hinge on a World Cup qualifier with Chile played on polling day. The pundits predicted that a defeat for the national team would favour the challenger, Abdalá Bucaram, who had been trailing in the polls. Chile won 4−1 and Bucaram was elected. (He was ousted within the year accused of corruption, but not before having installed himself as chairman of the Ecuadorean football club Barcelona.)

It is a commonplace to observe that football is a religion in Latin America, which presumably makes Roman Catholicism a contender as an Olympic event. Certainly both activities tend to take place on a Sunday, although, until recently at least, it is women who fill the pews while the men head for the terraces. Football can move great passions and reach vast numbers of people, as few other activities can. When Argentina won the World Cup in 1978, it is estimated that three million people congregated around the obelisk in central Buenos Aires to celebrate. But there are always dissidents. The great Argentinian writer Jorge Luis Borges quietly expressed his disdain for the national passion by organizing a literary seminar to coincide with Argentina's first game in the tournament. Elsewhere in Latin America whole countries have bucked the regional trend and given themselves to baseball.

In Britain and around the world, there is a need to believe in Brazil as the repository of football's soul. If Brazilian football did not exist, you feel it would be necessary to invent it. In the process the reality of Brazilian football can be hard to discern behind the myth. Each World Cup since 1970 has included a Brazilian team which has been described as seeking to recapture the glory days of Pelé et al. It is one of the most overworked clichés, after the one about describing any meeting between a British and a US leader in terms of 'the special relationship'. A little hyperbole is understandable,

15

particularly when Brazilians continue to produce moments of jaw-dropping skill, such as the incredible swerve Roberto Carlos managed to put on the free-kick from which he scored against France in the 1997 Tournoi de France. But the famous yellow shirts often seem to be a licence to abandon critical faculties. Commenting on a Brazilian 4–3–1–2 line-up in that competition, Sky TV's Andy Gray said, 'You might as well put Taffarel [the goalkeeper] and ten attackers.' Brazil are certainly a good team going forward, but to imply they care nothing for defence is ridiculous. In the 1994 World Cup Brazil had the best defensive record in the tournament (excluding the tedious Norwegians who played only three games to Brazil's seven). Even the great 1970 side, legendary for not caring how many they conceded as long as they scored more, was not as profligate at the back as is widely assumed. Of the top four teams in the tournament, they let in fewer goals than West Germany and Italy – the 'disciplined' Europeans – and only another South American side, Uruguay, had a better defence. In fact Brazil, for all their intuition and spontaneity, have long been at the forefront of tactical innovations (although admittedly Brazilian football benefited in the middle years of the century from the expertise of Central European coaches, such as the Hungarian Dori Kurschner).

But while Brazil have captured the world's imagination, it is to the River Plate that Latin America has traditionally looked for its footballing inspiration. Uruguay, its worldbeating teams of the first half of the century largely forgotten, is now mainly associated with dour defensiveness. Argentina is the country which best epitomizes the Latin American game in its blend of skill and ruthless determination to win, a mixture encapsulated in the stocky body of Diego Maradona. His performance against England in the 1986 World Cup – handling the ball into the net on the sly and then beating half the English team to score one of the greatest goals ever – summed up as well as any 90 minutes the Jekyll and Hyde nature of the Latin American game. This book recalls Latin American football's worldbeating triumphs and some of the lowlights of unsporting behaviour and corruption which – given the recent revelations involving Olympique Marseille, Porto, Anderlecht, Kiev, Tbilisi, Uefa referee Kurt Rothlisberger, the prevalence of transfer 'bungs' in English football and the FA charges against Bruce Grobbelaar and Hans Segers in the wake of their match-fixing trial – can be said at times to have reached European levels.

The Beautiful Game aims to give readers a taste of what football is like in Latin America, its history, its highs and lows, and how it is experienced by millions of fans. It makes no claim to be comprehensive or definitive. It deals principally with football in Uruguay, Argentina, Brazil, Colombia, Bolivia, Mexico and Nicaragua, based on visits during 1995–97, a period in which the region's international football was dominated by the qualification process for the France '98 World Cup.

Throughout this football century Latin America and Europe have vied for the distinction of being the game's true home, and if the record in the World Cup and World Club Championship is anything to go by, Latin America has the stronger case. In part this book is about what is special about Latin American football, but readers should be warned that it provides no simple answer. In most of Latin America, football is one of the foremost expressions of a country's culture. But if football is the Latin American game, it is also the world game. In Di Stéfano, Pelé and Maradona, Latin America has produced three players who vie for the title of the best ever, but Europe too has produced great players, Africa is doing so now, and in time the world's best may be an Asian. That other factor, the passion of the supporters, is also relative. Argentinians may love their football and worship Maradona, but how do you explain that when Argentina's No. 10 was kicked out of the 1994 World Cup for taking drugs, thousands took to the streets of Bangladesh to protest? It is a testament at once to the worldwide appeal of the game and the leading role that Latin America has always had in it. They say that the River–Boca derby in Buenos Aires is the fiercest, most passionate in the world, but the same too is said of the Fla–Flu in Rio de Janeiro, and of Real Madrid v Atlético Madrid, and of Rangers–Celtic. After a point, such comparisons become otiose.

17

During the writing of this book I was asked to do a radio interview about the disaster at a World Cup qualifier in Guatemala in which 78 people were crushed to death (I had been in the stadium in question just a few months earlier). What they were looking for, the producer said, was a discussion of why Latin Americans were so crazy about football that they ended up killing each other. I wasn't sure I could help. I told him that seven years earlier I had been living in Central America at the time of the Hillsborough disaster, in which 95 people were crushed to death in similar circumstances to the Guatemala tragedy. Then, people had asked me, 'Why are the English so crazy about football that they end up killing each other?'

1: One Hundred Years of Attitude

MONTEVIDEO, 12 JANUARY 1997. It was the day of the seventh round of South America's World Cup qualifying competition. Uruguay and Argentina, the continent's historic rivals, were about to renew their acquaintance.

The Argentinian fans, segregated in one corner of the stadium, let out a roar which belied their numbers, as the visitors, taking advantage of some sloppy Uruguayan defending, took the lead. Another two goals saw the Argentinian fans exultant, stripped to the waist, twirling their shirts above their heads as they bounced up and down, baying at the crestfallen Uruguayans on the other side of the line of riot police. Then, with just a few minutes remaining, one of the Uruguayan forwards sidestepped a challenge on the edge of the area and sent a shot crashing into the top corner. As the scorer knelt and made the sign of the cross, it was as if someone had hit the loudness button to reveal a new dimension in volume. The stadium vibrated with the noise of tens of thousands of voices singing out the glory of the goal and the misery that it must be to be Argentinian. At the final whistle and despite their defeat, the Uruguayan team saluted the crowd and headed purposefully to the Argentinian section where, amid much fist-clenching, they brandished their sky-blue shirts and taunted the visiting fans penned behind the high fence. It was the sort of gesture which might well have started a riot, or at least incurred the wrath of Fifa, had it not been for the fact that all the players were women.

Uruguay's women's team had lost 3–1 to Canada in a 60-minute warm-up match. The main event was still an hour and a half away.

In the interim the singing and chanting did not let up. Another line of police appeared to help keep the fans apart, but there was no real trouble. Everybody entering the stadium had had to pass through two police checks in which anything that might be handy in a fight was confiscated. Face-painting was banned because, it was said, it might hamper identification of suspects. The fierce rivalry between the two countries needs no encouragement. The idea of national anthems before the game had been abandoned, which was understandable given the deafening whistling which drowned out every name on the Argentinian teamsheet as it was read out over the loudspeakers. The atmosphere of fiery passion increased to a crackling intensity as the last few minutes ticked away towards kick-off. And that crescendo, culminating in the referee's whistle, was the real high point of the evening, as the hot midsummer air resounded to the two sets of supporters bellowing their pride in their team, their country.

After that, Uruguay and Argentina played out a 0–0 draw.

The River Plate, which separates, or links, Montevideo and Buenos Aires is the cradle of football in Latin America. They've been playing football here for almost as long as football has existed in its recognizable form. Uruguay–Argentina is the oldest international fixture in the world outside of the British Isles, and it is the one that has been played more times than any other. When Argentina and Uruguay contested the first World Cup Final in 1930 it was already a repeat of the Olympic Final of two years before. They stand together at the top of the list of South American Championship winners, a long way clear of third-placed Brazil. But whatever the competition in which these two old rivals meet, the fixture, like England–Scotland, always has a special savour. Like England, Argentina is the dominant partner in the relationship, being bigger and wealthier. Uruguay, a country of 3 million people and 27 million sheep, has, like Scotland, a long tradition of supplying key players to its neighbour. And like those diehard antagonists, England and Scotland, Uruguay and Argentina are in fact very similar, or at least have more in common than divides them, but this last fact is one you would be advised to whisper in the build-up to matchday.

This particular meeting came at an especially sensitive time for both teams. South America normally organizes its World Cup qualifying via two groups of four or five but for the 1998 Cup in France, Conmebol, the South American Football Federation, had hit upon the idea of a single round-robin group of nine, with each team playing 16 games over 18 months. With Brazil qualifying as champions and the top four going through, it seemed like a shoo-in for the continent's traditional football powers. However, Argentina's campaign to date had been lacklustre to say the least: after 6 games they had accumulated only 9 points, losing to Ecuador and drawing at home to Chile. Some people were beginning to think the unthinkable. Maradona predicted that a defeat or a draw in Montevideo would mean they could kiss France '98 goodbye.[1] Uruguay, equal on points and just behind in fourth place, had their own worries. Their failure to qualify for the 1994 tournament had badly dented confidence, and the prospect of the likes of Bolivia again usurping what they took to be their rightful place in the finals weighed heavily on Uruguayan minds.

The match was played in midsummer when neither the Argentinian nor the Uruguayan leagues were in action and *le tout* Buenos Aires had decamped to Punta del Este, the Uruguayan seaside resort which is a holiday mecca for the middle classes of the Southern Cone. Many would have bought tickets for the game there, so although only a disappointing 4000 or so tickets had been sold in Buenos Aires, there were probably 10–12,000 Argentinians in the ground. Fifa had designated this a high-risk fixture and the number of police on duty was more than double the normal allocation, at 1200. For security reasons, the travelling support were to be accommodated on the Amsterdam terrace, as it was nearer the car park and easier for the fans to make their getaway. But the Amsterdam, named after the scene of one of Uruguay's two Olympic triumphs, is traditionally where the home fans stand, and even the head of security who was responsible for the arrangements said it turned his stomach to have the Argentinians there.

These River Plate derbies have a reputation as tough, uncompromising affairs. This one started in a similar vein, with the game punctuated by a series of fouls. But they tended to be niggling infringements designed to break the opponents' rhythm rather than their legs. Uruguay had the better chances but were unconvincing in front of goal. The veteran Enzo Francescoli, who had been recalled from international retirement, was the worst offender, missing two good scoring opportunities. For Argentina, it seemed that if only the lively Ortega and Batistuta could find the same wavelength they could cause problems for the home team. Fortunately for Uruguay the two remained strangers, and Batistuta was rewarded for his woeful performance by being dropped for the rest of Argentina's qualifying campaign. The man of the match was, appropriately, a defender, Paulo Montero of Uruguay and Juventus.

Most of the frenetic and messy match was played amid an eerie hush; either the tension created by the possibility of losing was too much for the crowd or they were struggling to stay awake. Only towards the end did the home fans really make some noise, as the young substitute Abreu went close a couple of times. At the final whistle there was a sense of relief, that it was over and that everyone had avoided defeat. A draw more or less suited both teams in terms of the qualifying tournament and there had been rumours before the match of a fix to that effect[2] (although given the form, that would seem to be a waste of any fixer's money). The phrase 'honours even' on this occasion seemed more than a cliché. Each side had emerged with honour intact, the essence of all derby confrontations. The headline in one Uruguayan newspaper the following day summed it up: 'AT LEAST WE DIDN'T LOSE TO THE ARGENTINIANS,' it sighed.

Workmen were still putting the finishing touches to the Centenario stadium – whose dramatic tower still looks strangely futuristic – when Uruguay and Argentina contested the first World Cup Final on 30 July 1930. Even then it was a fixture with a long history. As early as 15 August 1888 teams representing Argentina and Uruguay had played a challenge match, and the first officially recognized international between the two countries took place on 16 May 1901.[3]

That first game in 1888 was played to mark Queen Victoria's

birthday and both teams comprised young British gentlemen, for at the time football in South America was still largely an amateur, élite and expatriate game. When Argentina beat Uruguay 6–0 in 1902, the goalscorers were Dickinson, Brown J., Morgan and Anderson (plus two own-goals). By the time of Uruguay's victory in 1930, the Brits were gone and in their place young South Americans were producing a distinctive and exciting version of the game.

In the late nineteenth century Britain was at the peak of its imperial power and, although South America was never formally part of the Empire (British Guiana and the Falklands apart), Britain had its fingers firmly embedded in the continent's economy. By the 1880s 20 per cent of British foreign investment was in Latin America, with Argentina leading the way. With a huge trade in wheat, beef, copper and nitrates, Argentina, Uruguay and Chile had much in common with the white dominions of Canada, Australia and South Africa. It was probably at the main ports, such as Buenos Aires, Montevideo, Santos, Rio de Janeiro and Valparaíso, where the continent's primary products were exported and British manufactures imported, that the first games of football were played in Latin America, as visiting British seamen relaxed in their spare time.

Britons were in at the birth of the game in Argentina, Uruguay, Brazil and Chile. But it was the resident British community either side of the River Plate which established football, alongside a range of other typical athletic pursuits of the British bourgeoisie, such as cricket, rowing, rugby, tennis and polo. The first really organized football in South America took place under the auspices of the Buenos Aires Football Club, formed in May 1867 by Thomas Hogg and other British ex-pats. On 27, 28 and 29 of June *The Standard*, one of two English-language newspapers in Buenos Aires at the time, carried the following advertisement:

On Saturday 29 of this month a football match will take place in Palermo and all those interested in playing are asked to procure from Messrs Galbraith and Hunter two caps, one red and one white, chosen to distinguish them during the game.

When the 12 o'clock train arrives a meeting will be held at the ground to consider the rules of the game, and the game will begin immediately afterwards. By order.[4]

It was, in fact, the club's second game; the first had taken place nine days earlier. (It was only four years since the formation of the Football League in England.) These and subsequent games benefited from a fierce rivalry between Hogg and William Heald, who could both marshal numerous team-mates.

At the end of that year Thomas Hogg wrote to Edward Mulhall, the editor of *The Standard*, saying: 'In my opinion this game [football] will take a long time to spread, even among the British: but even so I intend to persevere because I consider it the best pastime, and the cheapest for the youth of the middle class and also for that of the people . . .'[5]

Hogg was right in that his pioneering club would enjoy only a fitful existence before, having presumably given the rules thorough consideration, in 1873 it opted to play rugby instead. It took a generation for football to become established in Argentina. But Hogg also spotted one of the reasons for its eventual success in its low cost (requiring no sophisticated equipment or facilities), which made it accessible to the whole of society and which would help ensure that it would outgrow its privileged beginnings in South America.

Football, meanwhile, throve in the city's British schools, and it was a schoolmaster, Alexander Watson Hutton, who had the greatest influence on the early development of the game in Argentina. A graduate of the University of Edinburgh, he arrived in Buenos Aires in 1882 and, after working briefly at the St Andrew's Scotch School, set up his own English High School in 1884, employing a specialist games master to teach football. The first league, set up in 1891, soon foundered, largely due to lack of support from the clubs. Many of those early matches were essentially pick-up games between the likes of 'Mr B. B. Syer's team' and 'Mr J. O. Anderson's team'. Two years later Watson Hutton reformed it as the Argentine Association Football League (AAFL) with five clubs participating. The first two championships were won by Lomas Athletic Club, a team of Bedford School old boys resident in Buenos Aires. The English High School's old boys' team later changed its name to Alumni (the school name was retained by the schoolboy side, which played in a new second division) and completely dominated Argentinian football in the first decade of the twentieth century before disbanding in 1911.

British schools also played a prominent role in neighbouring Uruguay. William Leslie Poole, a teacher at the English High School in Montevideo, formed the Albion Cricket Club in May 1891 and soon its football section was playing matches against teams from across the River Plate. The first football match (in fact, a two-game series) between two Uruguayan clubs had already taken place between Montevideo Cricket Club and Montevideo Rowing Club in June 1881. The cricketers won both matches. Clubs also formed around British-owned businesses, such as the railways,[6] which in 1891 produced the Central Uruguay Railway Cricket Club, whose football section would later become known as Peñarol. In 1900 the CURCC won the first Uruguayan Association Football League title, a championship which at that time involved just four clubs. However, the distinction of the continent's second oldest championship (after Argentina) went to Chile, where in 1895 nine teams of mainly British origin disputed the first league title. The country's first football team, Valparaíso FC, had formed six years earlier, in 1889. The teamsheets for a challenge game held in Viña del Mar on 4 August 1893 between the cities of Santiago and Valparaíso gives an idea of the ethnic make-up of Chilean football at the time:

Valparaíso: Webb, McNoughton, Reynolds, Roberts, Bailey, Crangle, Baldwin, Woodgate, D Scott, Fleming, Simpson
Santiago: P Scott, McColl, Coast, Madden, Rogers, Anderson, Hood, Melrose, V Scott, Jones, Allen.[7]

That same year a team of Buenos Aires Brits crossed the Andes for a game in Valparaíso. But that was only part of the story because the year earlier a group of Chileans of modest means (Real, Avaria,

25

Hidalgo, González, Mujica, Alvarez, Acuña, Solar, Sánchez, etc) founded Santiago Wanderers – still a major club – in the city of Valparaíso, confusingly enough. Other homegrown teams soon followed in the capital, some linked to educational establishments (Atlético Escuela Normal) and some boasting of their social origins, such as Chile Obrero FC.

The founding father of Brazilian football was Charles Miller, born in São Paulo to British parents and educated in England, where he turned out for a Hampshire county side against the great English amateur team, Corinthians. He returned to Brazil in 1894 and the following year, he 'collected together a group of young Englishmen from the local Gas Company, the London and Brazilian Bank and the São Paulo Railway Company, picked two sides and played the first game of football in Brazil in the modern era'[8], supposedly using the ball from the Hampshire–Corinthians game of the previous year. At Miller's instigation, the São Paulo Athletic Club added football to its list of sports. But other foreign midwives attended the birth of football in Brazil. Hans Nobiling, an immigrant from Hamburg, persuaded an existing German sporting club in São Paulo to take on football, while the city's Mackenzie College, set up by American Methodists, was also taking to the new game. Sport Club was formed by young men of various nationalities, while Palestra Italia, later to become Palmeiras FC, was established by Brazilians of Italian descent. Rio de Janeiro was not far behind in setting up its own clubs along similar lines.

The late nineteenth century was also a time of frenetic urban growth in Latin America. Buenos Aires went from 178,000 inhabitants in 1869 to 678,000 in 1895 to 1,576,000 in 1914; São Paulo grew from 40,000 in 1880 to 800,000 in 1920; Rio de Janeiro went from 300,000 to over a million in the same period; Santiago's growth from 130,000 in 1880 to 507,000 in 1920 is almost paltry by comparison.[9] It was in these burgeoning cities that football would take hold and become a mass game.

With the formation in 1899 of a second division in Argentina, football began to be taken up in ever greater numbers by Spanish-speakers, a boom partly fuelled by sport in schools. What occurred was 'something like a revelation for the public and for the children themselves, on discovering in the numerous competitions which take place under the auspices of the colleges and schools, that football and other so-called English sports, were not the brutal and complicated games that had been supposed by universally accepted prejudice, and that neither were they accessible only to Anglo-Saxons. It was also clearly seen that Latin impetuosity could be submitted to the rigour of the laws of the game and the severe regulations in the clubs, without strange influences and without superhuman efforts.'[10]

In 1902, the president of the AAFL, Francisco Chevallier Boutell, could note that football was 'becoming the national sport' of Argentina.[11]

While England and the English were still looked on as the fathers of football and an example to the local game (in 1903 the renamed Argentine Football Association affiliated itself to the English FA), a creolization of football was well under way. A description in a local magazine of Juan Ramsay, one of the guiding spirits of early Chilean football, captures something of that moment: 'At all times he has shown himself to be a true gentleman, Chilean by birth and heart, but English in all the deeds of his glorious sporting life.'[12] Ramsay was not only a distinguished player and referee, he also founded Atlético Unión and did much to encourage the spread of the game beyond its patrician origins.

By 1903 the laws of the game had been drafted in Spanish and meetings of the Argentine Football Association also took place in the local language. Although it was 1912 before the name was finally changed to Asociación Argentina de Football, across the River Plate the Uruguayan Association Football League became the Liga Uruguaya del Football in 1905.

For one of Uruguay's two great clubs, Peñarol, full nationalization came a decade later. Indeed, until 1913 it was still known as the Central Uruguay Railway Cricket Club and its statutes and board meetings were conducted in English. Only those of English origin were allowed as members. Nacional, Uruguay's other great club, was formed by the merger of Montevideo Football Club and Uruguay Athletic Club, and from the start, as the name implies, pursued a policy of fielding Uruguayan players, albeit, in those early days, of the better sort.

The two clubs have become a sort of secular equivalent of Rangers and Celtic, completely dominating Uruguayan football. Peñarol and Nacional rank second and third respectively in the all-time list of winners of the Copa Libertadores, the South American Club Cup.

Nacional have their roots among college students, in contrast to Peñarol's more proletarian origins. Nacional's fans were known as *cuelludos* after the stiff collars worn by young gentlemen of the era. They had a cruder, equally class-tinged name for their antagonists, coined by Scarone, a Nacional player of Italian origin. They were called the *mangias*, as in *mangia-merda*.

Peñarol and Nacional are Uruguayan football. Between 1900 and 1994 on only 15 occasions was the league won by other clubs. From the start of the professional league in 1932 until 1975 no other club won the championship (Peñarol won 23 times to Nacional's 20, the latter including five unbroken years to 1939). Only AC Milan has won the world club title as many times as Peñarol and Nacional (three times each). Virtually every Uruguayan international player, no matter where he starts, will play for one of the big two (and if he is any good he will normally be sold to Argentina or further afield). In one of the first internationals against Argentina, the Uruguayan FA decided to dress the Nacional team in the sky blue national colours to represent the country. The match took place on 13 September 1903 and the Uruguayans won 3–2 in Buenos Aires, the country's first international victory. Every year Nacional marks this date with a big awards celebration.

Enrique 'Quique' Aramburu is an old man now and a little shaky on his feet, but his lively mind easily recalls the highs and lows of 68 years watching Peñarol. Just as well, perhaps. I'd made a special point of coming to see him as I'd been told that he had an impressive collection of rare football magazines stretching back decades. So naturally one of the first things I asked was whether I could have a look at this unique record of Uruguayan football. 'Oh, those,' he replied. 'I got rid of them a little while back.' Fortunately Quique Aramburu is his own living record. He saw his first game at 5 years old, became a club member at 12, and served for many years on the board of directors. Sitting in his dressing gown in his Montevideo home, he gave a partial account of the club's history between sips of Scotch.

'I got on very well with the children of Mr Moore. He was the representative of the British merchant fleet's victualler. His name was John "Jack" Moore and he married a Uruguayan woman. He took me to the football once. I fell in with love with Peñarol. So at that time I joined. I became a fan and finally a member. I'm a life member and also an honorary member, in recognition of my services to the club.'

The details of that first game are now lost in the mists of time but what remains fresh, naturally, is Quique Aramburu's first match against Nacional. 'The first derby I saw, we won 2−0. We played three *clásicos* that year and won them all 2−0. It showed I had chosen well.'

In the early British days football was played in an unsophisticated style. 'Everybody just chased after the ball. Until a Scotsman came – from Ferro Carril del Oeste in Argentina – Mr Joe Harley. He played No. 5. He began to introduce the short-passing style. It was short passing and long passing, but a pass directed at another player. That's why they used to call it playing *a la escocesa* [Scottish-style]. And he also brought another particular characteristic, which was fair play. Once, Peñarol won a penalty and Harley thought it shouldn't have been given. He deliberately kicked it wide, as if to say, "I don't want gifts."'

Peñarol's British roots are still remembered, and in some surprising quarters. 'In 1961 we won the Intercontinental Cup,' recalls Aramburu. 'The Prince Philip was here at the time and he made a speech that I heard on the radio, in which he said he was very proud of the success of Peñarol, which was a team with British origins and had become world champions.'

The name Peñarol comes from the area where the railway company had its workshops and where the club played its home games (the land was owned by an Italian immigrant who came from Pignarol, or whose surname was Pignarolo – this is still a matter of learned dispute). The reasons for the name change aren't hard to imagine: think of those Uruguayan fans turning out to cheer on the team and having to chant 'Come on Central Uruguay Railway Cricket Club'.

Until 1913 the chairman of the club was also the administrator of the railways, but eventually, inevitably, the British handed over control of the club to the locals, the *criollos*. It seems the accountants in London had increasingly come to see the sporting sideline as a loss-making distraction, particularly since angry fans had trashed the companies' carriages on the way back from an away defeat.

'The English weren't interested in carrying on. They found people were getting distracted and they were losing money. It was even a case of the fans damaging the rolling stock after games. They sliced up the seats, which were made of very nice leather, broke windows. And they did their sums in England and figured, this isn't good business.'

But for nearly half of Uruguay, the whole story of CURCC's metamorphosis into Club Atlético Peñarol is an insidious red herring. The CURCC, they argue, enjoyed a transient existence between 1891 and 1913, at which time, and coincidentally, another club called Peñarol was formed. This would mean Nacional, founded in 1899, would be not just older than Peñarol, but the oldest club currently playing in the Uruguayan league.

Aramburu, ever helpful in setting the record straight, points out a few salient statistics of a century of rivalry. 'We've got a statistical advantage over Nacional. More championships, largest number of victories, smallest number of defeats, more goals in favour, fewer goals against; it's the same story for over one hundred years. In this century they won't be able to catch us up. We've already got this century sewn up.'

★　　★　　★

30

Uruguay and Argentina have been locked in an antagonistic embrace for as long as the Oriental Republic has existed. Uruguay has always been a buffer state between Brazil and Argentina and has always struggled to assert an identity of its own. Most Latin American countries conjure up some sort of image in the mind of even the most uninterested observer – Paraguay may signify fascist generals; Peru, the Incas and Machu Picchu; Brazil, carnival, the rain forest or Ronnie Biggs (in Middlesbrough, of course, Brazil's national emblem is the Mexican sombrero) – but most people would be hard pressed to think of anything that Uruguay is famous for. Although the British-built meat cold store ensured Fray Bentos became a household name, how many know that it is a place, let alone that it is in Uruguay?

Uruguay is a country strikingly free of distinguishing marks. It has no mountains, volcanoes, precipitous waterfalls, pre-Columbian ruins or exotic wildlife. For a sheep or a cow, however, Uruguay's broad expanses of grassland will offer little cause for complaint. But maybe it's asking a lot of a country which is the size of one of Brazil's smaller states. For drama, it is urban Uruguay which has always led the way, and urban Uruguay really means Montevideo, where 1.3 million of the country's 3.1 million people live. Uruguay's next biggest city has a population of just 100,000. It was Montevideo which developed a vibrant culture in tandem with its bigger twin across the River Plate, Buenos Aires, and its two finest products were football and tango.

Even worse for Uruguayans than their country's relative anonymity is that wherever they go they find themselves condemned to be confused with Argentinians. They certainly know how Canadians feel. Although Uruguay received more immigrants from Spain than Argentina, where Italians were the main incoming group, they all speak a similar variety of Spanish.

So back in 1930 the World Cup was a way of putting Uruguay on the map – literally, for in some maps of the time it was depicted as a province of Argentina. Winning the World Cup would prove that Uruguay played the best football in the world and, just as importantly, that they were better than Argentina. The state-of-the-art Centenario stadium was named in honour of the one hundredth anniversary of the signing of independent Uruguay's first constitution. Uruguay would tell the world that it was a dynamic, young, democratic republic. The main portico of the stadium was dressed in Uruguayan marble and porphyry as a proud demonstration of 'the wealth and industry of the country'.[13]

Jules Rimet, the president of the International Federation of Association Football (Fifa), was effusive in his praise for the new construction. 'When they told me about the great Centenario stadium, I thought it would be one of the many that are continually being built, but once I saw it and could appreciate it I concluded that it ranks first in the world . . . There are some bigger ones in other countries, but these are designed for all sorts of sports, so that I do not exaggerate to say that it is the foremost in the world which is exclusively for football . . . Football, to be appreciated completely, should be seen close-up and in the Centenario stadium one can follow the match from any point in the ground.'[14]

At the Paris Games in 1924 Uruguay became the first Latin American side to enter the Olympic football competition. Argentina huffily stayed at home and could only watch from afar as the Uruguayans dazzled the European crowds, who were witnessing South American football for the first time. The skilful Latin Americans carried all before them, thrashing Yugoslavia, the USA and France in the early rounds, before disposing of Holland in the semis and beating Switzerland 3–0 in a one-sided Final. The speed, grace and exuberance of the South American team, not to mention eight goals from the tournament top scorer 'Perucho' Petrone, did to the Europeans what gunpowder and the horse had done to pre-Columbian America.

Having won four South American Championships – two more than either Argentina or Brazil – and now the Olympic title, Uruguay were clearly the best team in the world. The Argentinians, though, cannily invited them to a challenge match in Buenos Aires, noting that Uruguay had not had to face Argentina on its way to Olympic gold.

More than sixty years on, that still rankles Quique Aramburu. 'Politically, Uruguay handled that badly because they didn't need to go. They should have said: "Excuse me, we're world champions. What are you?" But they went and the Argentinians won 1–0 . . . It was a political error to go there. They claimed they were the moral champions.'

As with Scotland's victory over world champions England at Wembley in 1967, the Argentinians assured themselves of bragging rights for years to come. That match was also notable because Onzari, a winger from the Argentinian club Huracán, swung in the only goal direct from a corner. It was the first time a goal had been scored in such a way, which in South America is still known as a *gol olímpico* and still nobody believes it is ever intentional.

The two countries were to meet nine more times in the next four years (the Lipton and Newton Cups were annual challenge matches) before the question of who were the real champions could be properly resolved. This time it was in the Olympic Final in Amsterdam. Argentina had scored 23 goals in the 3 matches it took them to reach the Final. Uruguay had had a much tougher time, just beating Italy 3–2 in the semi, and had not looked the worldbeaters of four years earlier. But they knew their rivals well and after a 1–1 draw, Uruguay defeated Argentina 2–1 in a replay to take the gold medal for the second Olympiad running. It was the 103rd international between the two countries.

Two years later the old enemies faced each other again in the Final, this time of the first World Cup tournament organized by Fifa. There was little doubt they were the two best teams in the tournament: each had won their semi-final 6–1. The quality of the field taking part was, however, disappointing. Fifa had awarded Uruguay the World Cup in recognition of its Olympic triumphs and to mark its centenary over the claims of Italy, Spain, Holland and Sweden. Entry was by invitation, but in the event only four European countries appeared in Uruguay, as one country after another discovered reasons not to make the long sea voyage to Montevideo. Among the absentees were the four would-be hosts and all the British teams. In the end, it

33

didn't matter: Uruguay had shown and were to show again that they were the best team in the world.

Attendances for the early games not involving Uruguay were also disappointing. Just 1000 people watched the first match between France and Mexico at Peñarol's Pocitos ground. Five other first-round games attracted even fewer spectators. It was a different story when the Centenario stadium was inaugurated on 18 July with the game between Uruguay and Peru. A crowd of 70,000 saw Uruguay win 1–0 with a goal from Héctor 'Lefty' Castro, who had lost his left hand in an accident involving an electric saw. He claimed after the game that he had turned down a Peruvian attempt to bribe him.

For the Final, the crowd at the Centenario was swelled to 93,000, with many *porteños* having hired boats to bring them across the wide river from Buenos Aires. Still, the support was overwhelmingly for the home side.

Uruguay had the best of the early stages and scored first, Dorado putting the ball between the goalkeeper's legs. Argentina pulled one back through Peucelle but when, in the 37th minute, the Uruguayan captain Nasazzi stopped with his arm in the air appealing for offside, Argentina's Stábile carried on, driving a high shot past the keeper. It looked well offside but, after consulting with his linesman, the Belgian referee let the goal stand.

According to the official album of the tournament, 'Throughout the stadium a wind of anguish blew and hopes tended to vanish . . . Instead of encouragement [the Uruguayan team] received strong and clear evidence of reproof from their partisans.'[15] For a few minutes it was as if they were playing away.

After half-time they were transformed, scoring twice. At 3–2 the Argentinian Varallo was on the point of scoring but for the calm presence of Andrade on the goal-line, with the keeper Ballesteros beaten. Castro sealed the Uruguayan victory a minute before time. The team included four of the side that had set Uruguay on the path to glory six years before in the Stade Colombes in Paris.

It was a Final worthy of the first world championship and distinguished spectators were unstinting in their praise. The captain of the

Peruvian team, Antonio Maquilón, said it was 'The most exciting game I have ever seen in my life.' The president of the Chilean delegation, Aquiles Frías Ahumada, said: 'I have seen the strongest and most exciting match of my life, which will stay with me as a lasting memory. After the magnificent performances witnessed in this competition, to be a spectator at a Final of this quality is a pleasure which should be appreciated for all its immense value.'[16]

Fifa subsequently recognized the two Olympic triumphs as the equivalent of World Cups, making Uruguay the first three-time world champions (but try telling a Brazilian, or indeed any non-Uruguayan that). Sadly, Uruguay, perhaps mindful of the poor European attendance in 1930, did not, for political reasons, travel to Mussolini's Italy for the third World Cup in 1934 (nor did they travel to France four years later). With the hiatus of the Second World War Uruguay were not to appear in another World Cup until 1950, twenty years later, when they would again give the world a footballing lesson.

Uruguayans have traditionally put their success down to something called *la garra charrúa*. *Garra* (literally 'claw') means guts, fighting spirit, ferocity, and *charrúa* is a journalistic synonym for Uruguayan. The *charrúas* were the original inhabitants of what is now Uruguay before successive waves of Europeans came to make a killing or a new life there. The fact that the new Uruguayans killed off the last of the real *charrúas* in the middle of the last century has done little to dent a national self-image of indomitable battlers punching well above their weight.

While the national team's triumphs in the 1920s and 1930s were the product of a dynamic South American football fusion to which the Old World had no answer, their victory in 1950 was for Uruguayans the epitome of *la garra charrúa*. Before the match the Uruguayan FA directors had told their players that they had achieved their objective by reaching the Final* and that they shouldn't try

---

* The final round was played as a four-team league, but the last match, in which Uruguay needed to win while Brazil needed only a draw, is usually taken as the 1950 World Cup Final.

to ruin the Brazilian party. The players had other ideas. To snatch the title from the red-hot favourites Brazil in their own brand-new stadium was a feat of toughness and savvy exemplified by the Uruguayans' iconic captain, Obdulio Varela.

Varela was a colossus, directing the game from centre-half. It was he, more than anyone, who kept his head when in the decisive match Brazil went 1–0 up with the biggest crowd ever assembled for a football game urging them on to win. Two second-half goals stopped the Brazilian cheers in their throats. Uruguayans were still celebrating a couple of weeks later when the film of the World Cup victory appeared in Montevideo cinemas. The committeemen running Uruguayan football had gold medals cast for themselves. The players received silver medals and some money. Varela bought himself a Ford with his bonus but within a week it was stolen.

Varela went on to play in a national team which many people felt was even better than the 1950 champions. In Switzerland in 1954 Uruguay were one of the teams of the tournament and in the semi-final played the great Hungarians in what those who witnessed it said was one of the most thrilling games of football ever. It was 2–2 after 90 minutes but in extra time Hungary scored twice. Few could have realized that this dramatic encounter would mark the end of an era for Uruguayan football.

The first black man to captain his country, Varela had great human qualities, a keen sense of social responsibility and, despite his nick-names – 'The Black Boss' and 'The Caudillo' – he was committed to leftwing politics. In 1948 he was one of the leaders of the strike which paralysed Uruguayan football and which meant that the championship was not completed that year.

During the 1970s, when both Argentina and Uruguay were ruled by military regimes, Obdulio Varela went to Argentina to play a match in homage to a fellow member of the 1950 team. A journalist from Argentina's top sports magazine approached him and asked him what he felt about winning the World Cup, insisting that Obdulio Varela must have attached some importance to the fact that he was captain in the victory over Brazil in 1950. Varela said no, he was just one more fighter in the battle, and that was that.

'But you must have felt proud,' the reporter said.

'Yes, of course I felt proud,' he answered. 'I felt proud to be Uruguayan.'

'And now how do you feel as a Uruguayan?'

'Now I feel shame,' he said simply.

In the dictatorial atmosphere of the time it was a remark which could have cost Varela dear. A Peñarol official who was travelling with Varela overheard the conversation and asked the journalist to tone down what he had said, saving Varela from a potential problem – although whether he would have been grateful for the gesture is another matter.[17]

The 1950 team was still a very skilful side but in the long, slow decline which has been Uruguayan football in the second half of the century, la garra charrúa has at times translated into an ugly dependence on violence and intimidation to grind out results. The nadir came in 1986 in Mexico. Uruguay's final group game in Nezahualcóyotl was a travesty of football, and not just because it was against Scotland. With the match barely begun, one of the Uruguayan fullbacks, Batista, crossed over from one side of the pitch to the other to deck one of the Scottish players. The referee bravely sent him off. The ensuing 89 minutes were an exhibition of the meaning of the term 'ungentlemanly conduct', with the Uruguayans demonstrating their garra charrúa in a litany of foul play, running the gamut of kicking, tripping, shirt-pulling, spitting and time-wasting as the ten Uruguayans sought to spoil the game in the hope of hanging on for a point. The Scots were of course eliminated but, remarkably, the 0–0 draw meant Uruguay qualified for the second round as one of the best third-place teams on just two points from three games.

To the relief of Fifa, Uruguay didn't make it beyond the second round, dispatched, appropriately perhaps, by the old enemy, Argentina, who went on to lift the Cup. If there was one team to match Uruguay for the ability to sneak a 1–0 by fair means or foul it was surely Argentina, and in their manager, Carlos Bilardo, they came up against the master.

Uruguay has exported people – not least football players – over the years. Its population today is roughly the same as when it won the first World Cup in 1930. Chelsea's Gustavo Poyet is a perfect example of the sort of player who has made Uruguayans so sought after around the world: skilful, tough, disciplined and above all possessing an unquenchable will to win. Off the field he's a mature, cosmopolitan family man, but even when relaxed and smiling in his temporary home at an airport hotel, his face speaks of barely hidden depths of hardness. Definitely a man you'd want on your side when the going gets tough. The Uruguayan footballing character comes, he thinks, from having the important things drummed in at an early age.

'I'm a special case: I get on very well with the Argentinians. I've got many friends there. But we've got a tremendous football rivalry. When I was eight or nine I was playing against an Argentinian team in a seven-a-side, and as I was leaving the house my father said to me, "If you lose, don't come back." It was a case of going to sleep at my auntie's or a cousin's or wherever. It was an obligation for me to beat Argentina that day.'

Poyet, like most Uruguayan professionals, started playing seriously at an early age: 5 or 6. His father was a top-class basketball player, but for Gustavo there was never any doubt that football would be his game.

'In Uruguay, apart from being the main sport, it's also an everyday thing. The child is born, and from the start people are concerned that he should support one team or another. Some want him to be Peñarol so they give him a Peñarol shirt, others want him to be Nacional so they give him the shirt, or they make him a member, or they give him a ball in the club colours. My father was always Peñarol. But my mother's family was Nacional, so my uncles tried to lure me away. The only one they succeeded with was my brother. He's the only one who split from the Peñarol family. But as soon as I started playing professional football, I put the Peñarol stuff to one side. I used to be a great Peñarol fan, but once I had to play against Peñarol I pretty much stopped. I'd gone from being a fan to being a professional.'

At the age of 14 he left his local team to join a professional club, River Plate (not to be confused with the leading Argentinian club of the same name). Poyet is one of the few Uruguayan players to go abroad without having first passed through one of the two main clubs or Argentina. He was, in fact, on the point of signing for Peñarol when a French club, Grenoble, came in looking for a young centre-forward, as he then was. Language and cultural problems were to be expected, but even travelling to away games was a novelty for Poyet. What is called the Uruguayan league is in fact made up entirely of clubs from Montevideo. 'The interior' (i.e., the rest of the country) has its own football structures, separate and inferior. Good players from the provinces are obliged to graduate to the city. It's a division found in all areas of national life.* For Poyet it meant that while playing for River Plate the furthest away trip he had to make was to Atlético Cerro, forty minutes away across town. So coming to Europe and having to travel five, six, seven hours on a bus was a bit of a shock.

Poyet spent a difficult two years in France; a young player barely in his twenties playing for a club in crisis, lonely, at times not getting paid, and having a hard time from the press. But he came out of the experience – moving on to a successful stint with Real Zaragoza in Spain – demonstrating the sort of mental toughness for which Uruguayan players are renowned. It was a characteristic which marked him out for Ruud Gullit, under whom, until injury, he had become a fixture in Chelsea's midfield.

'This *garra interna*, this internal strength, makes the Uruguayan a player, I believe, who easily adapts to things and above all is a winner. I like to win everything. If we're sitting here playing cards I want to win. We may be laughing, enjoying ourselves, having a drink –

---

* For example, of the two traditional political parties, the Colorados are the more centralist while the Blancos have their base in the farms of the interior.

I want to *win*. And if I don't win, even though I might not show it, inside I'm screwed. I think all Uruguayans are like that. There's people who recognize it, there's people in Europe who know that Uruguayan players will die to win.' That has undoubtedly been a factor in the continuing marketability of Uruguayan players despite the failing fortunes of the national team. The strongest league in the world, Italy's Serie A, has throughout the 1990s seen a succession of Uruguayans at its top clubs (including Enzo Francescoli, Daniel Fonseca, Rubén Sosa, Paulo Montero and Alvaro Recoba).

Uruguay is a country steeped in football, where everyone is a football expert. During the 1990 World Cup the working hours in government offices were changed to accommodate the timings of games televised from Italy. But while past triumphs have helped forge a national identity, for Uruguay's players, the burden of history can at times weigh heavily.

'I played in the Copa América in 1995 in Uruguay,' recalls Poyet. 'Uruguay hadn't lost at home in the Copa América in its entire history. We couldn't lose. It wasn't a case of losing through an unlucky penalty or something – we *couldn't lose*. Because it was obligatory not to lose. It was a case of coming out on to the pitch not worried about winning, about being the champions – we could have still been champions having lost a game – no, no: we had to be champions and not lose. It was an amazing, unique pressure. I think you have to be there to live it, to feel it. There's no comparison with any game I've played in Europe – none! Perhaps playing the Final of the Cup Winners Cup with Real Zaragoza, but you don't feel that responsibility, the obligation, that pressure to say that if I lose today it remains etched for ever in history.'*

Of one of the national team's less illustrious episodes, Poyet has mixed feelings. Uruguay in the 1986 World Cup were widely perceived as a disgrace, a plain dirty team. Poyet recognizes that the whole episode saddled Uruguay with a bad reputation – before the 1997 Copa América the Uruguay coach, Héctor Núñez, felt obliged

* Uruguay beat Brazil on penalties in the Final, having not lost a game.

to assure journalists that 'we don't win games by poking other players' eyes and grabbing their testicles'[18] – but it's not clear he thinks it's deserved, and he's ambiguous about whether subsequent efforts to change the team's style have been worthwhile.

'Yes, Batista got sent off after fifty seconds, but that was an error of the French referee. The problem is that the reputation of the *garra charrúa* betrays you. As they know that Uruguayan teams are very strong and hard, referees are on the lookout to punish us. It's taking a lot for us to lose that reputation. It's something which still weighs on Uruguay when we play abroad. Sometimes you know you've got to be a little controlled because if you cross the line a little they're going to punish you more harshly than the opposing team. In that way it is handicapping Uruguayan football, but out of all that trouble at the 1986 World Cup we've been trying to change. But we haven't managed to attain a very good level at club or international level. Maybe we've got better in some respects, but our overall level has gone down. So I don't know what is better: being on the top with conflicts, or being a bit lower down without so many problems. You've got to get the balance right.'

For Uruguayans, even more so than the English, there is a palpable feeling of having lost their birthright as a pre-eminent football nation. With every passing year, Uruguay's golden age slips ever further into the past. Uruguay have won the South American Championship six times since their last World Cup win in 1950, although half their victories were recorded as hosts. But even their fourth place in the 1970 World Cup looks, in retrospect, like another step in a long decline.

Any team representing Uruguay is expected to display *la garra charrúa*, but while necessary, it is no longer sufficient and can at times be counter-productive. Says Poyet: 'On one hand it benefits us on the other it is a handicap. I think that in the past with this *garra*, you could go on to win things, but now it's not enough. Now you've got to hold on to the ball, have a serious tactical system, run much more – football's changed. But because of our past it's inside us, and it's that tradition that is still demanded of us. But I think

41

you've got to add other things to it because football has changed.'

Quique Aramburu thinks Uruguayan football has changed, but not for the better: 'I wouldn't say we've lost our character, but we don't play how we used to. Technically, the players are inferior . . . The Uruguayan style? The Uruguayan style now is to play badly.'

Uruguay's disappointing showing in the 1998 World Cup qualifying competition was certainly grist to the mill. But unfavourable comparisons with the greats of yesteryear have for some considerable time been the stock-in-trade of Uruguayan football criticism. In a discussion of Uruguay's football decline, the writer Eduardo Galeano described his country as one which preferred nostalgia to hope. 'It is not that the past is bad, it's bad when the past becomes the best of all possible times and above all when it becomes the inevitable fate for eternity.'[19]

His words find an echo in the rundown port area of Montevideo. The port market is still a wonderful place to watch various clearly recognizable animal parts being grilled for you in one of the smoky *parrillas* while sipping a *medio y medio* (half white wine, half sparkling wine), but in the neighbouring streets it feels like the boat left a while ago. Montevideo is a pleasant, easy-going city, especially for those arriving from Buenos Aires, but it also lacks a certain dynamism and a sense of being a forward-looking place. Uruguay has one of the most unfeasible pension systems in the world, as it continues to export its young people, including footballers, leaving a shrinking percentage of workers to pay for the ageing population. It all adds up to a place that feels like its bright future now lies in the past.

Where did it all go wrong? is the undercurrent of much discussion of the state of Uruguayan football. But perhaps more pertinent is: how did it all go right in the first place? In the days when Uruguay v Argentina was really Montevideo v Buenos Aires, the country could compete on more or less equal terms. But now that Uruguay's 3 million are pitted against the best of Argentina's 33 million, some disadvantage is inevitable. And when they have to face Brazil, which can pick from 150 million people, what is remarkable is how close those games always are, how much history and tradition counts for.

The France '98 qualifying tournament ended up marking another step in Uruguay's footballing decline. But while 1997 was a bad year for the senior side, there were some signs of hope triumphing over nostalgia. In Malaysia the Under-20 side drew much favourable comment from a string of good performances in the World Youth Cup. The young *charrúas* caught the eye of many observers and came within a whisker of becoming world champions – the first Uruguayan XI to do so at any level in nearly fifty years. They lost out narrowly in the Final . . . to Argentina.

2: The Sublime and the Malign

MY MOTHER WOULDN'T claim to be an expert about Latin American football, but growing up in the 1960s I can remember her having a firm opinion about one player. 'Ooh, that Rattín, he's a bugger,' I recall her tutting. It was a view that would have found few to contradict it in England at the time. Antonio Rattín – with the stress firmly on the 'Rat' – was a national hate-figure following a game in the 1966 World Cup watched by most of the country. It was the quarter-final played at Wembley, and Argentina barred England's path to a place in the semis. For an hour of a tough, ill-tempered game England had been unable to break down the Argentine defence. Then, with the Argentinian players surrounding the German referee, Rudolf Kreitlein, after another disputed decision, their captain was dramatically sent off. For several minutes he refused to go and then, stomping off with abundant bad grace, he continued the argument on the red carpet in front of the royal box.

'The arguing and gesturing went on for three minutes or so and it also became plain to me that, if no solution could be found soon, the match would have to be abandoned and awarded to England. That would have been catastrophic so I decided to go on and see what I could do,' recalled Ken Aston, responsible for referees' logistics at the tournament. Aston managed to persuade Rattín that to persist would be very bad for the Argentinian FA. 'In the end he went,' Aston told the *Evening Standard*, 'but not before making a lewd gesture to the crowd.'

England went on to win 1–0 against Argentina's ten men. 'In the tunnel after the match it was mayhem. Some of the Argentine squad were standing by the England team bus, kicking in the panels, and when Harry Cavan [a Fifa official] came down to the dressing-room area, one of them spat a half-eaten orange full in his face.' It was decided that it would be prudent to forget about selecting a player for the mandatory dope-test: Argentina were, in any case, out.

After the match, the England manager, Alf Ramsey, stoked the controversy, saying: 'We have still to produce our best football. It will come against the right type of opposition, a team who come to play football and not act as animals.' The English public, outraged at what they saw as the Argentinians' unsporting behaviour, largely endorsed Ramsey's view of them as animals. Rattín was the living, spitting proof of the odious instability of the Latin temperament.

The Argentinian public's outrage was equal and opposite. Feelings were running so high that the British embassy in Buenos Aires received hundreds of abusive calls and angry youths stormed the British stand at a trade fair. Extra guards were placed around the ambassador's residence as the team came home to a heroes' welcome. Relations didn't get this bad again until the Falklands War.

Antonio Ubaldo Rattín still claims to be baffled as to why he was sent off that hot July day at Wembley. Sitting in the office of his insurance business in Buenos Aires, its walls decorated with pictures of him in his playing days, Rattín's booming voice expresses a mixture of impugned virtue and genial exasperation.

'The first fifteen minutes of the second half the English had us on the rack. There were seventy thousand people cheering on their team, the referee giving non-existent fouls to the home side. He was giving everything to England, so I asked for an interpreter because I was the captain. I showed him the captain's armband and the referee told me to get off.'

What exactly was said in that brief conversation has been the subject of much speculation. Most people assumed Rattín was dismissed for swearing at the referee but, he points out, not unreasonably, 'He didn't understand a word of Spanish, I don't speak German . . . Many people said that I was giving him the *corte de manga* [the universally understood gesture of grabbing the upper arm and raising the fist sharply] but that's not true. I was just showing him I was the captain.'

For Rattín the real reason is clear: he is in no doubt that he and his team were the victims of a fix.

'When they had the draw for the referees for all the quarter-finals, the Argentinian and the Uruguayan representatives turned up and they told them, we've already done the draw. And just by chance the referee for our game against England was a German, who sent me off. The referee for the Uruguay v Germany match was an Englishman and he sent off three Uruguayans. And Germany won 4–0. Everything was set up.'

It is a view which in Argentina, indeed in Latin America in general, is entirely uncontroversial: England's day of glory is seen in much the same dubious light as, well, others see Argentina's in 1978. For the most part, the 'fact' that England were gifted the title in 1966 is accepted with a resigned shrug: these things are to be expected.

'England was the last World Cup before satellite television. In all the World Cups from '66 back, the host nation always won or was a Finalist,* because Fifa was always sweating that if the host nation didn't do well the tournament would be a failure. Now if France were to go out in the first round in 1998 it wouldn't matter – let them be knocked out. They've already sold the satellite TV rights for millions. So 1966 was the last World Cup before satellite, the president of Fifa was Stanley Rous, England, who had invented football, had the chance to be champions, which they had never been before, so you had a series of factors all pointing towards England being champions. And I'm not just saying it because of my position, because there were also problems in the Final with Germany, with the referee giving things in favour of England.'

But he harbours no bitterness against the host country. On the contrary, Rattín, the son of an Italian immigrant, is an avowed Anglophile.

* Not entirely true: France in 1938 and Switzerland in 1954 did not even make the semis.

'I'm a great admirer of England. In our history, in 1810, we threw out the English, but I think it was a mistake because we could have been like Australia or Canada, a different sort of country, without any doubt. If I had the chance to go to London to live, I'd do it tomorrow like a shot.'

He has been back to England on several occasions, most recently as Bobby Charlton's guest at Euro '96, and says he is always well received, that people who remember that Wembley game say they're sorry for what happened. In the 1970s he was hired as Sheffield United's representative in Latin America. In that capacity he arranged the transfer of Alex Sabella to the Yorkshire club, earning himself $70,000 in the process. Sabella didn't last long in Sheffield but the club made a tidy profit when they sold him on. Rattín was even involved in the initial contacts which led to the transfer of Osvaldo Ardiles and Ricardo Villa to Tottenham Hotspur.* His only regret is that he never learned the language.

As for Ramsey's 'animals' comment, Rattín laughs it off. 'We were a strong, hard team. I assure you that if we'd been playing at home we'd've been world champions. We had an average age of twenty-seven, twenty-eight. We have a saying here, which is a saying of mine, which goes: matches are won by kids, championships are won by men. You've got to have balls to be a champion. It's all right to have two or three or four kids in a team, but when the time comes for responsibility you need men. In our team we were men of character. What does being a man mean? To play calmly, to talk, to not feel the weight of responsibility, to do what you're told, that's character.'

Rattín wore the sky-blue-and-white stripes of Argentina for over ten years and was a stalwart of Boca Juniors for fifteen. Although he is synonymous with Boca, Rattín's association with Argentina's most popular club came about almost by chance. The most normal thing is for a boy to be indoctrinated by his father or other male relatives. But Rattín's father had no interest in football. Instead, it

* The final deal was done by their agent, Oscar Martínez.

was the club's blue and yellow colours* which caught his attention and secured his support as soon as he was old enough to think for himself. Long since retired, Rattín nevertheless knows that as long as there's a Boca fan around (which in Argentina is always) he need never buy his own drinks. With his jet-black hair and upright bearing, he remains an unmistakable figure. When I told my taxi driver I was going to interview Argentina's No. 10 of an earlier age, he gasped in awe. 'Rattín,' he told me solemnly, 'was a bulwark for Boca.' A tough, fearless character, Rattín embodied the type of player the Boca fans loved, and the Boca fans, as any Argentine will tell you, are The People. Their proud boast is that Boca are 50 per cent plus one of the population.

Boca were founded by Genoese immigrants in the working-class Buenos Aires neighbourhood of the same name. They are locked in an endless contest with River Plate, their rivals based in the north of the city, who are associated with the wealthy, although their origins too are in lowly Boca. For Rattín, the difference is not just one of class, it's a distinct outlook, a whole style of play.

'The Boca fan wants you to *transpirar la camiseta* [soak the shirt in sweat]. River fans, no. They want to see you play. Nutmegs, flicks, passes, while Boca fans are more after strength and character. The Boca fans, if you give your all on the pitch and you end up losing, they'll still applaud you. What they want is for you to give your all. If you come off sweating through your shirt, if you're dripping with sweat, they're happy.'

Rattín and Boca were made for each other. Together they won five Argentinian championships. He was a player for the big occasion – the bigger the stage, the more he revelled in the challenge, whether it was Wembley, the San Siro or the Maracanã. But for Rattín there is nothing to compare to the great derby of Argentinian football: Boca v River.

* According to the club's mythology, Boca's directors were divided on what the team colours should be and finally agreed that they would settle on those of the next ship to sail into the harbour, which turned out to be Swedish, bearing the national colours on its funnel.

'The whole country's paralysed, and I tell you sincerely, every time it comes around I wish I could go out and play in it, just for a little bit, just for fifteen minutes. It's something overpowering out on the field, and it's a rivalry which you can feel a week before and a week after the game. Boca–River is really a game worth seeing. I'd get friends of mine, people in other countries, calling to say, don't you lose now. Boca–River, the whole atmosphere – not the actual game, because the game is ugly, you're not going to see good football – but the overpowering atmosphere is something you never forget.'

In his 15 years with Boca, Rattín played in 27 *clásicos*, winning 12 and losing 5. Winning that one game could secure the team's position with their fans for a whole season. A defeat could be forgiven – eventually. 'In our times, if you lost, the week after – at least until Wednesday, Thursday – you didn't go out in the street,' Rattín recalls. 'Ah, but it was a lovely thing . . .'

Despite the intense rivalry, Rattín won the respect of River fans by not engaging in taunts and triumphalism when Boca were doing well. 'I believe that in life you reap what you sow. Don't do to others what you wouldn't like them to do to you. If I don't like you coming to Boca and doing a lap of honour, then I'm not going to do it when we win at another ground.

'One day in '65 we became champions, and we came to celebrate on a boat near the River stadium. People from *El Gráfico*, the most important magazine in Argentina, were there and they wanted to take photos of us with the River stadium in the background, where we'd won the championship a few hours before. I didn't want to. I didn't appear in the photo. The others did. I thought it wasn't ethical.'

The old dockside district of Boca is the poorest neighbourhood in Buenos Aires, with a quarter of its population living below the poverty line. It's always been a poor *barrio*, the first stop for the huddled masses arriving from Europe, particularly Italy. The football club's nickname, '*xeneixe*', is a word referring to the founders' Genovese roots. It's also famed as the artists' quarter and has enjoyed a second career as a tourist destination, with diesel-spewing coaches

49

regularly clogging the little streets with their tenement-style *conventillos*. But although the bright colours of the corrugated iron walls of the houses along the Caminito may have been freshly repainted for the benefit of the dollar-bearing visitors, the foetid stench wafting off the murky Riachuelo waterway is 100 per cent authentic: Boca can only stand so much prettification.

Boca's La Bombonera stadium rises up stark and unapologetic, not unlike Highbury, in the middle of residential streets. The locals wouldn't have it any other way. Inside the ground the feeling is similarly tight, close. The Uruguayan writer Mario Benedetti wrote that a stadium is 'the skeleton of a crowd'[1] and, even empty, La Bombonera gives a sense of the intimidating atmosphere that can be brought to bear on visiting teams. A high perspex screen completely surrounds the playing area.* Along one flank, the traditional stand has been dispensed with, and what looks like a block of flats takes its place, containing executive boxes and the like. Argentina's rulers have generally felt it wise to keep on the right side of the country's most popular club. The original ground was built with the help of a government loan granted by the president, General Agustín Justo, who laid the foundation stone, and two years later in 1940 opened the completed Bombonera. Justo cannily ensured that he was an honorary member of both Boca and River.

On one side of the ground Boca Juniors have their own small sporting complex, including a swimming pool and a training pitch. It's the second week of January and the first day of pre-season training for Boca Juniors. It should really be the halfway stage of the championship but, in 1991, the Argentine Football Association decided to split the season in two: the *Apertura* (Opening) and

---

* The first fence around a football pitch in Latin America – a 12-metre-high wire netting affair – was erected for the post-Olympic Argentina v Uruguay match at the ground of Sporting Barracas in 1924. Barriers between pitch and spectators were to become a fixture of Latin American football. 'It became a symbol, suggesting that the South American football crowd was more volatile than its Western European or North American counterpart.' Tony Mason, *Passion of the People?* (1995), page 34.

Clausura (Closing) championships. Boca were feeling the heat because not only had they had an indifferent *Apertura* campaign but River Plate had run away as champions. The first day of training is an event, and there seems to be a tacit agreement among the main Buenos Aires clubs to stagger its start so they all get a fair crack of the media coverage. All the main media organizations had turned out to witness the first signals emanating from the new coach Héctor 'Bambino' Veira, a Boca favourite as a player, who had replaced the former World Cup winning manager, Carlos Salvador Bilardo. Two hundred or so supporters sat in the training pitch's small stand beneath the blazing sun watching the squad being put through their paces, one or two shouting 'Shift that lard!' every time the players jogged around in front of their vantage point. After the session the media swarmed around Bambino Veira while the team got ready for the drive to the resort of Mar del Plata, where they were to take part in a pre-season tournament.

Boca would be starting the season without one of their most famous supporters, José Barritta, known as Grandad. He was awaiting trial with eight others for allegedly leading an ambush with guns of River Plate fans in 1994, killing two of them. (Barritta was subsequently jailed for thirteen years in May 1997 for heading an illegal organization and racketeering, but was cleared of murder.) Grandad was the leader of Boca's *barra brava* – a cross between a supporters' club and the mafia – having wrested control of the organization from its previous head, Quique the Butcher, in 1982. The *barras* are used, and surreptitiously financed, by some clubs to get behind the team at matches but also to get on a player's back if he's being troublesome over a contract or some other matter. The gangs are also freelance muscle for politicians and anyone else prepared to pay. Their Brazilian equivalents, the *torcidas organizadas*, operate in a similar manner,*

* In October 1997, Corinthians' 'Hawks of the Faithful' *torcida organizada* blocked the main Santo–São Paulo road after a 1–0 defeat in the port city and attacked their own team's bus with sticks and stones. Public prosecutors were seeking a court order to disband the fan club.

although the Argentinians are the undisputed continental leaders in the field.

The *barras bravas* got a major boost with the patronage of the military dictatorship. The generals were displeased by demonstrations of opposition when Argentina played abroad so they paid for several *barras bravas* in the early 1980s to be Argentina's loyal supporters at away games in Europe and to stamp on any dissent.

The *barras bravas* are a sort of Frankenstein monster which grew out of control. Now hooliganism is only a part of their repertoire as the gangs have diversified into various rackets. Barritta's Player No. 12 Foundation is reported to have amassed $3.5 million between 1991 and 1994 through extortion. But Boca is by no means the only club with a *barra brava* problem. The treasurer of Rosario Central, Roberto Muñoz, estimated that its *barra* was extorting $200,000 a year from the club in cash, free tickets and transport; a bizarre example of how Argentinian clubs have ended up actually paying their supporters. The *barra*'s members made even more money by selling on the free tickets the club gave them. 'They enter the stadium anyway because they know someone at the gate or they just push their way in,' said Muñoz.[2] Club officials and players alike are tapped for cash. Daniel Passarella, the current national coach, took the unusual step of thumping a fan who came pestering him for money while working for River Plate in the early 1990s. But for the most part, players pay up and accept the informal tax. Maradona is reported to have written out a cheque for $30,000 to the *barras* immediately after the 1986 World Cup triumph.

Diego Armando Maradona was the other notable absentee from Boca's roster as they faced the new season. Though on the club's books, he was at the time between comebacks. Boca's new chairman, Mauricio Macri, had said that Maradona would be welcomed back whenever he felt like turning up. To have said anything less of the club's, and the country's, living legend would have been to risk the outrage of the supporters. (For his part, Maradona said he had 'definitively broken off relations with Macri' in one of his periodic spats with authority.) But in January 1997 there was little danger of

Maradona turning up and jogging round the pitch with the others. Overweight, cocaine-addicted and, as he shortly afterwards told Chilean television, suicidal, Maradona was in no condition even to come and watch. Kicked out of the 1994 World Cup for testing positive to a mixture of five different substances, all variants of the banned stimulant ephedrine, he had served out a fifteen-month suspension from football protesting his innocence, always on the lives of his daughters, and with an unofficial (his ban applied to coaching too) and unsuccessful stint as a coach. His initial return to action had been shortlived as his old problems continued to swirl about him. A four-year prison sentence still hung over him for shooting at journalists with an airgun.

He eventually turned out for Boca seven months later. In the meantime, he had checked into a Swiss drug clinic to finally kick his cocaine habit, and then reached new levels of self-parody by hiring the disgraced Canadian sprinter Ben Johnson as his personal trainer. He also announced that he had had cosmetic surgery to remove a double chin, caused, he said, by his prodigious slimming regime.

On 24 August 1997 the 36-year-old Maradona finally made his long-awaited and spectacular comeback for Boca, scoring in a 4−2 win over Argentinos Juniors, his first club. Four days later the AFA announced that he had failed a dope test: traces of cocaine had been found in his urine. (A judge allowed Maradona to play on, pending his appeal.) Maradona himself said little, although he indicated that the choice of him for a supposedly random dope test had not been entirely coincidental. 'For a change they picked me. They were holding up the number 10.'

Maradona may well be paranoid but that doesn't mean they're not after him. The most popular view in Argentina is that his suspension in 1994 was payback for his criticisms of Fifa and for Argentina's performance in the Italian World Cup in 1990. In Mexico in 1986 Maradona had publicly criticized Fifa's arrangements which obliged players to perform in the searing heat of the middle of the day to accommodate European television schedules. Four years later a grimly determined Argentinian side had been a dark smudge on Fifa's showcase event. They qualified from their first-round group in third place, nicked a late goal after being outplayed by Brazil, scraped through their quarter-final on penalties after a 0–0 draw, knocked out the hosts on penalties in the semis and came close to repeating the feat against the Germans in the Final. The late penalty which stopped them has always looked iffy and, with the expulsion of two Argentinian players, is taken as further proof of an anti-Argentine conspiracy. After the game a tearful Maradona refused to shake the Fifa president's hand. With Maradona's approval, an Argentinian journalist who covered the 1994 World Cup wrote an imaginative account of the doping incident (in a novel called *Innocent*) in which Maradona was the victim of a CIA plot, with the drugs administered in a spiked communion host. The more sophisticated version suggests that as Maradona had been taking cocaine since his days at Barcelona in the early 1980s he could have tested positive, and probably did, in 1986 when he was the star of the World Cup, and at other times in the intervening years. According to this reasoning, when Fifa needed him, it was quite prepared to turn a blind eye to his peccadilloes.

Feeling discriminated against was nothing new for Maradona. Growing up in the slums of Villa Fiorito in a family originally from the provinces, he has said he felt looked down on as a *cabecita negra* – a little black face from outside the city. His lavish wedding in 1989 was sniffed at (by those not invited) as a gaudy, *nouveau riche* show. Ironically for a country which prizes its 'European' image, his dark, short, stocky Indian features would become an icon of Argentinian-ness, domestically on a par with Gardel, the great tango singer. Playing in Spain he would find himself referred to as a *sudaca*, a derogatory term for a Latin American.

Unlike most Latin American capitals, Buenos Aires looks like a European city, an artist's impression of a non-existent metropolis somewhere near the Franco-Italian border. Its broad avenues, its cosy coffee shops, its imposing buildings, all pay homage to turn of the century Paris and, like Paris, those who can, leave the capital in the heat of midsummer. The European impression diminishes when you get down to the level of the *barrios*, where most people live, and of which they tend to be fiercely proud.

Argentinians have got a bit of an image problem in the rest of Latin America. Across the continent the Argentinian is a byword for arrogance and condescension. Suffice it to say that a common euphemism for ego is 'the little Argentinian we all have inside us'. Argentinian jokes abound. (For example: How do you get twenty-four Argentinians in a Mini? First, you have to deflate them . . .) All of this is, of course, terribly unfair, a generalization based on a small sample of *porteños* from central Buenos Aires. Some people believe that something unpleasant happens to Argentinians as they go through passport control at Ezeiza airport, giving foreigners whose countries they visit a distorted impression of the national character. The main resentment against Argentinians derives from the impression that they believe they are Europeans marooned by a bizarre quirk of fate at the wrong end of the Americas.* In this mental geography the vast Atlantic Ocean is as nothing compared to the yawning chasm separating them from poor, backward and neighbouring Paraguay (where most people still speak the indigenous Guaraní language). They have a point, in that Argentina is probably the whitest country in Latin America, with a negligible black population, and its indigenous population is largely invisible in the capital, which is Argentina's face to the world. Argentinians either don't have, or don't care for, the knack of making themselves popular. When Argentina played West Germany in the 1986 World Cup Final, their fellow Latins in the largely Mexican crowd started cheering for the Germans. By contrast, when Brazil won the tournament in the same country sixteen years earlier they quickly won the hearts of their hosts. During the early stages of the 1970 tournament, the team appeared on the balcony of their hotel in Guadalajara wearing

* Argentinians, the saying goes, are Italians who speak Spanish and think they are English (and, it might be added, dream of Paris). In Italy it is said the Argentinians are Sicilians who speak . . . etc.

sombreros, and it wasn't long before Brazil were serenading the crowd with samba tunes. A grateful city responded by erecting a large monument to the Brazilian team outside the Jalisco stadium. In Sweden and Chile the Brazilians had courted local popularity by carrying a large flag of the host country around the stadium.

But if they are not loved, the Argentinians are certainly admired. The country has always been one of the most developed in Latin America and has been a leader culturally, economically and, with its sad history of military rule, politically. In football, Argentina is the team other countries on the continent have traditionally measured themselves against. Its players and coaches have been sought after in Latin America and beyond, which hasn't always been to the benefit of Argentinian football. One of the Argentina's biggest problems used to be that as soon as they got together a good team, Italy would come in and take their best forwards. Two of Argentina's 1930 World Cup finalists, Monti and Orsi, appeared for Italy in the 1934 Final in Rome while Argentina, understandably wary about having their players poached again, sent out what was virtually a reserve side in their one and only game and were consequently on the next boat home. Italy were still at it in 1957. Italian clubs snapped up Maschio, Sivori and Angelillo from the successful South American Championship team, and all three later appeared for the Azzurri. One of Argentina's and the world's greatest players, Alfredo Di Stéfano, 'the blond arrow', ended up playing for Spain.

Italy and Spain remain the destination of choice for virtually all Argentinians playing abroad. Despite the illustrious example of Ardiles and Villa and the ever-growing extent of the 'foreign legion' in British football, there is, at the time of writing, only one Argentinian playing in the English League. Mauricio Taricco plays full-back for Ipswich Town who bought him for £200,000 from Argentinos Juniors in Buenos Aires, the club for which Maradona made his professional debut at the age of 15. Before that Taricco had spent five years at River Plate having already played seriously for several years. Taricco's early start in the game is typical of Argentina, and Uruguay. Boys as young as five are taught not just basic skills, but tactical discipline and, in a sense, professionalism, in an environment of keen competition.

'I began at the age of 5 or 6, so I'm 23 now, and my experience runs from the age of 5 to 23,' states Taricco. 'In many other countries you start later. Believe it or not, when you start to play at 5 in a little club they make you mark your opponent, play the ball, so you start learning things that you'll use in the future. It's not a case of them putting you on a pitch at 5 years old and saying, Well, they're just kids . . . No. They give you an idea of how to get on a pitch and play.

'There they teach you to take good care of the ball. That's to say that the most important thing is to try to control it, to have possession of it, to make sure the opposition doesn't have it. When the opposition have it, to try to win it back. That's why you get a slower game, unlike here where you have the long ball sometimes and you're going forward. But there they say that the long ball is a pass to the opposition, because you can make a 10-metre pass which is safer than making a 50-metre pass. Here, the crowd often wants to see that. If you take too many touches in defence and you hold back too long, the people become impatient and want the team to push forward. Over there they don't pressure you so much about that. As long as you've got the ball the other team can't score. That's the way we think.'

Taricco enjoys his life in the Suffolk countryside but it's clear he has mixed feelings about English football. During his first season he found himself lucky to make it on to the bench in a team that was heading straight for the trapdoor to the 'First' Division. His new employers seem to have shared the traditional suspicion of the suitability of South American skills to an English winter, and a relegation dogfight. But those same skills would eventually make him a fixture at full-back.

Taricco is one of the few people in England who mourn the passing of the Anglo-Italian Cup, a competition for First Division teams more famous for small crowds and bad feeling than the football played in it. But for Taricco, who played in the final tournament, it was a chance to measure himself against the Italian clubs, some of them big clubs just visiting the lower division from Serie A, and also to get himself spotted. For Taricco, as for generations of Argentinians, playing in Italy (or Spain) remains the true index of footballing success.

'English football is good to watch, more exciting. Of course, if you boot the ball upfield and you've got the two or three players chasing after it, it's more exciting. Sometimes you look at Latin football, Argentinian football, and it's boring. You might go five minutes without the ball crossing the halfway line.' Taricco says that as a spectator he prefers the 'English style', but clearly to play that way offends his professional self-respect.

The attitude to possession is not the only cultural clash the Argentinian defender has come across in England.

'In Argentina when you're playing with the juniors, what they teach you, the coaches, is to win. You have to win. It doesn't matter what you do on the pitch as long as you win. They teach you that the result is what's important. And also it's important to play well. If you play well you'll get results. But sometimes it's not a question of playing well, it's a question of getting results, and taking advantage of every situation to get a result. In Argentina, and in loads of Latin countries, a team goes one up and they go on the defensive. Or someone taking a free-kick will take his time about it. Things that aren't done here. The people want you to carry on quickly. I'm against that. I believe that if you're winning it's the other team that's in a hurry.'

The issue took dramatic form in Taricco's first season in England, in 1995, when he was involved in an altercation with Sheffield United's captain, Billy Whitehouse, who was sent off after Taricco fell to the ground clutching his face. Taricco was accused, not least by United's then manager Dave Bassett, of having deliberately got Whitehouse sent off by feigning injury. 'It's a disgrace,' said Bassett. 'He pushed him away and he went down as if he had been punched.'[3] About this, Taricco is admirably candid.

'I had a problem with an opposing player and he pushed me. And when I got up he raised his hand to me and I threw myself to the ground. I talked to him. I said something to him. And he grabbed me and threw me to the ground. The ref saw him and sent him off. So everyone told me, "You're a cheat."'

Even Taricco's team-mates didn't disguise their disapproval. He can understand, but not sympathize with them.

'The mentality of the people is different. Here they don't accept that. I understand that. While I'm here I accept it, but I can't completely agree with it. If I have the chance to dive or to put it in with my hand without anyone seeing, well, fine, no one saw. If someone is really important in their team, I'll try to provoke him so that he retaliates and gets sent off. That's really disapproved of here, to get the other guy sent off. But that's an advantage that you can give the team because if you're playing against ten men, you've got an advantage. In Argentina it's accepted. If you get someone sent off, after the game the coach will see it as a good move.'

Of course, this sort of thing is not the exclusive preserve of the Argentinians. One of the most audacious feats of gamesmanship came in a vital World Cup qualifier between Brazil and Chile in 1989. Chile, needing a win to qualify ahead of Brazil, went behind to a Careca goal and were facing the end of their World Cup hopes. With 65 minutes gone, a flare from the Maracanã crowd landed in the Chilean penalty area and the goalkeeper, Roberto Rojas, went down poleaxed. He was stretchered off bleeding and his team-mates refused to play on. Serious consequences threatened for Brazil until it was discovered that the flare had landed nowhere near Rojas, who had cut himself with a blade concealed in his goalkeeping gloves. Chile's manager and physio were found guilty of complicity in the goalkeeper's deception and all three were banned. Brazil were awarded the match 2–0 and Chile were barred from taking part in the next World Cup.

Taricco's team-mates, he says, watched Argentina win a penalty from a dive in the Olympic Final against Nigeria, so they understand it's nothing personal: it's an Argentinian thing.*

---

* Anglo-Argentine cultural misunderstandings on the football field go back a long way. Playing against a Buenos Aires XI in 1929 Chelsea were booed for their tactic of shoulder-charging, viewed as unsporting in Argentina, and for which they were constantly penalized. The crowd, however, cheered when

Do Argentinians then see the English approach to fair play as a little stupid?

'Yes, totally. Not stupid, naïve. What we say is: what have they won? The title in 1966, that's all. That's the point of view in Argentina. You'll maybe say that we only won in 1986 because of the handball. OK, but we won. Many people will answer you that way.'

The quarter-final against England in the 1986 World Cup was in many ways the defining moment of Maradona's career. His first goal, handled into the net over the advancing goalkeeper, Shilton, fixed his image in the minds of many English people as a cheating Argie. Asked whether he handled after the game, Maradona replied: 'Maybe it was a little bit the hand of Diego, maybe a little bit the hand of God.' His manager, Carlos Bilardo, was similarly ambiguous. 'When it happened I felt it wasn't handball. But then after watching the playback, I thought, well, there was some doubt. Put it that way. I'm not saying yes or no,' he said. 'I never question referees' decisions,' he added, completely untruthfully.[4] What made it worse for the suffering English was Maradona's lack of remorse and his countrymen's unapologetic exultancy in the act. There, Maradona was seen as a playful kid – a *pibe* – who had tried it on and got away with it – therefore, good luck to him.[5] Craftiness, guile and ducking and diving (often literally) are the traditional skills in football, as in life, of the kids from the edges of society. Maradona was the Artful Dodger.

His second goal, in which he beat half the English team before slipping the ball into the net from close range, has been hailed as the best ever scored in a World Cup. Maradona takes up the story after receiving the ball in his own half: 'When I got the ball I saw that Reid could not catch me. And I felt the urge to run with the

----

the Argentinian international Luis Monti kicked Chelsea's centre-half in the groin, the latter fainting and having to be carried off. The Chelsea players were also showered with missiles, including stones and oranges. Brian Glanville recorded that 'A Chelsea defender showed his scorn for the barrage by catching one of the oranges, peeling it and then proceeding to eat it.' Brian Glanville, *Soccer Nemesis* (1955), pages 87–8; Tony Mason, *Passion of the People?* (1995), pages 105–6.

ball. I seemed to leave everyone behind. No one could touch me. When Fenwick tried to stop me I pushed the ball forward. He tried to foul me but I just kept going. When I faced Shilton I kept control of the ball for as long as I could. He couldn't work out which way I was going to turn. When I passed him the blond No. 6 tried to foul me but I had so much momentum that I held him off and I pushed the ball into the net with my left foot. It was the dream goal everyone wants to score in any game. I have to thank God that I scored it in a World Cup.'[6]

Maradona scored a somewhat similar goal in the next round against Belgium, and was the outstanding player of the tournament. The official World Cup film was called *Hero*, and was a homage to the little Argentinian who had made their competition a success. No one, including Fifa, was inclined to judge his first goal harshly. The July 1986 issue of *Fifa News* was unequivocal: 'Diego Maradona's football in Mexico was honest.'[7] Maradona was a football genius and could be pardoned his little lapses.

Argentina were on the end of some poetic justice for the Hand of God goal in 1995 when they faced Brazil in the quarter-final of the Copa América in Ecuador. At 2–1 up, Argentina were minutes away from a place in the semis when the Brazilian forward Tulio grabbed the equalizer. Grabbed was the appropriate word, since everybody in the ground except the referee and his linesmen saw that he had pulled the ball down with his hand before shooting. Brazil went on to win on penalties and the unrepentant Brazilian press celebrated the 'Hand of Tulio' goal. Few in Argentina appreciated the irony.*

It was all a long way from the first meetings between the countries, which took place in 1914 in an altogether more Corinthian era. Brazil lost the first official encounter in Buenos Aires by three goals

---

* President Carlos Menem called it 'monumental robbery'. 'Have a look at the video. Not only was the goal offside, the Brazilian striker also controlled it with his arm and then scored.' Many Argentinian newspapers referred to the 'hand of the devil'.

to nil but did better in the next match, which took place the following day after a hearty evening banquet at the La Plata Fencing and Gymnastic Club. Brazil were one up when, late in the second half, Argentina put the ball in the net. The referee gave a goal but the Argentinian captain, Gallup Lanús, refused to accept it, saying that the Argentinian scorer had controlled the ball with his hand. Brazil won 1–0 and the sporting *porteño* crowd chaired the Brazilian goalkeeper from the field.

Argentinian and Brazilian sides had met before then but in circumstances which had yet to acquire the status of a formal international. One such game took place in Rio de Janeiro when Argentina's President Julio Roca brought a football team with him on an official visit to help cement friendship between the two countries. At half-time the Argentinians were leading the locals 3–0. Roca descended from the stands to congratulate his players on their splendid performance. But as he left he pointed out that the Brazilians would take it very badly if they lost, particularly by so many. More diplomatic, he said, to let them win. 'Do it for the fatherland, lads!' he urged. There are different accounts of the final score: some say it ended 3–3, others that Argentina went on to win 4–0. But all agree that the astute old soldier had ordered his team to take the fall. It would not be the last case of political interference in Argentinian football.*

Roca was the first Argentinian leader to realize the potential of the new mass game. He was the first head of state to attend a football match, between the visiting English professionals Southampton and the local champions Alumni, in 1904. Also in attendance was his minister of war, General Pablo Ricchieri, who had promoted this and other 'English exercises' with a view to forging a 'strong, manly' population. Eight thousand people saw the visitors win 2–1, but for Roca the event was a success, placing him publicly among Buenos Aires high society at a fashionable international sporting occasion. The press were struck by 'the enthusiasm of the ladies for the beautiful game'.[8]

* Roca later donated a cup bearing his name to be contested in challenge matches between Argentina and Brazil.

The political potential of football is obvious. A mass activity, accessible to all, which moves great passions and can unite vast numbers of people to a common purpose. In Argentina, the close relationship between football and politics is taken as a given. It is said in jest[9] (probably) that after the leaders of the Senate, the Chamber of Deputies and the Supreme Court, the head of the AFA is fourth in line to the presidency. Many on the left have traditionally seen football as another opium of the people, a mixture of alienation and escape valve. But no politician is going to get very far in Latin America taking a negative attitude to the game. The generals who snatched power in Argentina in the mid-1970s found in their in-tray the 1978 World Cup which had been awarded to the country under the government of Isabel Perón, widow of the strongman of Argentinian politics. Quickly they seized upon the tournament as a means of rallying the population to the national 'process', as their rule was known. In doing so, they were taking their cue from the greatest politician-in-uniform in Argentina's history, General Juan Domingo Perón, who throughout his career was adept at associating himself with sporting success.

Perón had the European examples of Mussolini and Hitler (the 1934 World Cup and the 1936 Olympics were the most high-profile examples of their use of sport for political ends) to inspire his vision of a nation strengthened by sport and united behind their leader, the 'first sportsman', as official propaganda had it. One of his many sporting pronouncements stressed the nation-building qualities of sport: 'We are going to set to work to form sportsmen . . . In this it is necessary that all of us – government, people, teachers, army, all the forces of the nation – set ourselves to the task of forming good and strong men; in this way, we will triumph.'[10]

Perón set up many of Argentina's sporting organizations, including the Olympic committee. Perón's first love was fencing, a sport at which he had excelled as a young officer (he was also a handy boxer). His football sympathies are disputed. Some say that as an aspiring politician he adopted Boca Juniors as a populist gesture to bring him closer to the masses. But for most people he was and always will be a fan of Racing, a club which won the title three times (in 1949, 1950 and 1951) at a time when Perón was at the height of his powers. Still others say he favoured no team in particular, although he did enjoy good football. The mystery is appropriate to a man who built his political career on being all things to all men, the people's dictator, combining apparently contradictory political forces. The president's wife naturally did her bit: the Eva Perón Foundation organized an annual national championships for children's teams – and supplied all their kit – which brought together hundreds of thousands of youngsters.

Curiously for a government which paid so much attention to sport, Argentina under Perón failed to take part in the 1950 and 1954 World Cups and missed several South American Championships in the period. Valentín Suárez, the president of the AFA, said there were many reasons why Argentina did not travel to Brazil in 1950. The AFA was in dispute with the CBD (Brazilian Sports Federation) and some also felt that with so many of its best players abroad (particularly in the wake of the 1948–9 strike which saw many players go to Colombia) Argentina was not in a position to field its best team. 'Also,' Suárez added, 'mixed with these reasons were the political ones . . . and even though the government's opinion wasn't decisive when they suggested that Argentina stay out of the Cup, the suggestion was respected.' One reason for the government's 'suggestion' was that having built up such an aura of sporting success around Argentina, the possibility of defeat in an important international event held potentially serious implications. They had a point. Having thought themselves worldbeaters in their splendid isolation, Argentina's participation in the 1958 World Cup in Sweden turned into a national trauma, with the team knocked out in the first round after losing 6–1 to Czechoslovakia.

But still, for the junta of the 1970s the World Cup was a great opportunity, and they were far from the first to hit upon the idea that sporting success could be turned to political advantage. The military regime in Brazil had tried its best to capitalize on the national team's success in Mexico in 1970. The squad's theme tune '*Pra Frente*

Brasil!' (Forward Brazil!), with its references to 'ninety million in action' and the whole of Brazil lending a hand and feeling the same emotion, expressed the military's ideal of a society moving as one disciplined force and was used as a general pro-government rallying cry.*

Following the Argentine example, Uruguay, with its own murderous military junta, tried to repeat the trick by staging a *Mundialito* of former World Cup winners in 1980 (only England failed to turn up). They, like their counterparts across the River Plate, were out of power within five years.

A stadium full of Argentines rallying behind the nation in the form of the *selección* (national team) was greatly to be desired, but crowds can also be unpredictable, undisciplined. When President Miguel de la Madrid opened the 1986 World Cup in Mexico, his speech was drowned out by boos from a packed Aztec stadium. But the Argentinian crowds devoted themselves to cheering on their team, an activity the military sought to direct for the national 'process'.† After Argentina's 3–1 victory over Holland in the Final, President Videla addressed the nation, summing up the junta's fascist aspirations for the World Cup win. 'The shout of "Argentina" that came from our hearts, that blue and white flag that we had in our hands, are signs of a profound reality that exceeds the limits of a sporting event. Do not let these feelings fall in the daily routine, because they are the best proof of our identity and our will to succeed. The entire nation is triumphant. The entire population

---

* Brazil's dismal showing in the 1974 World Cup produced alternative lyrics: '*Todos juntos de revólver na mão/Esperando o seu Zagallo descer do avião*' ('Everyone together with guns in their hands/Waiting for Zagallo to get off the plane').

† In 1979 a Maradona-led Argentina won the World Youth Cup in Japan. It was the same day as an Organization of American States committee arrived in Buenos Aires to investigate the junta's appalling record of abuse, and human rights protesters had gathered in the Plaza de Mayo in front of the presidential palace. Pro-government radio called on the people to come to the Plaza de Mayo to celebrate the team's victory, thus swamping the show of dissent.

should now assume a new goal: creativity and hard work. Argentinians: we have been able to succeed. Let's also be capable, with the help of God, to drive the Nation to larger objectives.' This spirit of national unity generated by the World Cup victory was later channelled into the reconquest (or invasion) of the Malvinas (or Falklands).*

The Montoneros, the Peronist urban guerrilla movement which served as the pretext for the arrest and disappearance of thousands of so-called 'subversives', called a truce for the World Cup, arguing that world attention would thus be focused on the junta's crimes. A boycott by foreign teams never seemed likely, although four years earlier the Soviet Union had forfeited the chance of a World Cup place by refusing to play an eliminator in Santiago's National stadium where political prisoners had been interned, many never to reappear, after General Augusto Pinochet's 1973 coup.

The organization of the '78 tournament was not without violence. General Omar Actis, the head of the Ente Autárquico Mundial '78, responsible for organizing Argentina's World Cup, was assassinated on the way to his first press conference, but he was probably the victim of inter-service rivalry over the kudos of leading the great national project than an attack from the left. Responsibility for organizing the event passed to an admiral, Carlos Alberto Lacoste.

No expense was spared to present the best image of Argentina to the world. Despite inflation running at 165 per cent, three new stadia were built, at Mendoza, Córdoba and Mar del Plata. Television, telephone and telex facilities had to be completely overhauled. A US public relations company, Burson-Marsteller, was given a million-dollar contract to buff up Argentina's lamentable image. The finance minister, Juan Alemann, put the cost of the project at $700 million, much more than the subsequent cost of the 1982 Cup in Spain. He called it 'the most visible and indefensible case of non-

---

* Likewise, when Maradona was suspended at the 1994 World Cup, the Argentinian press found the scenes of grief comparable only to the death of Perón and the surrender in the Malvinas/Falklands. *Clarín*, 20 October 1996.

priority spending in Argentina today'.[11] Mindful of Perón's example, the generals decided that it was worth it, but only if the national team were successful.

The generals had put their faith in a talented young manager, César Luis Menotti. They also took out a little insurance. Eight years later the *Sunday Times* published what it said were details of how Argentina bribed Peru on the eve of a crucial match. Argentina needed to beat Peru by at least four goals to overtake Brazil and so reach the Final. The Argentinians knew the precise scale of the task in front of them because Brazil's match against Poland had conveniently been scheduled for earlier in the day. Peru had looked a decent side but on the night in Rosario they were torn apart 6–0. Some Peruvian players were dropped, others played out of position. Peru's Argentinian-born goalkeeper was a flimsy barrier. The newspaper's anonymous sources said that Argentina's central bank released $50 million in credits to Peru and that Argentina shipped 35,000 tons of grain, and possibly weapons as well.*

It is impossible to say with any certainty where the truth lies. But an air of suspicion has always hung around this game, starting from the timing of the kick-off, which conferred an advantage on the host nation before a ball was kicked. On the other hand, Argentina had a good team that had been closeted together for months before the tournament and played before fervent crowds to a dazzling tickertape welcome. They also had the shortest shorts of the post-war era (since the Argentinians' silky black hot pants, shorts have been in a long, slow process of expansion). In Mario Kempes, recalled from his Spanish club, and Leopoldo Luque they had a formidable strike force, while Ardiles in midfield and René Houseman on the wing gave them a touch of class. The flair of that team, wrapped up in the tickertape exuberance of the fervent home crowds, has in Argentina come to represent the highest aspirations of artistic football.

The team was a testament to Menotti's footballing philosophy,

---

* A Colombian drug mafioso, Gonzalo Rodríguez Gacha, also tried to influence the result, but a suitcase full of cash was intercepted in the United States.

which he pointedly said drew on the finest traditions of the Argentinian style. But another manager, Carlos Salvador Bilardo, showed that a very different but, in many ways, equally Argentinian approach could be successful.[12] Under Menotti, Argentina won the World Cup on home soil in 1978; eight years later his successor, Bilardo, repeated the feat in Mexico. And as far as most people are concerned, that's where the similarity ends. Menotti is associated with teams in which players with skill and flair are given free rein; Bilardo's teams are dedicated to winning at all costs. Menotti is the articulate, left-wing intellectual, the philosopher-prince of football; Bilardo, who lists his hobby as watching football, is the tough soldier who has risen through the ranks and knows that it's not about the taking part, it's the winning.

Bilardo's single-minded desire to win is almost painfully apparent in his frenetic touchline performances. He has abused his players for kicking the ball off for an injured opponent to receive treatment. When details of one of his post-match harangues at his players appeared in the press he was so furious he wanted to haul in the journalists who covered the club to find out which of his team was a 'squealer' (the club directors had to talk him out of that one). One of Bilardo's big bugbears concerns the swapping of shirts after the match. He is against it. As manager of Boca in 1996 he went on the radio during a losing streak fresh from giving his players a seventy-five-minute earbashing. 'Today I told the players: the Boca shirt costs $30,000, the price of a car . . . They must wear it with pride, take the field with it. Whoever swaps it must pay $30,000 for it. And whoever swaps it I'll report to the police for robbery and theft. Because the team belongs to Boca. If the opposition want a Boca shirt let them go to the shop and buy one . . .'[13] (Sir Alf Ramsey perhaps knows how he feels: after the England–Argentina match in the 1966 World Cup he ran on to the pitch to stop Roger Hunt swapping his shirt with an Argentinian opponent.) Menotti took a more relaxed attitude: 'The Independiente shirt costs 30 pesos and we have them in all sizes,' he quipped. 'We'll listen to offers.'[14]

Bilardo played in the extremely successful Estudiantes de La Plata side of the 1960s. Estudiantes had been an undistinguished team until the arrival of a new manager, Osvaldo Zubeldía. He galvanized the team and took it to the Argentinian title, then on to win the Copa Libertadores, the South American Club Championship, four years on the trot and ultimately to become World Club Champions, beating Manchester United in 1968. But while the team was successful, many found its methods distasteful. Its was a wrecking style, designed to do everything to stifle the opposition, provoke them and put them off their game. When Bobby Moore spoke of 'the South Americans' of the 1960s, he was talking about a style which reached its apogee in Estudiantes: 'They were sure as hell not very pleasant to play against. They did do nasty things. They did tug your hair, spit at you, poke you in the eyes and kick you when the ball was miles away and no one was looking . . . their attitude was simply not to lose. Not at any cost.'[15]

Reporting on the first leg of Estudiantes' 1968 meeting with Manchester United, the *Guardian* wholeheartedly endorsed Ramsey's 'animals' comment of two years earlier. 'It is not the philosophy of the Argentines so much as the cynical execution of their ideas that rankles so badly. Their twin aims here last night were to intimidate and destroy.' The tackling 'was at times waist high' and was accompanied by provocative pinching of arms, ruffling of hair and whacking across the head. Nobby Stiles, who had been butted and punched in the eye, was sent off for disputing an offside decision. 'If you held the ball you were in danger of your life,' said United manager, Sir Matt Busby. The *Guardian* singled out two 'villains of the piece' – Carlos Pachamé and Bilardo.[16]

A dogged midfielder, Bilardo was an integral member of that side. 'I played against him many times,' recalls Antonio Rattín. 'He was *tramposo* [sneaky]. He was always up to something. Tricky: he'd pull your shirt, pretend to be hit, anything.

'The law is like this,' Rattín explains, drawing a line with his hand. 'Bilardo was always here [just over the line], never here [on the line], never here [just behind the line], and you get to the point where it wears you out.'

Bilardo put the lessons he learnt from his master Zubeldía into practice in the 1970s when he took over at Estudiantes, having hung up his boots at the age of 30. Meanwhile, Menotti, who had played for his hometown club of Rosario Central, was making his name at Huracán, bringing the championship to a club that had won nothing for forty-five years. It was his success at Huracán which caught the AFA's eye. After the 1978 triumph Menotti led the team again in 1982, but the Argentinians' defence of their title was a disappointment and ended early. Bilardo was appointed to succeed him.

Today the Menottistas and the Bilardistas are as implacably opposed as Swift's Big-Endians and Little-Endians, but it was not always so. On 30 January 1979, for example, Bilardo said: 'At home I've got a tape of the 1978 Final and every two or three days I watch it again. *That's* football.'[17] Bilardo, though never a friend, was an admirer of Menotti, despite his background. In 1983 Bilardo took a trip to Europe and used the opportunity to talk with some of the world's great football authorities, such as Di Stéfano, the Italian World Cup winning manager Enzo Bearzot and, in the Hotel Arena where his Barcelona team were staying before their match with Betis, Menotti. It was Saturday 12 March and it was the last time they had anything like a civilized conversation.

Although Menotti told him that Zubeldía's Estudiantes had set back the development of Argentinian football by at least ten years, the two parted on good terms. Menotti urged him to call up Tarantini, briefly a Birmingham City player, and Gatti, whom he called a phenomenon. Bilardo listened intently. Menotti had kind words for his successor in the run-up to his team's first match in a friendly in Chile. But when the teamsheet appeared, neither Tarantini nor Gatti were on it. The team's next match was a warm-up for a tournament in Toulon against the Spanish club side, Valladolid, a game they lost. Afterwards, Menotti criticized the new manager in caustic terms.

'That day,' Bilardo later recalled, 'everybody asked me if I'd read [the Buenos Aires daily] *Clarín*. I took the phone off the hook and sat down to read the story. I got mad. The next day I had training and I went to bed and took a Lexotanil just to make sure. It had no effect. I got up and took another, and to make sure, I read the report again. After that I couldn't sleep the whole night, I was poisoned.'[18]

Since then Bilardo's and Menotti's status as leaders of what are effectively two opposed theological schools has informed the way Argentina thinks about football. Bilardo preaches justification by results alone, while Menotti insists on the importance of doing good works. Both men expressed their ideas at a recent seminar of managers in Argentina. Menotti spoke in philosophical terms:

'I maintain that a team is above all an idea, and more than an idea it is a commitment, and more than a commitment it is the clear convictions that a trainer must transmit to his players to defend that idea.

'So, my concern is that we trainers don't arrogate to ourselves the right to remove from the spectacle the synonym of festival, in favour of a philosophical reasoning which cannot be sustained, which is to avoid taking risks. And in football there are risks because the only way you can avoid taking risks in any game is by not playing . . .

'And to those that say that all that matters is winning, I want to warn them that someone always wins. Therefore, in a 30-team championship, there are 29 who must ask themselves: what did I leave at this club, what did I bring to my players, what possibility of growth did I give to my footballers? . . .

'I start from the premiss that football is efficacy, I play to win, as much or more than any other egoist who thinks he's going to win by other means. I want to win the match. But I don't give in to tactical reasoning as the only way to win, rather I believe that efficacy is not divorced from beauty . . .'

Bilardo made clear that his approach to football was based in his own intense competitiveness: 'I like being first. You have to think about being first. Because second is no good, being second is a FAILURE . . .

'For me, it's good that if you lose you should feel bad; if you want you can express it crying, shutting yourself away, feeling bad

71

. . . because you can't let people down, the fans, everyone, the person who signed you. I'd feel very bad if we lost a match and that night I'm seen eating out calmly in some place. I can't allow it. That's why you have to make sacrifices and work hard to improve constantly in football where there are fewer and fewer spaces . . .

'I'm an optimist. For me football will get better and better. But I also know that it will make more and more demands. I even believe that the difference between defenders and attackers will disappear. I see the teams of the twenty-first century made up of a goalkeeper and ten players. Without fixed positions. Without specialists. Each one of them knowing everything. In that sort of football the ones who know most will prevail. And they will need to know more and more, because space will be closed down more and more. The one who has the most technical resources will win. And the one with the technical resources will not stick to one style. He'll have all of them at his disposal. And if they don't exist, he'll create them.'

So far, so straightforward. But contradictions abound. The most obvious one was that in winning the World Cup Menotti, the leftwing intellectual, carried out the wishes of the military dictatorship. On this most touchy subject, Menotti has defended himself over the years, arguing that his free-flowing brand of football expresses the opposite of the military's regimented approach to politics.* There is an element of justification after the fact in this, but there again, was Menotti to abdicate his career because of the political climate in which he found himself?

Menotti is the great prophet of skill, of the football genius, but in 1978 he left out of the World Cup squad the most skilful player of his, and possibly any other, generation: Maradona. True, he was only 17 at the time, but so was Pelé in 1958. By contrast, Bilardo, the hard-faced pragmatist, won the World Cup precisely by giving Maradona his head and came within a dodgy penalty of repeating his success four years later. Critics argue that without Maradona the

* As Simon Kuper (1994) observes, Argentina's exciting style was in fact just what the military would have wanted.

team would have won nothing, but it's also true that Bilardo recognized what he had on his hands, made him captain and fashioned a team around him.* When Menotti had the chance to work with Maradona in 1982 in Spain, his star player was a muted presence, ending the tournament by being sent off after jamming his studs into a Brazilian's crotch in frustration. And Menotti's team was no stranger to a bit of chicanery. The start of the 1978 Final was delayed as the Argentinian team left the Dutch standing around on the pitch for five minutes before they finally came out. Then the Argentinian players protested for several minutes about the lightweight cast René Van de Kerkhof wore on his injured forearm, even though he had played with it in an earlier round. The pliable referee forced the Dutch player to have the thing bandaged up, although what this was supposed to achieve is something of a mystery.

Strangely, since their bust-up in 1983 Menotti's and Bilardo's teams had never met in competition. That was until Sunday 3 November 1996. What would normally have been a fairly run-of-the-mill mid-table fixture in the Argentinian *Apertura* championship became the centre of a feverish media build-up because of the identity of the two managers. It was a fixture that had been awaited for years, and at one stage had seemed unlikely to occur. Menotti had only just returned to managing three months earlier, having spent two years out of the game working for a television station. For days the newspapers devoted pages to the impending duel between 'Big Nose' Bilardo's Boca and 'Skinny' Menotti's† Independiente, retailing the two men's less than complimentary views of each other.

Menotti: 'All our lives we were different ideologically. I do remember my first confrontation with a different style. It was with Osvaldo Zubeldía. But we had a different relationship. Our differences were to do with football and nothing more ... In this case, we're divided on everything.'[19]

* Maradona later played for Bilardo at Sevilla in Spain and at Boca Juniors.
† Bilardo's own nickname for Menotti is 'Little Radish' because, he explained, 'he's red on the outside and white on the inside'. *Olé*, 30 October 1996.

Bilardo: 'Menotti failed in '82. He failed at Barcelona, at Atlético Madrid and at Boca. And at River he sold Pumpido and Ruggeri because they were "our" players.'[20]

Menotti: 'With Bilardo we're irreconcilable. Never in my life will I say hello to him.'[21]

Bilardo: 'Football is played to win. Or not? Shows are for the cinema, for the theatre . . . Football is something else. Some people are very confused.'[22]

Menotti: 'Would I sit down to have a discussion with Bilardo? No, I'd sit down with Alsogaray and discuss a model of society. As Sábato said, some things you don't discuss, you punish.'[23]

Friends and allies of both men were consulted for their view of the debate. Angel Cappa, manager of the Spanish team Las Palmas, summed up the Menottista view of the Bilardistas' pragmatism: 'They just eat and defecate.'[24]

Before the match, Bilardo was hyperactive. You got the impression that if teacups were to be found in Argentinian changing rooms, Bilardo would smash them. When the game started Bilardo was his characteristic self, gesticulating, spitting, screaming at his players. Menotti, equally characteristically, was the opposite. Sitting, almost reclining, wearing jeans and a grey jacket, he only stirred to light himself another ciggie.

The game was close-fought and decided by a single goal. The referee booked nine (five Boca, three Independiente) and sent off three (two Boca, one Independiente). After 21 minutes of the second half Burruchaga swung over a well practised free-kick, Arzeno, the big centre-half, nodded it down at the far post and Guerrero scored from close range. Menotti's team won the victory in classic Bilardo fashion, with a training-ground set-piece. Menotti uncharacteristically leapt to his feat to celebrate the goal. For Bilardo it was a particularly bitter blow. After winning the World Cup Final he said he hadn't enjoyed it at all because the Germans had scored twice from dead-ball situations. When Guerrero missed a sitter, a furious Menotti − in best Bilardo style − pulled him off, in all sending on three subs in the later stages to defend the lead. Twenty-three years earlier, when Menotti and Bilardo had last faced each other as managers, the result was the same, with Huracán's Carlos Babington securing victory over Estudiantes from a free-kick.

As a showdown it settled little, except that Menotti's team won. But then, as he would say, that's not entirely the point. Bilardo lost, which for him is everything. What it maybe showed is that it's not so easy to keep these two apparently opposite approaches to the game apart. For his followers, Menotti is the Dr Jekyll of Argentinian football; Bilardo, its Mr Hyde. But Jekyll and Hyde were, of course, two sides of the same man.

3: The United Colours of Football

SOMETIMES IT'S NOT the football which makes a game memorable. The visit of São Paulo's Portuguesa to the crumbling Edwardian elegance of Fluminense's Laranjeiras ground in September 1995 produced little in the way of action to excite the crowd. In a game played largely at walking pace, neither goal was seriously threatened. The rhythmic skills, the flicks, feints and dribbles for which Brazilian football is famous, were sadly absent. Then, with 15 minutes to go, the visitors scored, provoking a belated sense of urgency in the home side, a handful of chances, but no goals. And so it finished 1–0, but the incident that drew the biggest cheer all afternoon had little to do with the players' efforts. Shortly before the goal, a visiting player had gone down injured. The Portuguesa trainer, a black man with a bald head, had to jog all the way around the pitch to the opposite touchline to administer the magic sponge. As he reached the far side, beneath the home terraces, empty plastic bottles, litter, bags of talcum powder and assorted other projectiles began to land around him, and on the line of policemen, who looked on indulgently. Then, almost as the trainer reached his injured man – plaf! – a big bag of talc caught him full on the head, turning his black pate white. The crowd roared.

It was no coincidence that the Fluminense fans were lobbing talcum powder. Talc or, more accurately, rice powder – *pó-de-arroz* – has been the club's unofficial emblem for years. Fluminense was one of the last clubs to accept black players. But even before it fully abandoned the colour bar, the pressure for results meant that gradually some light-skinned mulattos who could pass for white were taken on. In 1916 they signed Carlos Alberto, a mulatto, from

América. Before the game he would talc his face with rice powder to lighten his appearance. Despite the pre-match ritual, as he sweated, so the rice powder would be washed away. Even without the perspiration, his freakish pallor was all too obvious. Spotting this, the opposition fans began shouting *'pó-de-arroz'*, a cry which greeted his appearance on the pitch ever after. The nickname soon became transferred to the team as a whole.

Fluminense has the most aristocratic roots of all Rio de Janeiro's teams and retains its upper-class image to this day. Its great rivals are Flamengo, the most popular club in Brazil, and therefore in South America. Flamengo's mascot is the *urubu*, the type of scraggy black vulture which can be seen circling over the shanty-towns on Rio's hillsides, where the bedrock of the club's support lies. Why a vulture? Well, it's not because it scavenges, not because it flies and not because it's ugly. The *urubu*'s key characteristic in terms of Flamengo was that it is black, and so, its rivals sneeringly maintained, were most of its supporters.

Both *pó-de-arroz* and the *urubu* started out as terms of abuse but both were quickly adopted as a badge of honour by the intended targets. The *urubu* even became a popular cartoon character, drawn by the cartoonist Henfil. What they also have in common is their allusion to race, the issue which goes to the heart of Brazilian society and which has undoubtedly been a key factor in the formation of Brazil's distinctive brand of football.

'Samba', as in 'samba skills' or 'samba stars', has become a journalistic commonplace, inseparable from stories about Brazilians and their football. But, like most clichés, it has its grain of truth. As one Brazilian sociologist has written, 'A country that has samba, capoeira, *frevo* and *chorinho* has to play a different kind of football.'* In Latin America, Brazil is almost a case apart. It's not just that they speak Portuguese and not Spanish, and that as the fifth-largest country in

* *Frevo* and *chorinho* are samba-based musical styles, the former lively, the latter slow and sentimental. Capoeira is a style of dance-cum-martial art, like the drum-based samba, brought over by African slaves.

the world it dwarfs its neighbours. Brazil is such a huge country, with such contrasting topography and with such a diverse population – including Africans, Portuguese, Germans, Poles, not to mention the indigenous people – that it's a wonder the whole thing hasn't split asunder into its component parts long before now. Pretty much the only thing that all Brazilians have in common is that they all speak Portuguese and they all want Brazil to win the World Cup.*

As well as being the biggest, Brazil is also the blackest country in Latin America. At first glance Brazil looks like a country that has got it right on race. Unlike the United States, race is not a political fault-line. Race riots are virtually unheard of. Generations of mixed marriages between various ethnic groups mean you can find skin tones in almost any shade you care to choose, and all of them are represented on the football field, arguably the most integrated area of Brazilian society. The problem, in a country with one of the most skewed income distributions in the world, is the correlation between race and class. It's true that there is no shortage of poor whites alongside the millions of black and mixed race people below the poverty line. But if you're black and rich, then your name is probably Pelé.

Pelé, for many the greatest footballer ever, sums up a lot of Brazil's contradictions about race. Pelé became a successful businessman after his playing days were over and is at the time of writing Brazil's special minister for sport and the only black person in the cabinet.

Of 513 congressmen, only 11 are black. But, as Pelé noted, 'the lack of black congressmen has a good side in that today, politicians have a bad reputation of being corrupt. At least blacks don't carry that burden.'

Blacks and mixed race Brazilians make up nearly half of the 155 million population, although many believe the real figure is higher – maybe 60 per cent – because of the imprecision of racial categories and a general reluctance among people to identify themselves as

* It also shows why the isolated Amazonian Indians are only Brazilian in a formal sense.

black or 'coloured'. They are the descendants of some three to six million African slaves brought to Brazil (America's biggest slave importer) to work on sugar and tobacco plantations and in the gold and diamond mines.

Average black income is half that of whites; almost half of the black and mulatto population subsists at levels at or below the minimum wage. Black families make up 60 per cent of the 10 million poorest Brazilian families. This is in a country where, according to a recent UN report, the richest 10 per cent earn 30 times as much as the poorest 40 per cent (in neighbouring Argentina the ratio is 10 times). And it is getting worse, not better.* The result is that almost any index of deprivation you care to take shows a sharp correlation with skin colour, with blacks at the bottom of the heap. A quarter of white Brazilians are illiterate, while approximately 40 per cent of their black counterparts cannot read. And black Brazilians die on average 13 years younger than white Brazilians. As one columnist in the Rio de Janeiro daily *Jornal do Brasil* wrote: 'When Nelson Mandela was here he said he felt at home. He was being nice . . . He might also have been saying he felt he was in a disguised South Africa.'

The link between class, or at least social status, and race remains strong. Nearly all apartment buildings in Brazil have two lifts, and black people tend to find themselves directed by the porter to the 'service' elevator. But a rich and famous man like Pelé does not have to suffer such indignities. Success can whiten a black man's image. A famous story is told of Robson, one of the few black footballers to play for Fluminense in the 1950s. He was driving with a white team-mate, Orlando, when a black couple, rather the worse for wear, stepped in front of the car without looking – even as the vehicle screeched to a halt they carried on oblivious. Orlando began shouting at them, but Robson calmed him, saying, 'I was black once and I know what it's like.'[1]

* The 1993 census showed the richest 10 per cent held half the country's wealth, up from 48 per cent a decade earlier. The poorest 10 per cent owned just 0.7 per cent, down from 0.9 per cent.

Nevertheless, the myth of the racial democracy is strong, not least among those who appear most disenfranchised. Brazilian blacks, despite their successes in those areas traditionally for the marginalized – sport and entertainment – have not forged a strong racial consciousness. Working-class black people will tend to identify themselves in class terms rather than racially. This is, of course, an impeccably Marxist line.

In Salvador, the capital of Bahia state, the black heart of Brazil, it is Bob Marley whose face adorns T-shirts and whose music blares from ghetto blasters around the old colonial district of Pelourinho. Bahia has no shortage of its own black music, and socially conscious music, but it seems to be Marley's status as an international champion of the black man which has secured his cult status in Salvador so many years after his death. There is no comparable Brazilian figure.

The beginnings of a racial consciousness in politics have developed in the aftermath of the transition to civilian rule in 1985. An important landmark was the three-hundredth anniversary of the death in 1695 of Zumbi, the last leader of an independent black state at Palmares, which lasted for a century. It was at the commemoration of Zumbi's death in an ambush by Brazilian colonial forces that a Brazilian president said the unsayable: that the myth of a racial democracy was false. 'Yes, there is prejudice,' said President Fernando Henrique Cardoso, announcing the establishment of a commission to improve the quality of life for black people. 'For years we have denied the existence of racism and discrimination in Brazil.

'It is not just a bureaucratic or legal problem,' he went on. 'It's more. It is a cultural, a social problem.'

It was probably this, rather than a lack of valid cases, which explains why it was 1997 before the supreme court upheld a case of racial discrimination for the first time. Vicente Francisco do Espírito Santo was sacked from the state electricity company because, his supervisor told him, he 'wanted to whiten the department'.

Whitening the department, society, the country, has a long tradition in Brazil. In the early part of the century it was an officially promoted policy to be achieved by encouraging European immigration. Many Brazilian leaders looked enviously southward to Uruguay and Argentina, each of which had a much whiter population.

In 1921, when Brazil went to Argentina to contest the South American Championship, President Epitácio Pessoa ordered that the team should contain white players only. He was worried that to have a dark face representing the nation would bring shame on Brazil in South America's whitest, and most 'civilized', country.

The only player directly affected by the president's injunction also happened to be the team's star and top scorer, Artur Friedenreich. The first real star of Brazilian football, he was the son of a German father and an Afro-Brazilian mother, a mulatto. Nicknamed 'The Tiger', he was born in 1892, just four years after the abolition of slavery in Brazil (the last country in the world to do so). He had green eyes and crinkly hair. The hair caused him no end of trouble. He was always the last one out on to the field as he strove to slick down his rebellious thatch, smothering it in brilliantine and then stretching it flat against his scalp under a towel until the very last moment. But his talent could not be disguised. When he scored the winning goal in the 1919 South American Championship – Brazil's first international tournament victory – an exclusive jeweller's shop in Rio put his boots on display in its window alongside diamonds and pearls. He played until he was 43 and scored a career total of 1329 goals, 10 more than the great Pelé, the world's top scorer in the professional era.

Despite President Pessoa's efforts, dark faces have been synonymous with Brazil's football prowess ever since, a fact not lost on the Argentines. Some elements among the Argentinian *barras* have a few unpleasant ditties in their songbook reserved for visits by the Brazilians.*

* For example: *Ya todos saben que Brasil está de luto/son todos negros, son todos putos.* (Now everybody knows that Brazil's in mourning/they're all black, they're all queers.) *Y siga, siga el baile/al compás del tamboril/que esta noche los cogemos/a los negros de Brasil.* (And the dance goes on and on/to the rhythm of the drum/because tonight we fucked over/the blacks from Brazil.) Julián García Candau, *Épica y Lírica del Fútbol* (1996), page 227.

Black players were at the forefront of the European experience of South American football. José Leandro Andrade played in the midfield of the Uruguayan side which won the 1924 Olympics in Paris. He was a big hit with the crowd; Europeans had never seen a black man playing football before. The press called him The Black Marvel. After the Games he stayed on in Paris and became a celebrity among chic society. But the reception was not always so warm. In 1916 in Argentina, Uruguay beat Chile 4−0 in the first South American Championship. After the game the Chileans called for the result to be set aside, protesting that Uruguay had fielded two Africans. The two in question were Isabelino Gradín and Juan Delgado, both great-grandsons of slaves. Gradín, who was also the South American 200 and 400 metre champion, had scored two of the four goals. At the time Uruguay was the only national side in the world with black players. Gradín's displays on tour in Brazil helped inspire local black players to challenge the racist status quo.

The fact that football in its early years was dominated by educated whites was taken, at least by educated whites, as evidence of their innate superiority in football, as in much else. It's an attitude rich in irony in these days when it is commonplace − but of equally dubious value − to hear black people's sporting successes ascribed to an innate athletic prowess. 'Innateness' can only explain so much. The poor and the dark may have democratized Brazil's top sport away from its élite origins, but the country is also proud of its world-beating reputation in another field: Formula 1. And when did you last see a black racing driver?

Until the mid-1920s black players were a rarity in Rio de Janeiro. The first was reputedly a footballer named Epaminondas, who played for São Cristóvão. This scarcity was hardly surprising, because until 1918 the Federação Brasileira de Sports banned blacks from participating in any sports teams. Football teams were still largely clubs for young gentlemen, many of them students, where the players were also club members. Even without a formal ban, black players just wouldn't 'fit in'.

In 1921 América signed Manteiga (his nickname meant 'butter'), a black sailor, on the basis of his footballing talent, even though this was before professionalism was recognized. Many members and players at the club were deeply unhappy with the situation and nine of the playing members, from some of Rio's leading families, resigned. It was something of a pyrrhic victory for Manteiga. He was still not allowed into América's club hall. The same year, worn down by the hostile atmosphere, he 'defected' while on a club trip to the north-eastern state of Bahia. The source of their displeasure removed, the other members returned. That was not the only indignity Manteiga had to suffer. When he joined the América club, Miranda, a light-skinned, mixed race team-mate, took to wearing a cap so that his curly hair would not associate him with the black man.[2]

For the few black men in the game, such as Manteiga, it was a trying time. Even in the changing room there was no escape from the deference due to those who in everyday life were your betters: there, Manteiga would doff his hat when anyone spoke to him.[3] On the pitch you would have to tread carefully, as a black man's offence would always be treated more severely by players and crowd alike. And black players were routinely those accused of taking bribes when their teams lost.

Being Brazil, it was as much a case of class as race. The early clubs were equally social and sporting bodies. The Flamengo team which won the Rio title in the years 1914–15 was composed almost entirely of students, mainly medical students. Fluminense's successful team of the same era was also full of undergraduates.

Change came, dramatically, in 1923 when Vasco da Gama came from nowhere to win the Carioca (Rio) championship with a team dominated by black and mixed race players. The reaction was immediate: the other big Rio clubs formed a new strictly amateur organization, the Associação Metropolitana para o Esporte Amador (AMEA), which not only banned any player who had no other job outside football, but also proscribed those who worked in low-paid jobs, such as waiters, drivers, etc.

Players were required to sign their name on a teamsheet before each game, a major hurdle for the ill-educated poor. Clubs got round this stipulation by employing teachers whose sole job was to tutor players in forming the letters of their own name. Some players even had their names changed for them to make the strange patterns easier to copy. Thus Pascoal Cinelli became Pascoal Silva.[4]

It could only delay, not prevent, the change that was coming, and eight years later Rio de Janeiro accepted professionalism,* opening the door to the democratization of football. Ironically, it was Fluminense, the most hidebound of the august societies which were Rio's football clubs, which promoted the change. For years the other clubs had been more flexible about admitting those who were not of good family, particularly mixed race players, as club members, but Fluminense still found this a hard pill to swallow.

Professionalism meant that the club could establish two categories – members and players – with the players as the hired hands (or feet) of the members, a relationship the latter felt more comfortable with.

Another of the factors which hastened the introduction of professionalism was the fact that after the 1930 World Cup a number of players of Italian origin, mainly from Argentina and Uruguay but also from Brazil (particularly São Paulo), had been lured back to Italy by the prospect of well-paid contracts. Some players falsified Italian papers to qualify. For the obviously non-Italian black players this option did not exist, and they had no choice but to stay and develop their football in Brazil, in the process developing Brazilian football. The big stars of the 1930s would be black: Leônidas da Silva and Domingos da Guia (although both would resume their careers at home only after spending a year in Argentina, which went professional before Brazil). They were hired by Flamengo, Fluminense's great rivals, and their tremendous popularity transferred to their new club, which eclipsed Vasco as the leading club among Rio's poor, dark majority, a position it has never lost.

* The professional Carioca Football League was formed on 12 January 1933, two years after Argentina went openly professional.

Flamengo is the people's team. (Or maybe that should be 'Framengo', as Fluminense supporters mockingly imitate the supposed mispronunciation of the uneducated.) It's hard to walk far along the streets of Rio without seeing someone wearing the characteristic red-and-black hooped shirt. And unlike almost any other team in this vast country, Flamengo attracts considerable support outside its home state (Corinthians of São Paulo is the only club that comes near). Fluminense on the other hand has a reputation as the toffs' team. The reality is naturally more complex: there is no shortage of affluent 'Mengão' fans and the terraces at Fluminense games are not choc-a-bloc with yuppies. But class associations are central to both clubs' identities.

Flamengo and Fluminense have the most celebrated rivalry in Brazilian football. Fluminense supporters taunt that they have won the Rio championship more times than Flamengo; Flamenguistas point to their greater haul of national titles. The fixture has its own nickname/trademark/logo: the Fla–Flu. It holds the record for the highest ever attendance at a club game: 177,020 watched a 1963 Fla–Flu at the Maracanã stadium. Like all good derbies, it is a fixture best won with a flukey goal or an outrageous refereeing decision. In 1995 the Rio championship went down to the final minutes of the last game. Flamengo had fought back to 2–2 against Fluminense, who ended the game with eight men after three of their players had been sent off. With three minutes left the title appeared to be within Flamengo's grasp. Then the Fluminense midfielder Ailton picked up the ball, beat a couple of defenders and hit a speculative shot into the area where it took a telling deflection off the stomach of veteran striker Renáto Gaúcho – an ex-Flamengo player – securing the title for Fluminense. This rich combination of circumstances was celebrated as the 'gol de barriga' (the belly goal).

Flamengo fans laughed longest though in 1996, when Fluminense fell through the trapdoor of the national league for the first time ever. Relegation is almost unheard of for a big club – normally a league restructuring is introduced which has the side-effect of leaving the club back among the big boys. In one of their final, crucial matches, Fluminense faced Atlético Paranaense – a club from the city of Curitiba* in Paraná – who fielded a former Fluminense player, Ricardo Pinto, in goal. With the away team winning, Pinto took great pleasure in taunting the crowd behind his goal at Laranjeiras about the imminence of their descent to the second division. It was not a wise move. The outraged fans invaded the pitch and mercilessly assaulted the visiting keeper, who was rushed to hospital suffering from a blood clot on the brain.

On the last day of the season, three clubs were trying to avoid one relegation place: Fluminense, Bahia and Criciúma. If Fluminense beat Vitória they would only go down if Bahia managed to beat Flamengo *and* Criciúma beat Atlético Paranaense. Fluminense won 3–1 but few of their fans were there to witness the event as they had gone along to watch Flamengo, finding themselves in the almost unthinkable situation of cheering on the *rubro-negros*. Surprisingly, Flamengo lost 1–0 at home and their supporters celebrated the defeat. Flu supporters' last hope was the game in Curitiba. Atlético Paranaense were fourth in the table at the time, with a recent excellent record, and it was no surprise when they took the lead. But Criciúma scored twice, the second near the end of the game, to stay up and condemn Fluminense to the second division. Despite the defeat the Atlético fans were cheerful, and mindful of the game at Laranjeiras, serenaded their journey home with the chant '*Eu, eu, eu, o Fluminense se fudeu*' ('Fluminense are fucked').

A scene witnessed by a friend shortly afterwards said much about perceptions of the two teams. A Flamengo supporter started giving some grief about enjoying life in the second division to a Fluminense supporter who was selling books on the street in a square near Fluminense's home ground. Eventually the bookseller turned to his tormentor with a look of disdain and said: 'Listen, son, I'm a Fluminense fan. It's not a poor man's team. You try and get into Laranjeiras

* The city's other main club is called Coritiba because for many people the name Curitiba was considered indelicate, as *cu* in Portuguese is a vulgar word for backside. This has never seemed to bother Arsenal.

dressed like that and see how far you get.' The curious thing was that they were both dressed almost exactly the same.

The Fla–Flu rivalry goes right back to the clubs' origins. In 1911, after winning the Carioca championship, virtually the entire Fluminense first team walked out in a dispute with the club. The team without a club sought a new home across town in the Flamengo Rowing Club on the shores of Rio's circular lagoon. Flamengo didn't have a football section at the time and weren't entirely sure that they wanted one, but agreed to let the Fluminense refugees join. Even so, the new arrivals were not allowed to wear the same red-and-black hooped shirt as the rowers. It was only when Brazil entered the Second World War and the footballers' improvised red, black and white shirt was thought to resemble the Nazi flag that the club finally did away with the business of separate shirt designs. Flamengo thus became the *rubro-negros* (Fluminense, with their maroon, green and white shirts are the *tricolores*). To this day the name of the club is Clube de Regatas Flamengo.*

The following season the most eagerly awaited confrontation was the match between Fluminense's championship-winning side, now playing as Flamengo, and the makeshift team of Fluminense reserves who had hurriedly taken their place. To everyone's surprise the new Fluminense won the first Fla–Flu, a fact that lurks as the last, crushing resort of a 'Nense' fan in any argument with a *rubro-negro*.

But the most famous Fla–Flu of all is the Fla–Flu da Lagoa. It took place on 23 November 1941 and it was the game which decided that year's Carioca championship. The whole season boiled down to this one game, but nobody remembers anything other than the closing minutes. When Flamengo scored to make it 2–2, there were six minutes left on the clock. The clock, in those days, was not held by the referee but by a timekeeper who sat on the touchline. Flamengo needed to win, but for Fluminense a draw was good enough. So with six minutes remaining the Fluminense players hit

* Likewise, Clube Botafogo de Futebol e Regatas; Clube de Regatas Vasco de Gama; and Fluminense Football Club.

upon a tactic perfectly adapted to Flamengo's lagoon-side Gávea ground. Every time the ball came to them the *tricolores* punted it high over the crowd and into the lagoon. The Flamengo staff rummaged through their stores to find more footballs until every last scuffed training ball had been hurriedly pumped up, pressed into service and then booted into the lake. All the resources of the club's rowing section were pressed into service to retrieve the balls from the water and return them to the pitch. Meanwhile, representatives of each team stood over the timekeeper, Flamengo's man urging him to stop the clock while the ball was out of play and Fluminense's man insisting that it should keep running. The Fluminense players were desperately waiting for the final whistle which would give them the title, but the more they kicked the ball into the lagoon the more those six minutes seemed to stretch out into an eternity as the watch was stopped again. Trying to waste time, one of the Fluminense players, Carreiro, was sent off for taking a dive and remonstrating with the referee for not giving a penalty. The Fluminense players surrounded the ref and minutes passed before Carreiro finally left the field and play resumed. It was beginning to get dark. Finally, Fluminense's Romeu Pelliciari, who wore a cap to cover his bald head, received the ball and set off on the mazy run to end all mazy runs. He meandered down the wing as if to cross and then wandered all the way back to his own half, holding the ball, shielding it, until at last the timekeeper blew his whistle, the referee spread his arms and the championship went to Fluminense.[5]

A game at the Maracanã starts, like *Star Wars*, long before and far away. The first time I visited the historic old ground was for a match scheduled to kick off at 9 p.m. But from early evening onwards all around Rio de Janeiro, from the drab industrial suburbs of the Zona Norte to the swanky beachfront districts like Leblon, knots of young men sporting their colours stand on street corners drinking *chopp*, the country's ubiquitous weak lager, at open-fronted bars. Then the poor jumped on buses, while those who could piled into cars for the breakneck drive across town to the stadium. I don't know if

Brazil has drink-driving laws, but if it does no one seems to give them a second thought, although God knows how much *chopp* you would have to drink to actually impair your performance. Outside the stadium was the familiar bustle of people, mostly youngish men, meeting up and grabbing a last drink before going in. For the Maracanã the crowd, on this particular night, was modest, just 35,000 or so. Even so, getting in felt like being the sand in the hourglass. As far as I could tell only one turnstile was open and so, as if to sort out the men from the boys, anyone wanting to get in would have to squeeze, push and jostle for fifteen or twenty minutes past a few hundred others with the same idea. Fortunately friction was kept to a minimum by the copious amounts of sweat lubricating the writhing mass. Once beyond the turnstile a long concrete ramp leads up to the stadium itself, where finally getting in is like some sort of near-death experience, as access is via a narrow passageway with a bright light at the far end. In this case you should give in to the impulse to walk towards the light (the floodlight) to behold the vision beyond. Even with the great gaps among the crowd the Maracanã is an impressive sight, not for any architectural nicety, but for its sheer size. The cheapest section, standing at pitch level, has long since been closed off, and apart from a sort of 'royal box' where rich Cariocas have their debenture seats, the whole ground is one big sweep of stepped concrete. For a big match it would be standing room only, but this night all but the diehards were sitting. The concrete steps were still warm from a day of sunshine. A couple of weeks before I had watched Chelsea beat West Brom with the snowflakes swirling under the roof of the West Stand at Stamford Bridge, which added a certain savour to the sensation of watching a football match on a January evening and having to take my T-shirt off because it was so hot. It was easy to see why football scarves never really caught on in Brazil. Even so, I was still the most overdressed person I could see around me – shorts were *de rigueur* – as the shirtless multitude racked up the *arquibancada* (terrace) presented a soft mosaic of a hundred shades of brown. As at a children's party, people passed among the crowd giving out balloons to be inflated and burst. Vendors offered drinks and ice cream. One man was wandering the terraces selling plastic cards with a scurrilous depiction of Flamengo's superiority over its city rivals represented by the Mengão *urubu* in intimate congress with a Lord Snooty figure (Fluminense), a swarthy Portuguese (Vasco) and, oddly, Donald Duck (Botafogo) – a dollar for the set of three.

But what really makes the Maracanã special is its history: for half a century it has been the home of Brazilian football, and therefore the world game's spiritual home. It has seen many famous games and many famous goals, including Pelé's thousandth. A plaque commemorates another Pelé goal for which he beat half the opposing team before hitting the net. Halfway through the game the man sitting next to me explained that he had witnessed John Barnes's famous goal for England in the stadium in 1984 and that, after the initial shock, he, like many in the crowd, had stood and applauded.

The stadium was built for the 1950 World Cup and, as Brazilians proudly boasted, was the largest in the world. The World Cup seemed destined to mark Brazil's accession to the top table of world football. In 1938 a Brazilian team featuring Leônidas, the 'Black Diamond', had come third after narrowly and controversially losing to Italy in the semi-final. But in 1950, with the European teams still recovering from the war years, Brazil had home advantage and built the magnificent new ground by the murky Maracanã river as a vast showcase for the national team's expected victory.

Brazil's path to the final game was a triumphal procession. In their first-round group they swept aside Mexico, Switzerland and Yugoslavia, and in the final four-team league they beat Sweden and Spain by 7–1 and 6–1 respectively. To clinch the title, they only needed a point from their final match against Uruguay, which was widely seen as a formality.

Uruguay had only drawn with Spain and beaten Sweden by the odd goal in five. But the Uruguayans were fresher: because of other teams' withdrawals, the Uruguayans had only had to play one game – an 8–0 demolition of Bolivia – to qualify for the final group.

It was said that 200,000 people – well over the official capacity

– crammed into the Maracanã stadium on that historic Sunday afternoon, the biggest crowd ever at a game of football. Later it would be suggested that 'only' 174,000 were in the ground, but, if only on poetic grounds, the former figure just has to be true: a total that represented 10 per cent of the population of Rio at the time.

Everything seemed to be going to plan when Brazil scored just after half-time. But on 66 minutes Schiaffino equalized. Brazil only needed a point but their fast, fluid team was never designed to play for a draw. When, with 11 minutes remaining, Ghiggia beat the Brazilian goalkeeper at his near post the vast crowd went into shock. At the final whistle there was pandemonium. The elaborately planned Brazilian celebrations were still-born in that cauldron of national humiliation. The newspapers, already printed with the headline 'BRAZIL, WORLD CHAMPIONS', would never be read. Amid the confusion as the thousands of desolate Brazilian fans trooped away down the stadium ramp, Jules Rimet almost furtively shoved the trophy that bore his name into the hands of the Uruguayan captain, Obdulio Varela.

That evening Varela went drinking in several bars in Rio. Everywhere he saw desolate Brazilians mourning their team's defeat. He said if he had realized that Uruguay's victory would cause so much misery he would have preferred to have lost. Playwright and sportswriter Nelson Rodrigues said later: 'In the tragedy of '50, we paid for all the sins of the last 45 generations.'[6]

The recriminations began almost immediately and the scapegoats were quickly identified as Bigode, Juvenal and the goalkeeper Barbosa.[7] Commentators in the press spoke of a lack of fibre, of character, of discipline. Bigode was a coward; Juvenal a boozer. They even retailed an old story that on his debut in 1945 against Russia, in which he let in two goals in ten minutes, Barbosa had been so terrified that he had had to leave the field to change his shorts. Needless to say, Bigode, Juvenal and Barbosa were the team's three black players. Barbosa in particular was never allowed to forget that day in 1950. When he turned up in Teresópolis at the Brazilian national team's training camp for the 1994 World Cup he was shunned as a Jonah.

91

El Seleccionado Brasileño

(O Terror do Mundo)

Q. E. P. D.

Falleció el 16 de Julio de 1950.

Su padre, Obdulio Varela, sus hermanos políticos, Gastón Máspoli, Matías González, Eusebio Tejera, Rodríguez Andrade, Schubert Gambetta, Alcides Ghiggia, Julio Pérez, Omar Miguez, Juan A. Schiafino, Ruben Morán, invitan al sepelio que se realizará por la calle 18 de Julio.

Casa de duelo:

Enterrador: Estadio Méndez Moraes

Alcides Ghiggia Rio Janeiro

A mock funeral notice commemorating the death of Brazilian football, following Uruguay's triumph in the 1950 World Cup.

Barbosa and the other two were not the only scapegoats. In the 1950 Final the Brazilian team played in white shirts. So in the 1954 Final against Sweden, who played in yellow, they opted for blue shirts rather than play in the 'unlucky' kit (the World Cup had been won by teams in blue shirts on four out of five occasions, they reasoned, and in any case, blue was the colour of the Virgin Mary). The 1958 squad had no end of little rituals – the order of getting on the bus or of entering the field, etc – but the guardian of the team's superstitions was the delegation leader, Paulo Machado de Carvalho. Throughout the tournament he carried an image of the Virgin Mary and wore a 'lucky' brown suit, only taking it off to sleep. The same suit, by now fraying somewhat at the seams, was pressed into service four years later in Chile. But fair do's to him, they did win, twice.

Footballers in general tend to be superstitious but Brazil has overlaid a level of African mysticism with rites and beliefs taken from the Afro-Brazilian cult of *macumba*.

Carlito Rocha, at one time chairman of Botafogo, was associated with the club during the 1940s and 1950s. He believed that his pre-match rituals were essential to the team's success. When Botafogo won the Carioca title in 1948 he personally distributed mangoes to the team before the game which had to be sucked in his presence. He also personally brought milk and biscuits to each player in his room.

The rituals became more elaborate. At kick-off time he would have the curtains at Botafogo tied up (to tie up the legs of the opposition); he would make the players take a shower in water scented with a lucky herb, then lie on the ground and eat three apples; and he recommended that the club always buy an ex-Flamengo player as a talisman.

But the real key to Botafogo's success in 1948 was a stray dog, which one of the reserves brought into the ground one day. That week the little mongrel, by now named Biriba, watched from the dugout as Botafogo won. Carlito Rocha immediately recognized him as a lucky mascot. Thereafter Biriba would sit on the bench and if the opposition threatened, Carlito Rocha would order him to be released on to the pitch to run after the ball and break up play. As Botafogo kept winning, so Biriba's stock rose. Macaé, the reserve who had first found him, now had to sleep with Biriba under the stands and taste his food.

Before one important game Biriba urinated on a player's leg. Botafogo won, so the unfortunate player, Braguinha, had to suffer the same indignity every week. Biriba was given a gold collar with the club badge, champagne, and even his own win bonus. Carlito Rocha once even kicked a player off a team trip so that Biriba could go in his place.

But in the 1949 championship, Botafogo did not do so well. As the team started losing, so Biriba became less and less central to the matchday routine until finally, his magic gone, he was forgotten.[8]

Not every Botafoguense was convinced of the value of super-stition, notably João Saldanha, who managed the club in the 1950s. 'If *macumba* won games,' he said, 'the Bahia state championship would always be a tie.'[9]

The débâcle of 1950 – the *Maracanazo*, as it was known to the Uruguayans – also contributed to Brazilian football's general inferiority complex. Brazil still trailed behind Uruguay and Argentina in titles won and, despite the national team's successes against them, European teams still held an almost mystical aura of toughness, discipline and athleticism.

At the 1954 World Cup in Switzerland Brazil came up against Hungary in the quarter-finals. In 1952 the Hungarians had won the Olympic football title, and a year later the same team, featuring Puskas, Hidegkuti, Kocsis and Czibor, had given England a footballing lesson at Wembley, winning 6–3. To rub in the end of the myth of English invincibility, Hungary repeated the treatment with a 7–1 scoreline in Budapest. The quarter-final should have been a classic but it went down in history as the Battle of Berne.

Hungary scored twice in the first ten minutes, as they had done in most of their matches over the previous three years. Their explosive starts were down to a then-startling innovation: they actually warmed up before a game, so much so that when they ran on to the pitch at Berne their shirts were already damp with sweat. Brazil equalized with a goal from their right-winger, Julinho, to keep them in touch at half-time. But the game is remembered for the events which followed the award of a penalty against the Brazilian defender Pinheiro for handball.

The Brazilians protested loud and long but to no avail. Patriotic Brazilian journalists scampered on to the pitch to remonstrate with the referee and had to be escorted away by Swiss policemen. Hungary scored from the spot and thereafter the game degenerated into a series of fouls, off-the-ball assaults and brawls. The Swiss police found themselves back on the field of play several times during the many stoppages, as three players were sent off. After the final whistle (Hungary won 4–2) the teams dissolved into a mêlée and the fisticuffs continued in the tunnel, with the Brazilian manager captured on film in the changing-room corridor brandishing a football boot at the Hungarian team. Press photographs also recorded the cuts and black eyes of several of the participants.

On their return home, the Brazilians were well received: they had shown they were '*bem machos*' (well hard). The headline on one

94

paper (*Ultima Hora*) proudly proclaimed: '*GLÓRIA AOS QUE SOUBERAM LUTAR*' ('GLORY TO THOSE WHO KNEW HOW TO FIGHT').[10] Defeat was put down, not to the quality of the Hungarian side, but to the alleged bias of the English referee, Arthur Ellis. The Brazilian delegation in Switzerland made a formal protest to Fifa alleging that Ellis was part of a Communist plot to aid the Hungarians. As one writer noted, in Brazil 'the name Ellis became a swear word for many years thereafter',[11] unlike in Britain, where it was more likely to conjure up images of Mr Ellis's later career as the avuncular arbiter of races between Rotarians dressed as gorillas on *It's a Knockout.**

A more sober consideration was offered by the head of the Brazilian delegation, João Lyra Filho, in his report on the team's performance in the World Cup. He put the team's relative failure down to the country's miscegenated make-up, which called into question the players' mettle: 'The Brazilian players lacked what is lacking for the Brazilian people in general . . . The ills are deeper [than the game's tactical system, etc] . . . They go back to genetics itself.

'In Brazilian football, flashy trim lends artistic expression to the match, to the detriment of yield and results. Exhibition jeopardizes competition. It would be easy to compare the physiognomy of a Brazilian national team, made up mostly of blacks and mulattos, with that of Argentine, German, Hungarian, or English football. Brazilian football goes to great lengths with the flashy surface of effects (exhibition), while outstanding players [must] develop the profitable depth of results (competition) . . .'[12]

This contrast between artistic football (*futebol arte*) and the dour, disciplined tactics deemed appropriate for getting results (*futebol de resultados*) remains a fault-line in Brazilian conceptions of their own

* British referees in general had enjoyed a good reputation as being fair and impartial in Latin America. In 1937 the Argentine Football Association turned to a former Football League referee, Isaac Caswell, to help raise the low standard of refereeing. By 1948 all league matches were officiated by British referees. The 1950s also saw British referees at work in Colombia, Brazil, Chile, Peru and Uruguay. See Mason (1995), pages 108–11.

game, although subsequent history would diminish its racial overtones.

Brazil won the World Cup in 1958 with a style which incorporated the best of both worlds, as 'artistic' greats, such as Didi, Garrincha and the 17-year-old prodigy Pelé, beat all-comers. But while that team is remembered for setting the benchmark of a free-and-easy Brazilian style, enormous attention was paid to preparing the squad from a physical, medical and psychological point of view. The team doctor spent a month in 1957 visiting twenty-five towns as potential training bases in Sweden, marking them for weather, facilities, transport, food, entertainment, accommodation and health services. All the players were given a thorough medical check-up that revealed a woeful litany of ill-health, which was no doubt indicative of the social groups from which the squad was drawn. Among the 33 players, dentists found 470 teeth with problems and extracted 32. Most of the players had worms or parasites, many had anaemia and one had syphilis. In addition to rotten teeth and gammy gall bladders, chronic digestive and circulation problems were common. The football authorities also contracted a psychologist to conduct tests on all the players. Garrincha, the mercurial winger, scored 38 out of 123, which would not have qualified him to drive a bus. The psychologist,* João Carvalhaes, recommended that Pelé should not be selected. His report stated: 'Pelé is obviously infantile. He lacks the necessary fighting spirit. He is too young to feel aggressions and react in an adequate fashion. Beyond this he does not have the sense of responsibility necessary for team spirit.'[13] Pelé was selected and the rest is history, as too, in his own way, was Mr Carvalhaes.

For Chile, four years later, the Brazilians held their *concentração*†

---

* To be precise, a sociologist licensed in psychology.

† The *concentração* (*concentración* in Spanish) is an article of faith in Latin football, designed to concentrate a player's mind and keep him from any distractions, particularly women and booze. The 'concentration' can mean several nights sequestered in a hotel even before home games. As manager of Botafogo, João Saldanha, who didn't share the general enthusiasm for the *concentração*,

Kick-off at the first World Cup Final, 1930. Some 93,000 crammed into the Centenario stadium to see Uruguay overcome neighbours Argentina, 4–2 (*Football Archive*).

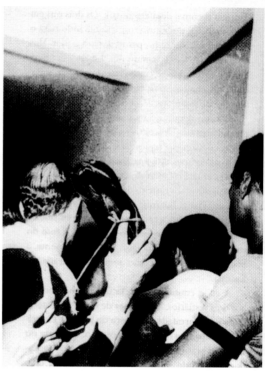

Pelé nutmegs an opponent in the
Maracanã (*Popperfoto*).

Violence in the tunnel after the 'Battle of
Berne', 1954, the legendary ill-tempered
encounter between Brazil and Hungary.

Rattín refuses to leave the field at Wembley, 1966 (*Football Archive*).

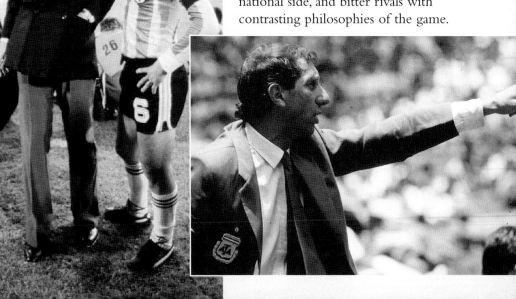

(*Above*) Chilean goalkeeper Rojas lies apparently injured by a firecracker in a 1989 match against Brazil. Chile were kicked out of the World Cup when it was found he was faking (*Popperfoto*).

Leftwing intellectual César Luis Menotti (*left: Popperfoto*) and hard man Carlos Salvador Bilardo (*below: Football Archive*); two former coaches of the Argentine national side, and bitter rivals with contrasting philosophies of the game.

A Bolivian street seller at the Copa América, La Paz, June 1997 (*Alistair Berg*).

(*Right*) The beautiful game in the shanty towns of Santos, Brazil (*Julio Etchart*); (*far right*) Zico, 1997.

Kick-off at Nicaragua's crucial home-leg World Cup qualifier against Guatemala.

(*Above, left to right*) Colombian drug barons and football bosses Miguel Rodríguez Orejuela and Pablo Escobar, respectively in jail and dead (*both Popperfoto*).

(*Below*) A picture to be ejected for: Faustino Asprilla takes to the field in the rain at a World Cup qualifier in La Paz.

The Aztec Stadium, Mexico
City (*Popperfoto*).

Gustavo Poyet, Chelsea's
Uruguayan midfielder (*Popperfoto*).

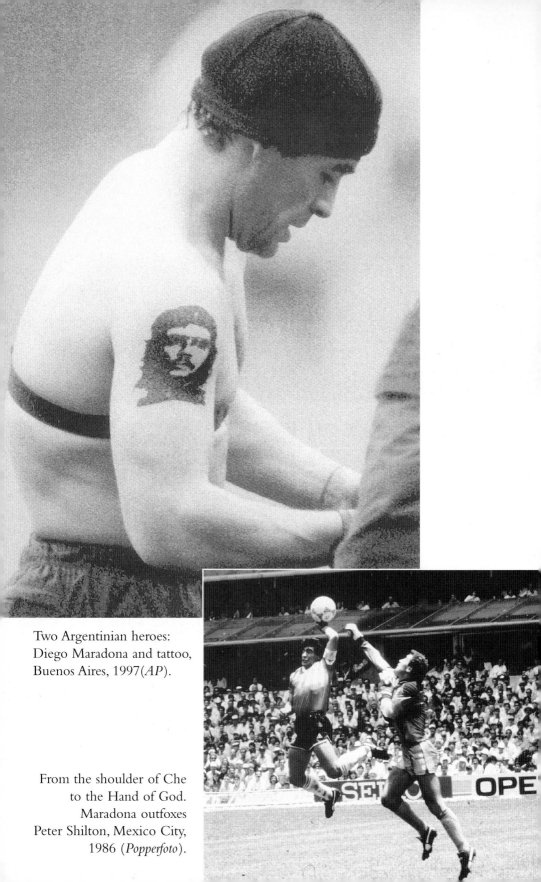

Two Argentinian heroes:
Diego Maradona and tattoo,
Buenos Aires, 1997(*AP*).

From the shoulder of Che
to the Hand of God.
Maradona outfoxes
Peter Shilton, Mexico City,
1986 (*Popperfoto*).

(training camp) at altitude to increase lung capacity and red corpuscles after the team doctor, Hilton Gosling, found the atmosphere in Viña del Mar deficient in oxygen. Carbon impressions were taken of the players' feet to determine alterations to their boots and studs, a precaution credited with drastically cutting the number of strain injuries. Care was also taken with food and Dr Gosling could boast that in two World Cups Brazil had suffered no cases of stomach upsets.[14] Finally, Dr Gosling went to Madame Chabela's brothel in Viña del Mar and passed twenty-four girls as medically fit to serve the World Cup holders.[15]

For the Maracanã, being football's spiritual home is all very well, but it doesn't pay the rent. After years of mismanagement, neglect and physical deterioration of the structure, the city authorities who owned the stadium decided to privatize it.

When the winner of the tendering process was announced in January 1997 it turned out that, despite predictions of fierce competition between Brazilian companies and big US leisure conglomerates, only one bid had been received, from a Brazilian consortium, which promptly announced plans to install a running track so they could cover the adjoining athletics stadium with a car park. The ensuing outcry led the governor of Rio to order the consortium to go away and think again.

There was, though, a consensus that the place needed doing up. In 1992, 3 spectators died and at least 50 were injured when a section of the topmost level fell down. The stadium reopened the following year with its capacity cut to 125,000. João Havelange, the Brazilian president of Fifa, said it might be better if they just bulldozed the whole thing and started again. Today's stadia needed to be smaller,

---

nevertheless would look in on Garrincha's room at night to check the winger – a famous drinker – was sleeping in his distinctive checked shorts. Years later Garrincha told him that he used to pay his team-mate Domício to wear his shorts and sleep in his bed while he slipped out of the window for a night on the town. Castro (1995), pages 190–1.

he felt, and the Maracanã's open terracing was out of place in the era of all-seater stadia.* The *geral*, the pitch-level area where the groundlings used to stand, had already been closed, partly, it was believed, to put a stop to the phenomenon of *arrastão*, in which groups of young men would steam through the undifferentiated crush, relieving spectators of their money, jewellery, watches and any other items of value. Sadly this also put an end to the taunting chant of other teams' fans when playing Flamengo: '*Au, au, au, Flamenguista é na Geral*', an allusion to the Flamenguista's supposed poverty.

One of the problems with a stadium the size of the Maracanã is that it's hard to fill. For the big, important derby games that's not a problem, but most games played in Rio are neither big nor important. The home grounds of the main Rio clubs are, with the exception of Vasco da Gama's 40,000-capacity São Januário stadium, unbelievably tiny. Fluminense's Laranjeiras ground holds about 10,000. Behind one goal is a blank wall, and on the other three a modest construction of two tiers of half a dozen steep concrete steps serves as the *arquibancada* (terracing). On one flank, what looks like a cricket pavilion rises stately above the directors' box. Given the fact that in the early days Carioca football was an offshoot of expatriate cricket clubs, and that the ground dates from 1908, that's probably what it is. Even Flamengo's Gávea ground only holds 13,000, although visitors to the sports complex attached to the stadium can marvel at the architect's model of what the redeveloped Gávea will look like, complete with a football pitch built on the roof.

* Havelange appears curiously out of step with Brazil's footballing traditions. Asked by *The Times* what virtue he most admired in football, the octogenarian former water polo player answered 'discipline'. He has also fought a running battle with Brazil's greatest star, Pelé – first banning him from the draw for the 1994 World Cup because of a row with Havelange's son-in-law, Ricardo Texeira, the head of the CBF, and then publicly berating him for legislative proposals, as Minister of Sport Edson Arantes do Nascimento, to reform the structure of Brazilian football.

Historically, such modest surroundings were no handicap since big games were routinely transferred to the mighty Maracanã. But when the city started jacking up the price, the clubs started staying away. The ground needed to raise money for repairs, but money was frittered away in inefficient and probably corrupt bureaucracy. Hence the privatization idea.

Brazil has twenty-five states, but in football terms two of them dominate everything. Both Rio de Janeiro and São Paulo consider themselves the capital of Brazilian football and, as most of the important media are based in one of the two cities, it's an impression that's hard to escape. This is despite the fact that some of Brazil's most successful teams of recent years, such as Cruzeiro (from Minas Gerais) and Grêmio (from Rio Grande do Sul) – Libertadores Cup winners in 1997 and 1996 respectively – give the lie to this. In the 1980s the Brazilian national championship was won by teams from Bahia, Paraná and Rio Grande do Sul. According to the stereotype, teams from black Bahia are languid and indolent, while those from white Rio Grande do Sul are tough and physical – European, or more specifically, Uruguayan.*

But the predominance of the Rio–São Paulo duopoly has got everything to do with the rivalry between Brazil's two biggest cities. For centuries Rio de Janeiro was the capital of Brazil and although the title was switched in the 1960s to Brasília, a sort of vast Milton Keynes carved out of the jungle, nobody seems to have told the Cariocas, who swagger on in the belief, the certain knowledge, that everywhere else is the provinces. And they have a point.† Rio de Janeiro – its beaches, its Carnival, the Sugarloaf Mountain, the statue of Christ, even the Maracanã stadium – is an image that is instantly recognizable around the world. São Paulo, on the other hand, may be one of the biggest cities in the world, it may be

* Grêmio, from the south, have won several titles but few friends in the 1990s with their dour, 'Uruguayan' style of play.
† The headquarters of the Brazilian Football Confederation (CBF) remains in Rio.

the country's industrial and financial heart and it may serve the best sushi outside Japan,* but what it lacks is Rio's glamour. Topography has a lot to do with it. Rio is fashioned by the sweep of Guanabara Bay, its mountains, its beaches and lagoons, with the city wantonly moulding itself to the twists and folds of the landscape. It's a city which still has lush forests and waterfalls within its limits. São Paulo hasn't so much absorbed its natural setting as bulldozed it.

Even Rio's poverty is more attractive. The city's *favelas*, where a fifth of the population lives, cling to the hillsides that loom over the chic beach districts of the Zona Sul, meaning rich and poor are forever cheek by jowl; São Paulo has largely banished its poor to the periphery.

But more than anything, Rio is an adolescent city, its culture centred on its beaches, obsessed with sex and with having a good time. São Paulo is its sensible big brother who appreciates good food and high culture but always knows that it has to get up for work in the morning.

Partly because of the difficulty of drawing together players from all over such a huge country, Brazil didn't play an international until 1914 and throughout the 1930s managed just twenty-two matches against foreign opposition. More common were games involving state representative XIs. Even when a national team did take the field, until relatively recently its composition would be heavily influenced by where the match was taking place. Games in São Paulo would invariably be dominated by *paulista* players who would be conspicuous by their absence from matches staged in Rio. A classic example of this tendency occurred in the 1950 World Cup when Brazil played all their games bar one in the new Maracanã stadium in Rio. The exception was the match against Switzerland, played in São Paulo's Pacaembu stadium. The team was changed completely from that which had thrashed Mexico in the first game,

* Immigration, particularly in the early years of this century, has made São Paulo the biggest Japanese city outside Japan.

100

with the entire São Paulo half-back line of Bauer, Rui and Noronha implanted for the only time in the tournament. Brazil drew 2–2, the only game up to the Final they did not win. Needless to say, this was only fuel to the fire for the Cariocas.

Brazil's brilliance at international level has for years been counter-pointed by the chaos of its domestic leagues. Being a country the size of a continent implies obvious logistical problems for a national league. But Brazil has taken this relatively straightforward handicap and built a whole edifice of dizzying disorganization upon it that has teams criss-crossing the country to fulfil fixture after fixture in various competitions often played before minuscule crowds.*

Politics, inevitably, plays a part. The state of Rio de Janeiro has only a handful of teams capable of winning the league. The title is usually a fight between Flamengo, Fluminense, Vasco da Gama and Botafogo. The league, though, contains twelve teams, most of them surviving on tiny crowds and precarious finances. In 1996 one team, Londrina, from the ranching country of Paraná, was reduced to paying its players in cows.

In addition to the state championship, there is the national championship, the Rio–São Paulo interstate championship, plus various Cups and, for the more successful clubs, the South American tournaments, which in 1997 were increased to four. In the twelve months before he was transferred to PSV Eindhoven, Romário played 108 games for his club in Brazil.

The 1997 São Paulo state championship, for example, was played in two groups of eight teams each. The teams played once against the other teams in their own group, then twice against the teams in the other group. At the end of this the top two in each group

---

* Picked for a recent international friendly away to Russia, two São Paulo players had to be substituted and leave a match early to catch a private jet from São Paulo to Rio in order to join up with the squad. Their match's kick-off time had been put back three hours when it was picked to be the day's live television game.

qualified for a knockout stage. This is one of the simpler formats.*

This begins to explain why only the really big games attract big crowds. For most of the season the fans of the big clubs just can't be bothered to turn up for apparently meaningless fixtures. In December 1997 Juventude set a new record by playing against Portuguesa in the national championship quarter-finals for the benefit of a grand total of 55 spectators. Gates such as this led Pelé to comment with pardonable exaggeration: 'More people attend rodeos than football matches.'[16] He proposed sweeping changes which, among other things, would probably do away with 40 per cent of the uneconomic professional clubs. Matters came to a head in January 1997, when the Rio de Janeiro state championship kicked off without three of the top sides. Flamengo, Fluminense and Botafogo refused to turn out in protest at the organization of the competition with its endless, loss-making fixtures. Only Vasco, of the big four, played its opening games.

Despite the dramatic gesture, the league structure remained unchanged and, after a two-week delay, the clubs resumed their participation. The only tangible effect of the protest was to increase the fixture congestion later in the season, as the initial, missed games were rescheduled.

Tension between the big clubs and the Rio state federation continued. At the Fla–Flu of 20 April 1997, the two teams took the field at the Maracanã wearing black shirts over their normal strips in protest at the chaotic organization of the state championship. Botafogo did the same before their game against Madureira. The fans in the Maracanã waved banners demanding the resignation of Eduardo Viana, the president of the Rio de Janeiro football federation. Viana replied, tersely: 'I will only leave the presidency dead.'

The influence of the smaller clubs does not only extend to their voting weight on the committees of the football association. In May

* In Rio the championship is in three stages: after the first stage the bottom four teams are eliminated; after the second stage the bottom two drop out; then the winners of the three stages play off against each other, unless the same team wins all three stages.

1996 Brazil's national Globo television network broadcast the tapes of a conversation between Ivens Mendes, longstanding head of the national football confederation's refereeing committee, and Mario Celso Petraglia, the president of Atlético Paranaense, a team from one of Brazil's less renowned footballing states. In the conversation, the man identified as Mendes offered to ask a referee to give Atlético a helping hand in the home leg of a Copa Brasil match against Vasco da Gama.

'I need you to send me 25,000 reais [about $25,000],' he said. 'If I get a chance I will even ask the referee to give you a little bit of a hand.'

'Tell your players to mark Edmundo closely,' he added, 'he gets angry easily.'

The man identified as Atlético's president replied that Mendes should get in touch with his secretary, who would 'take care of it'.

Sure enough Vasco's temperamental striker Edmundo (nickname: 'Animal') and the Atlético defender Andrei were sent off for fighting during the first half. Edmundo, whose name is no stranger to referee's notebooks, called his dismissal 'a huge injustice'. This time he may even have had a point. Atlético won 3–1 and went on to take the second-round tie 7–6 on aggregate.

Mendes had had similar conversations with other, bigger clubs, including Corinthians. Globo claimed that Mendes was using money given by club directors to finance his bid for election to congress. Mendes himself admitted taking the money but saw nothing wrong in it. 'What is wrong with me as a Brazilian citizen . . . who is trying to start a political career accepting help from my friends?'

In the ensuing scandal, Mendes resigned, and the CBF banned Atlético Paranaense for 360 days, but no other clubs were punished. Atlético Paranaense's suspension would mean that the *tricolores* could be reinstated.* This was good news for Fluminense's Renáto Gaúcho,

* In the end, typically, the league granted Atlético Paranaense's appeal and in a crazed Salomonic judgement decided that no teams would be relegated that year although the top two in the second division would be promoted, increasing the size of the first division by two.

103

as he had promised to walk down Copacabana beach naked if Flu had to play in the second division.

In 1997 Mendes and Petraglia were both banned from football-related activity for life. The Corinthians chairman received a two-year ban.

One effect of the boycott was that Fluminense launched their 1997 campaign against São Paulo FC in the Rio–São Paulo inter-state championship, a tournament with a venerable though intermittent history but one which, in the Brazilian way of things, had barely kept the same format for two years running. This year it was to be a knockout competition with ties played home and away by the top teams from each state.

São Paulo's vast Morumbí stadium has an official capacity of 105,000, but for Fluminense's visit large areas were roped off awaiting repairs. Even so, there was plenty of room for the 7000 paying customers to rattle around in. In fact, 7000 looked like an exaggeration, as almost the entire crowd huddled together high up on the roofless, sunbaked *arquibancada* trying to generate some atmosphere. The locals – there was no travelling support – were disappointed, as Fluminense's young team, fresh from relegation in the national league the previous year, held the home side to a 2–2 draw. Only the quicksilver display of their young left-winger, Denílson, offered hope for São Paulo in the return leg (which they won, on penalties, in a three-quarters-empty Maracanã).

Partly in an attempt to bring the crowds back, the Rio–São Paulo tournament in 1997 sported a number of rule changes designed to keep the ball in play and encourage attacking football. The innovations, which had previously been tried out in São Paulo, included: the right of each coach to call a five-minute time-out in each half; a basketball-style personal limit on the number of fouls that could be permitted – five fouls and the player is expelled; and a team limit of 15 fouls – for each subsequent foul the opposing team is awarded a free-kick from the D of the penalty area without a wall or indeed any other players at all between the kicker and the goalkeeper.

The first rule change clearly had less to do with keeping the game moving (indeed, it's hard to think of anything more obviously counter-productive) than with a desire to squeeze more adverts into TV and radio coverage of matches. But the limits on fouling could and did have a big effect on the character of games, although whether for better or worse is a moot point.

It might seem that Brazil is the last place in the world that needs help in producing attacking football, but in fact the domestic Brazilian game is burdened by a high proportion of dull, defensive and often violently negative matches.

The tactic of *matar o jogo* (killing the play), whereby as soon as possession is lost one player commits a foul to allow his team-mates to regroup, is commonplace. A more sophisticated spoiling approach involves different players on the same team taking it in turns to foul the other team's most dangerous player, thus reducing the risk of a man-marker being sent off. All too often such dirty tactics go unpunished by referees, and even if players are cautioned or sent off, the arcane workings of the disciplinary system frequently work to the benefit of the offender.

Until 1996, if a player accumulated three yellow cards in the Rio state championship it meant an immediate suspension, but a red card required a trip to the disciplinary tribunal, which frequently resulted in a let-off or a postponement of the suspension until a more convenient time for the club. This led to the farcical situation of players who had been booked, deliberately trying to get themselves sent off.

In the first leg of the Brazilian championship play-off in December 1997, the Vasco striker Edmundo received a yellow card. It was his third since his last suspension and should have meant that he would automatically miss the second leg against Palmeiras. However, in the second half Edmundo was sent off for fighting. Exploiting the rules, Vasco appealed against his dismissal (there is no appeal against yellow cards) which meant that Edmundo could continue playing until the appeal was heard. Vasco's vice-president denied the widespread speculation that the club had told Edmundo to deliberately get himself sent off. Edmundo himself answered a similar question from a television reporter with a volley of foul-mouthed abuse.

105

Nevertheless, his action had the effect that the striker, who had just broken the Brazilian all-time record for the most goals in a season, could play in the return leg. Not that he could add to his tally – both matches finished 0–0, but Vasco won the title because of their superior record over the season. Ironically, while playing for Palmeiras in 1994, Edmundo had put off a four-month ban by exploiting the appeal mechanism.

In the Carioca league a red card now means an instant suspension, but in the case of a player accumulating three yellow cards clubs can buy off the suspension by paying just $500.[17]

'This will just encourage violence and it will be the clubs who start whingeing when one of the star players gets hurt,'[18] said the 1970 World Cup star Gerson. 'The referees here overlook everything and the disciplinary tribunals overlook everything too.'

Flamengo played their first game under the new rules beneath the floodlights at the Maracanã stadium before a crowd of some 30,000, including a small but vocal away contingent. Corinthians of São Paulo provided the opposition but they were more like extras in a one-man show by Romário. Two-and-a-half years before, he had been the star of the Brazilian team which had won the World Cup for a record fourth time and was voted the best player in the world. Since then the temperamental striker had had a series of public disagreements with his club in Spain, culminating in his being sent back to Brazil on loan, and had been dropped from the national squad after failing to turn up for a friendly. Romário found himself watching Brazil's progress in the Atlanta Olympics on television while his striking partner from 1994, Bebeto, led the attack with the new sensation, Ronaldo. Starting the new year in the red-and-black hoops of Flamengo, Romário played like a man with something to prove and displayed his typical quickness of thought and feet that makes good defenders look like park footballers. Romário scored two and his striking partner and fellow international Sávio helped himself to another as Corinthians struggled to contain their darting runs. But the most remarkable aspect of the game was the last five minutes. Suddenly, it was as if the game had been belatedly declared a charity match. Like a dream in which everything appears normal except for one nagging detail, the players continued to pass, run and cover, but something was wrong: nobody tackled. It was blindingly apparent, even to those of us who had not been keeping count, that Corinthians had committed their fifteenth foul. Rugged defenders daintily tiptoed alongside their dribbling opponents, ultimately stepping aside if there was a danger of getting too close. It was like watching a game between twenty-two haemophiliac Romanovs: football reduced to a non-contact sport.

But that was just the half of it. Corinthians cleared the ball into the opposing penalty area. A Flamengo defender, running towards his own goal, had the ball covered, but the Corinthians' forward had a little snap at his heels and brought him down. Clearly he had not been paying attention at the pre-match team-talk when the defenders had the implications of the 15-foul rule drummed into them. The referee picked up the ball, tucked it under his arm and marched the 80-odd yards to the opposing penalty area where he placed the ball for a Flamengo free-kick.

Romário's free strike at goal was saved, denying him a hat-trick, but in other games in the tournament decisive goals were scored this way.

With understandable self-interest, Romário himself thought the innovations a good thing, as they would give more protection to attackers. 'Perhaps with these rule-changes Sávio will be able to show his real football,' he said.[19] The Flamengo coach and World Cup veteran, Júnior, told his players to deliberately set out to win fouls as a tactic with the aim of creating a tackle-free environment for the skilful Sávio to run riot in. All very well, but poor preparation for a meeting with a team from one of the 191 other Fifa members who still play by the old rules.

As one newspaper columnist observed, the changes put more responsibility on the shoulders of referees, 'a discredited class in Brazil'.[20]

Fortunately, though, it was a referee who stopped at least one of the new ideas going any further. The Canadian referee Sonia

Daroncourt refused to allow time-outs in the São Paulo champion-ship match between Palmeiras and São José, pointing out that they were not sanctioned by international rules. It was the first time a woman had refereed a top-division game in South America and an advert for feminine good sense (although Palmeiras, who had a goal disallowed and a player sent off, didn't see it that way).

The Brazilians haven't only tinkered with the rules but even thought up their own variant on the game. What could be more Brazilian than beach football? In January 1997 a team of barefoot Brazilians led by the now grey-haired Júnior and featuring current and former internationals such as Edmundo and Edinho won the world beach football championship at a specially constructed stadium on Rio's Copacabana beach, just as they had won every other world championship. Not content with being the best in the world at football the Brazilians have invented a game in which they are even more certain to beat all-comers. It's hard to imagine an English team, even one drawn from such seaside hotbeds of football as Blackpool, Brighton and Scarborough, rivalling Brazil any time soon. Of course England tried the same trick of inventing their own game by coming up with football in the first place, the only problem being that everyone else learnt how to play it better than us.

I had wanted to talk to one of Brazil's top football pundits, Washing-ton Rodrigues. The best place to catch him, he said, was during his physiotherapy session at Filé's clinic. When Brazil's top players get injured, it is to Nílton Petroni that they turn. Petroni, whose nick-name is Filé (as in fillet steak), runs a physiotherapy clinic in Rio's Barra da Tijuca, which has the atmosphere of a sweat-stained gentle-man's club for Brazilian football personalities and wannabes. All around, young (and not so young) men are building up wasted muscles by lifting weights, riding exercise bikes or exercising in the pool under the supervision of the clinic's team of physios. Else-where, it is massage and ultrasound. But everywhere there's the buzz of discussion about football, about players, their injuries, their lifestyles, their transfers, their problems with managers or women, about who should be in the team, about what some commentator said or wrote.

Filé, diminutive, fast-talking and energetic, flits around offering words of advice, checking the level on the ultrasound machine, but mainly, it seems, helps to whisk up the soufflé of gossip. He has plenty to talk about. He rose to prominence with Romário, who installed him as his personal physiotherapist at PSV Eindhoven and then at Barcelona. He accompanied the injured Romário to the 1990 World Cup in Italy but was not always held in such high esteem by the national team management.

'It was there that the problem, the political problem, began. I went as an observer. In fact I went to the World Cup as an observer of Romário's work. Because PSV wanted someone there to see that no one fucked him up. I went as an observer, but when I arrived Careca was injured, someone else was injured, then another. As the team didn't have a physio, everyone was calling, "Filé, Filé, Filé," and so I saw one, two, three, four, five, six, seven players, all the players. I got to the point where they couldn't send me away.'

The team doctor resented his presence, and Filé says he now recognizes that the manner of his arrival in the camp was not ideal. But battles with doctors are Filé's daily bread. Not surprisingly, Filé thinks physiotherapists are a neglected breed in Brazil and rattles off arguments as to why their (or, more particularly, his) labours should be valued more.

'I went to Europe. I was in Portugal, working with complete autonomy. I worked with six doctors. I was the one who went out on to the pitch. I was the one who treated the player on the pitch. At the end of the season, the chairman of the club said to me: "You make a profit for us. Because you get the players recovered really quickly." A top player, Sávio, for example, gets $100,000 a month. If Sávio spends a month not playing, that's $100,000 that the club has invested without seeing a return. Not only that but the player suffers because he quickly gets stuck with the label of injury-prone. Sávio should have been out for two months but I got him back in two weeks. How much did the club gain? Let's see: $150,000. A hundred and fifty thousand dollars might be the salary of a physio-therapist for four or five years.'

Filé pauses to exchange a few words with one of his clients, a player building up his fitness after returning from a stint in Japan, the new happy hunting ground for Brazilian footballers.

The new star of Brazilian football, Ronaldo, or Ronaldinho as he is known in Brazil, followed the same route as Romário to PSV and then on to Catalunya, and, like Romário, he took Filé along with him. Filé helped him to get back playing after a career-threatening knee injury suffered at PSV. Even though Ronaldinho was back and scoring freely for Barcelona at the time, Filé worried that he hadn't recovered the explosive force in his leg muscles, even though his thighs had regained their previous muscle bulk. He compared it to topping up half a pint of milk with water: in the end you've got a pint, but it's not the same as before.

'The difference [between Romário and Ronaldinho] is that Romário is a football genius. Ronaldinho is a great player but relies on his physique to do well. Romário, if he's not in good shape, drops back, goes into midfield, gives a pass, threads a ball through. He has that capacity. Ronaldinho doesn't have that because he's about physical strength all the time. If he loses the quality of his physical strength, just the quality of his muscular strength, his performance level begins to drop. He's playing because he's 20 years old. When he's 25, 26, if he hasn't recovered, he'll begin to fall and fall dramatically.'

Washington Rodrigues, doyen of Rio's football commentators, was spending a relaxed morning at Filé's clinic when I met him, getting some treatment on a troublesome knee. With an impressive white quiff and wearing only a pair of shorts, Rodrigues displays the proud brown belly of a Polynesian prince. He lies, beached, on a treatment table, as an ultrasound machine stimulates his aching joint.

Washington Rodrigues has been commentating, and commenting, on football for 35 years. He is a football celebrity of a type which does not exist in many other countries. Brazil has produced a string of football commentators/writers/philosophers who are held in high public esteem and whose newspaper columns are collected in books.

In Brazil, Mario Filho, Armando Nogueira, Nelson Rodrigues, João Saldanha, João Máximo and Washington Rodrigues are all household names, all the more remarkably so because none played the game at a high level. They are seen not so much as football writers as intellectuals whose specialist subject is football.

He may not have been writing about it then, but Rodrigues can well recall the trauma of the 1950 Final defeat. 'The atmosphere was one of absolute consternation and sadness. Because all of that happened at the same time as the birth of the Maracanã. I could feel in the country such a great euphoria because we had the biggest stadium in the world. And we really had a very good team at that time ... In the Final, if Brazil and Uruguay had played ten times, Brazil would have won nine. Unfortunately, the one we lost was the one we couldn't lose, which was that one.

'Whenever Brazil play against Uruguay – it could be a simple friendly – Brazil want to win because of 1950. It's the "revenge for '50", always the revenge. We've beaten them more than fifty times by now, but each time it seems like it's the first time since '50, because nobody could come to terms with that defeat.'

For Rodrigues, it is natural that sports journalists and commentators should reflect Brazilians' passion for the game.

'Brazilians have football in their blood. And nobody gets into journalism without first having their phase as a fan. I was a fan on the terraces, I used to go to see Flamengo's games wherever they were playing. I'm Flamengo, I like Flamengo a lot, I ended up manager of Flamengo, so that's how far my passion led me. And this is something that I think people shouldn't try to hide, unlike the European journalists who maintain an unbiased position. Here we've got no reason to hide it because the start of everything is you as a fan.

'I was the pioneer but I wasn't the first. Before me, Ari Barroso was a radio commentator who broadcast the game openly cheering for Flamengo. When the opposition was on the attack, he'd say: "There goes Vasco! I don't even want to look" and he'd stop commentating and look away because he was so worried that Vasco

111

might score. As this passion forms part of our lives, I think that the journalist has an obligation to show his preference, to establish an honest relationship with his listeners, with his readers.'

Washington Rodrigues himself is comparatively restrained when commentating. 'I try to stay as impartial as I can. But away from the microphone I'm Flamengo through and through.' That's certainly true. Lying there on the treatment table he refused to accept – despite all the evidence to the contrary – that Flamengo had been bested in the Fla–Flu da Lagoa. 'No, Flamengo won the game, Fluminense lost. Flamengo won the Fla–Flu da Lagoa. It was the Flamengo players who booted the ball into the lagoon.' True devotion to the cause.

While there may be an attempt at impartiality in domestic games, no such restraint applies when the *seleção* is representing the country. Two of Brazil's top football writers who attended the infamous Battle of Berne in 1954 as spectators felt that the controversial penalty for handball conceded by Brazil which started all the trouble was clearly awarded quite correctly. But when they got back to Brazil they felt it prudent to keep their thoughts to themselves because of the ferocity of public opinion at the 'injustice' which had been whipped up by Brazilian radio.

Brazilian commentators tend to start the game at the top and proceed to go right over it. In 1954 the stolid Swiss spectators were so amazed by their shrieking antics that they turned their backs on the game to watch the hot-blooded, hyperactive Latins in their open-air commentary positions at the back of the stands. Then, as now, the transcendent moment came when a goal was scored, provoking the exultant, endlessly extended cry of '*gooooooooooooooooool!*', a bullish bellow that can last half a minute, occasionally finishing with the added flourish of an '-*aço!*' if the goal is particularly good, or the commentator particularly enthusiastic.* In the 1994 World Cup one Brazilian TV commentator became a regular on US chat

---

* So arresting is this Brazilian contribution to sports broadcasting that Channel 4 adopted it, only slightly incongruously, for its coverage of Italian football.

shows, whose many viewers generally found the strangled Portuguese of his exuberant goal celebration much easier to relate to than all that business about kicking a ball around.

The fans in the commentary box are an essential complement to the action on the field. Until the advent of broadcasting via satellite in 1970, all Brazil's exploits abroad, including winning two World Cups, were followed back home on countless local radio stations. The 1962 World Cup was played in Chile which, although relatively close (lying on the other side of the Andes), was still beyond the broadcasting technology of the time and so might as well have been on the other side of the world. The videotapes had to be physically transported from the stadium in Viña del Mar to Santiago then on to Brazil for broadcast a couple of days later. The country, as it had in Brazil's previous World Cup forays, followed the game next to their wireless sets. Brazil's win over England in the quarter-finals had been conveyed vividly to the legion of listeners. The eleven Brazilian heroes had put on a footballing show rarely equalled, humbling the opposition and providing the Chilean crowds with a sporting education. Words could barely describe the brilliance of the display, but somehow they did, leaving little doubt that Brazil's team of worldbeaters would retain their title, would win '*o bicampeonato*'. That was, until the pictures arrived. Then television viewers were disappointed to find that the exhilarating bravura of the games they had heard on the radio had somehow evaporated leaving behind a more prosaic reality.

One of Brazil's top football pundits, Nelson Rodrigues (no relation), explained the discrepancy: the television pictures were wrong, he said; it was the radio commentators' imagination that had told the real story. He compared the videotape to a sort of passport photo, recording what was physically there but emptying the image of its essence, its character. The commentators had said Brazil put on a dazzling exhibition against England. It was pure imagination, but therefore, eminently true.[21] As if to bear him out, Brazil scored seven goals in their subsequent two games to win the '*bi*', with the mercurial Garrincha becoming the star of the tournament. Rodrigues summed up his view of objectivity thus: 'Only idiots are objective, they don't understand that a game of football obeys the rules of excitement!'[22]

Commentators are so much a part of the football furniture that it did not seem strange that Flamengo should appoint Washington Rodrigues their manager in 1995. In Britain the more normal route is for ex-managers to move into the broadcasting studio, but in Brazil the reverse route is not unique. One of the country's best loved commentators is also revered by many as its greatest manager. João Saldanha was the man credited with assembling the 1970 *tricampeão* team. A lifelong communist and inveterate fabulist, he claimed to have been to every World Cup finals. It wasn't literally true but he went to most, and died in 1990 at the World Cup in Italy. His informal style and his direct manner of addressing his audience had brought him huge popularity, and he brought his credibility to a national team still labouring under the disaster of 1966.

Saldanha had managed before – again on the strength of his reputation as a commentator – when Botafogo appointed him in 1957. With a team including Garrincha, Didí and Nílton Santos, he led them through one of their most successful periods. As coach of the national team, Saldanha's basic idea was to assemble all the best players and let them get on with it. On the day he was appointed, 4 February 1969, he announced two teams: his first team and his reserve team. The team that won the World Cup sixteen months later was the first team he named that day, plus three moved up from the reserves.

His team's form in the World Cup qualifying competition in 1969 was unstoppable. They had a record of played 6, won 6, scoring 23 goals, and conceding just 2. But as 1969 became 1970 the team seemed to go off the boil and Saldanha appeared powerless to turn things round.

An atmosphere of crisis was growing. The team had begun to play badly, losing a friendly to Argentina; Tostão, the top goalscorer in the qualifiers, had to undergo surgery on a detached retina and was doubtful for Mexico; and Saldanha himself was alluding darkly to 'political pressures' on him. Saldanha's position was in question

114

and Yustrich, the Flamengo manager, thought that he was the man to take over and missed no opportunity to criticize Saldanha in the press in the most insulting terms. For Saldanha, never a man to shirk a fight, it was too much. On the night of 12 March he appeared at the gates of Flamengo's *concentração* in São Conrado with a revolver in his hand demanding to see Yustrich. Fortunately, perhaps, he was not there, but a startled goalkeeper who was with the team on trial left the following day never to return.

Matters came to a head two days later when the team lost a warm-up game against the Rio club Bangu. After that game Saldanha caused a furore by insinuating that Pelé's eyesight was failing – that he was myopic – and saying he would rest him for the next match against Chile.

Three days later, the Brazilian Sports Confederation, led by João Havelange, sacked Saldanha.

Later the story would grow up that Saldanha was sacked because of his politics. Brazil at the time had a rightwing military government and the last thing they wanted, the theory ran, was an eloquent Communist representing the country in Mexico. If Brazil won the World Cup all the credit would go to the personable João Saldanha and not the fascistic regime. In a newspaper interview, the new president, General Emílio Garrastazu Médici, let slip that he was a great admirer of a particular forward, Dario. Saldanha was not. Even when injuries and illness ruled out two members of the squad, including a forward, Saldanha refused to call up Dario, preferring a midfielder. Asked about the Dario controversy, Saldanha replied that 'the president picks his ministers, I pick the team'. When he was sacked and replaced by Mario Zagallo, the new manager's first action was to call up five new players, among them Dario.

But the reality was a little more complicated. Saldanha, although an adoptive Carioca, came originally from the southern state of Rio Grande do Sul, as did General Médici. Both were big football fans, both followed Grêmio, and Médici had even played for Bagé, a team from his home state, in his younger days. Crucially, Médici was an admirer of Saldanha, despite the political gulf which separated them.

As for Dario, Médici never ordered him to be put in the team and probably never would have done. He was merely expressing his preference as a fan, the God-given right of every Brazilian. It may be true that Zagallo called up Dario, like Henry II's zealous knights, because he thought that was what the president wanted, but it is interesting that although Dario travelled with the squad to Mexico, he never played. 'Dario stayed at my side in the commentary box in Mexico the whole time. He never even made the substitutes' bench,' recalls Washington Rodrigues.

What seems most likely is that Saldanha realized things were going awry and, rather than suffer the fate of every other unsuccessful manager, he helped stoke a crisis to cover his exit. Ever after he would deny he had ever questioned Pelé's eyesight (Pelé used glasses to read, but if he really had a serious problem it only begs the question of what he might have been like if he had been able to see properly).*

Washington Rodrigues certainly thinks that Saldanha used his savvy. The manner of his departure meant that 'nobody knows exactly if he was sacked because he dropped Pelé or because his number was already up. He was very intelligent, so he left that doubt.'

Inevitably, perhaps, the João Saldanha controversy was, and to a great extent still is, swamped by political arguments. João Máximo, Saldanha's biographer, recalls those politicized times. 'The press was very censored. We couldn't say anything about the government. We used football sometimes. It was sometimes a code for talking about politics.'

The Dario episode and Saldanha's dismissal were a gift. 'We who were against the government used this. Not dishonestly, but we saw in this substitution, João Saldanha–Zagallo, a change of politics . . . We hated Zagallo: "He's the wrong man, he's not clever. He doesn't know anything about football." And that was a political position of the press, it wasn't the reality. Because Zagallo was a good coach too.'

João Máximo thinks that in the end things turned out for the

---

* Saldanha later denied he had questioned Pelé's eyesight, but João Máximo insists Saldanha told him personally.

best. 'I loved João Saldanha, but this is the real thing: it would have been a bad performance in the World Cup if at that time we had had João Saldanha as manager.'

It's a debate which continues to this day, not least because at the time of writing Zagallo is once again in control of the national team. For some he is the talisman of success, the man who won two world titles as a player, turned round a faltering team to win in 1970 and who was Carlos Alberto Parreira's right-hand man in the victory in USA '94. For others he is a lucky non-entity who had the good fortune to play alongside great players in 1958 and 1962, who inherited the world-beating team of 1970 and who produced one of the most unrecognizably negative teams in Brazilian history in 1974.*

The victories in 1958, 1962 and 1970, in which black and mixed race players such as Didi, Garrincha and Pelé showed that their *futebol arte* could win in style, changed Brazilians' attitudes to football and let them take pride in a distinctly Brazilian style. Back in the 1940s, Mario Filho, one of Brazil's greatest football writers, observed that nostalgia for the good old days of Brazilian football meant a hankering for the bygone time when Brazilian football was white. Nowadays, nostalgia is for the Pelé era, when the greatest player in the world was black and the national team captain was a mulatto (Carlos Alberto). Certainly Afro-Brazilian influence was important in forging the style of play, but it was a cultural rather than racial influence: as players, Zico and Juninho are as recognizably Brazilian as Pelé and Garrincha.

But still, even after the triumph of 1970, the doubts persisted, especially with regard to the Europeans' supposed superior discipline and professionalism, and grew during the subsequent twenty-four years in which Brazil failed to repeat its success.

The doubts are at the centre of one of the other great old chestnuts of Brazilian football: the question of the 1982 team which carried

---

* Zagallo recognized his own strengths and weaknesses. As a young player he was an inside-forward but, seeing that Brazil had several better players in that position, he switched to outside-left, where he won World Cup winners' medals in Sweden and Chile.

all before them until three goals from Paolo Rossi sent them home from Spain at the quarter-final stage. Tele Santana's team, which included Socrates, Zico, Júnior, Cerezo and Falcão, is generally rated alongside Holland '74 as one of the greatest teams never to win the World Cup. For many, the '82 side, after the dismal efforts of the 1970s to produce a more 'European' style, represented a return to Brazil's best traditions of *futebol arte*.

Washington Rodrigues is not one of them. 'The '82 team was one of the best teams that Brazil produced, but it didn't have a philosophy of play compatible with the evolution of football. We think that football has to be a show. So we were praised by everyone, but I don't even know in what round we got knocked out.

'They had marvellous technical skill, but it wasn't well used because Tele didn't do what Parreira did: that is, the important thing today is to win. You have to find the best way. If the best way was to put on a show, fine. But if not, if the important thing is the result, you have to play for the result. That's what Brazil did in '94.

'I criticize the '82 team and I approve of the '94 team. I want to win! For me what's fundamental is the result. You can put on a show when the game is already won. But if putting on a show stands in the way of the result, I'm against it.

'This Baron de Coubertain came up with a terrible idea: that what's important is the taking part. What's important is winning, not taking part. You always have to win. And Brazil played to win in '94 and won. In '82 we played to put on a show and lost.'

Washington Rodrigues's view of the relative merits of the '82 and '94 sides is not universally shared, certainly not by Zico, the star of the '82 team and the *seleção*'s top scorer after Pelé:

'I think that it was really one of the best teams Brazilian football has produced. Unfortunately, Brazilians are very concerned with results. So this mentality means that the '82 team is seen as a losing side. Abroad everybody recognizes it as a great team, but in Brazil, few people do. I think that that team's defeat was bad for world football. Because if Brazil had won, football would have changed.

'The '94 team played just to get the result. Brazil didn't attack,

Brazil just defended and counter-attacked with two players, Bebeto and Romário. Without Bebeto and Romário, Brazil wouldn't have won the World Cup.

'So he [Carlos Alberto Parreira] banked everything on two players and maintained a totally defensive set-up. He wasn't worried about taking a risk, he preferred to play for a 0–0 and try to win the game on penalties than to risk trying to win the game.'

Zico, a fit-looking 44-year-old, remains for many Brazilians the best player the country has produced since Pelé, although abroad his image has had to cope with the underachievement of the Brazil sides he played in and the fact that his time in Italy was spent with unfashionable Udinese. He was speaking in his office, a short drive from Filé's clinic at the Zico Football Centre. Wearing the centre's own kit, with its ubiquitous logo of a silhouetted Zico in action, the white shirt and shorts offset by an incongruous black briefcase, he looked relaxed and businesslike.

The son of a Portuguese immigrant father, Zico was born Artur Antunes Coimbra. He spent 22 years at Flamengo, before and after his two-year stint in Italy, and is still closely associated with the club. In 1981, a Zico-led Flamengo won the South American Club Championship and then went on to beat Liverpool – then at the peak of their powers – 3–0 in Tokyo to claim the world club title.

His last game in the World Cup came in 1986 against France. With the scores level, Brazil were awarded a penalty. Zico, who had only just come on as a substitute, took it and missed. Brazil eventually lost the game on a penalty shoot-out.* I'd always wanted

---

* This match provoked much discussion in Brazil about their players' penalty-taking ability. Partly to address this, the vice-president of the national league, Nabi Abi Chedid, decreed that penalty shoot-outs would settle all drawn games (the winner getting two points, the loser one – winners in 90 minutes would get three). Some clubs refused to accept this, so the first games produced several 'unresolved' draws. When the recalcitrant clubs came on board a few weeks later, the shoot-outs had to be replayed. So, for example, hundreds of people were let in free to the Maracanã to watch the delayed shoot-out between Fluminense and Botafogo.

to know why he took it when he had only just stepped on the pitch, but I felt a bit awkward that from a career of such outstanding achievement I was choosing to dredge up his most public moment of failure.

'I don't have any problem in talking about that. I lay my head on the pillow and sleep soundly because that's part of life and part of football. Whoever takes a penalty has to be prepared to miss. It's this Brazilian mentality of always wanting to find a scapegoat: this happened in other eras, in other World Cups. I didn't shoot well, but it wasn't because of that that Brazil were knocked out. Brazil lost in the shoot-out, in which I scored; Italy in '82, Cabrini missed a penalty, but they won the game. Do you remember who missed the penalty for Brazil in the '94 World Cup? Because Brazil won, no one remembers. If Brazil had not won everybody would have remembered.'

But why had he taken the penalty?

'As I was on the pitch, everyone left it for me to take the decision. At that time nobody was going to think that I was coming on just at that moment and wasn't into the swing of the game . . . in the previous game we had a penalty and Socrates took it, so when I placed the ball I even went and had a word with him, and he said: "Fine, go ahead." And I thought: you should be taking it, dammit. But imagine if I had been on the pitch and hadn't taken it and someone else did and missed. It would have been a problem.'

Another thing that Zico and Washington Rodrigues don't agree about is Romário. Rodrigues was Romário's manager during his brief stint at Flamengo. With him, he says, Romário, notoriously a hell-raising bad boy, was as good as gold: 'Contrary to what they say, Romário doesn't drink, doesn't smoke . . . With Romário I never had any problem. I was his best man, he just got married for the second or third time. He never missed a day with me, didn't turn up late, never failed to fulfil his obligations. Neither him nor Edmundo.'

Zico, on the other hand, has on a number of occasions criticized Romário, who now occupies the role he once had as the idol of the

Mengão masses. After 22 years at the club Zico remains a Flamengo institution whose views are taken seriously.

'In professional terms, Romário and Maradona are good examples because they are winners, they won titles,' Zico says. 'In social terms, without a doubt they are terrible examples because of the life they lead. Maradona is a bad example because of the drugs and Romário is a bad example because he's a party person, a nightclub man.

'But Romário's changing, he's living a different sort of life from the one he used to, because he understands that he needs to look after his body to be able to perform on the field. If not, he'll never be the player he's capable of being.'*

In his playing days Zico was a model professional, a clean-living family man devoted to his wife. On the wall of his office is a framed certificate from something called the Father's Day Council of the Japan Men's Fashion Unity, praising him as a role model. It's a souvenir of his lucrative Indian summer in Japan when he helped launch the J-League with Kashima Antlers. His off-field image was just as important as his playing ability for his Japanese employers. He is still technical director of Kashima Antlers and divides his time between Rio and Japan, and it was his Japanese earnings which allowed him to build the Zico Centre, with its excellent grass pitches and enviable facilities.†

Traditionally, of course, the youth of Brazil doesn't need such luxuries to refine its footballing skills. The *pelada*, a game played in rudimentary conditions on an improvised pitch, was the nursery of new talent where boys honed their skills. But Rio, like most Brazilian cities, has grown enormously over recent decades. Many of those open spaces have simply disappeared.

* Romário's lifestyle does not appear to have changed that much. A few months after Zico spoke, Romário, starting the new season with the Spanish club Valencia, responded angrily after being upbraided by his coach for staying out until 4 a.m. two days before a league match. 'The night is my friend,' Romário said. 'In my private life I do what I like . . . my team-mates can get stuffed.'

† In March 1998, Zico was appointed Zagallo's assistant for the World Cup.

'Over in Quintino [a Rio suburb] where I used to live there were eight grass pitches. Now it's all buildings, flats and housing. In my day there were many football pitches throughout Rio. I think we have lost the chance to have many great players because of the lack of space to play football in the street, so many people look for another route. If you're not going to play football, you're going to go for basketball, for video games, for volleyball, or go to the beach to surf.'

Of course, Rio still has its beaches where young Cariocas can show off their football skills, but even there you are as likely to find a game of volleyball, or that Brazilian hybrid, *fute-volei*.

Zico says the reason he built the centre – in Barra, a new addition to Rio's beachfront sprawl, twenty-odd miles down the coast from Copacabana – was that he had a boys' team with nowhere to play in the area. The football school takes boys from the age of 6 up to 17, separated into five age-group categories. The parents pay a fee but there is a sliding scale of bursaries, and some pay nothing. About 700 kids have been signed up for this year's course. Several pitches of various sizes boast some of the best-looking turf in Rio. There is a gym and an administration block, including the inevitable shop selling Zico merchandise.

'The first objective is to give these kids the opportunity to play real football, on grass, on a field, because here isn't just a place for those who want to go on to play professional football. We've got many kids who come here, play, and don't have any interest in being professionals. Their parents send the kids here because it's a nice, pleasant place; they're safe and the place has a positive attitude. We want to prepare citizens, not just footballers.'

For those kids with ability who want more out of their time at the Zico Centre than just becoming better citizens, Zico has another project bubbling away. 'If they've got talent, we're not just going to spend all our time coaching them for someone else. So I created a football team, Rio de Janeiro FC, that's going to take part in the Rio de Janeiro state championship. What I want to do is, in three years' time, have a professional team of kids who've graduated from here.'

The idea was to enter Rio de Janeiro FC in the third division of the state championship and progress up the divisions to break the dominance of the big four Rio clubs – Flamengo, Fluminense, Botafogo and Vasco da Gama. Already, in 1997, the club achieved promotion to the second division. Plans are afoot to build a couple of stands around the centre's main pitch that should provide room for 4000 spectators. One of Zico's sons is carrying on the family tradition in Rio de Janeiro's juniors.

Zico's ambition is that in ten years' time the game between Flamengo and his own Rio de Janeiro FC will rival the status of the Fla–Flu.

'Right now my team's supporters are the parents and friends of the players. When they start doing well, they could attract a lot of people, a whole set of youngsters who aren't committed to any club. So I hope that in ten years we could have a great match between Rio de Janeiro and Flamengo. It's hard to say who I'd support.'

Despite the diminishing space available for kids to play the game and despite the often brutal tactics used to stop skilful players, somehow Brazil continues to produce great players. Many Brazilians talk of the current generation as the best in years. Zico feels ambivalent about Brazil's young players who leave the country to play abroad at an ever earlier age. Over 300 have gone abroad in the last decade. In Spain alone, nearly 30 Brazilians are currently plying their trade, even after the departure of Ronaldo to Italy. 'Footballers are Brazil's main raw material, and much sought-after,' Zico says, matter-of-factly, and as a man who has made millions from his sport he doesn't begrudge others making their fortune with a football. But he worries that money is now coming to dominate football in a way it didn't before.

'Nowadays it's more about seeking fame and financial reward, not just the pleasure of playing. I hear a lot of parents say they want their son to play and be as good as so-and-so and make money, have this year's car, an apartment, women, all these things. So these days football is another way of making a living. Before it wasn't. It was a sport, a pleasure, a joy. It didn't get the same media coverage, footballers didn't appear on the society pages, they weren't headlines. It was just football.'

4: High Anxiety

On 12 December 1995 a curious item was carried by Reuters news agency. Bolivia, it reported, had come to a standstill. For five minutes in the middle of the day people in the streets of La Paz and other cities stopped what they were doing: shops stopped trading, buses stopped running. It was a scene reminiscent of the days when, at the eleventh hour of the eleventh month, Britain would come to a halt to remember in silence the millions who died in the Great War. But the Bolivian stoppage was far from silent – radio stations blared out the national anthem, people chanted – and it was not a commemoration of war or mass slaughter. To paraphrase Bill Shankly, it was something much more important than that.

The cause of the commotion was a decision by international football authorities to ban international matches from being played at altitudes above 3000 metres (approximately 10,000 ft). The ruling was based on a recommendation by Fifa's medical commission that playing at high altitude was a health threat to players. And the only stadium above 3000m where international football is regularly played is in the Bolivian capital, La Paz, which stands at 3600m (12,000 ft) above sea-level. Bolivian outrage was fierce and genuine.

'It is remarkable that from the plains, to the *altiplano* and the valleys, everyone has been united against this veto,' said the Bolivian president, Gonzalo Sánchez de Lozada, who personally led the campaign to keep football in La Paz, the world's highest capital city. His government announced that it 'would support with the greatest determination and energy the actions of the Bolivian Football Federation to repair this injustice'.[1]

Although Fifa's concerns were couched in health terms, the real reason was that some of the visiting teams felt Bolivia were gaining an unfair advantage by playing in the thin air of La Paz. A glance at Bolivia's results in the qualifying tournament for the 1994 World Cup would appear to show they have a point. Away from home Bolivia managed only one victory, against Venezuela, the traditional whipping boys of South American football. At home, Bolivia's record was played four, won four, including a historic 2–0 result against Brazil, their first ever defeat in a World Cup qualifying tournament. (Brazil beat Bolivia 6–0 in the return game in tropical Recife.) Bolivia went on to qualify at the expense of two-time world champions Uruguay.

Bolivia's only other important international triumph came in 1963, when it won the South American Championship. The tournament was played in Bolivia. The isolated nature of this success is perhaps indicated by the title of a book published in Bolivia in the 1970s: *Does Bolivian Football Exist?*

So Bolivia may have benefited from playing at altitude, but nobody likes a bad loser. The chairman of the Bolivian Football Federation, José Saavedra Banzer, for one was unimpressed with the arguments against La Paz. For him, the altitude issue was above all a question of sovereignty. 'Each country is sovereign over the question of where to play. In which city, at what temperature, at what altitude and all the rest,' he says. 'We didn't build a stadium here to gain an illicit advantage. That stadium has been there for more than one hundred years.'

Sovereignty. It's a touchy subject in Bolivia. No one consulted Bolivia when the world price of tin went through the floor in the 1980s, wiping out one of the Andean country's main industries at a stroke. One of the poorest countries – if not the poorest – in the continent, it's pretty much resigned to the fact that its opinion doesn't count for much in international affairs, but it naturally resents outsiders telling it what to do within its own borders. And the outline of its borders is another reason why national sovereignty strikes such a nerve for Bolivia. A hundred and fifty years ago there was a lot more of Bolivia than there is today. Between 1879 and

1883 Bolivia and Peru fought a disastrous war against Chile for control of the vast Atacama Desert, which had been of little interest to anyone until its enormous mineral potential became apparent. The result of the aptly named War of the Pacific was that Chile became that much longer and thinner and Bolivia lost its access to the sea, a fact it has not ceased to mourn bitterly to this day. Bolivia still maintains a rather sad little navy which putters around Lake Titicaca, high in the Andes, in half-hearted pursuit of smugglers and the like. To listen to Bolivians you might think the war ended some time last week instead of in the days before the horseless carriage was even a twinkle in Mr Daimler's eye and the Old Etonians were still appearing in the FA Cup Final. It's a folk memory, which football fans have done their bit to preserve. The most famous chant in support of the Bolivian team – first heard during the victorious 1963 South American Championship campaign[2] – is the distinctive '*Bo-bo-bo; li-li-li; via-via-via; Vi-va-Bo-li-via-to-da-la-vi-da-con-su-li-to-ral!*' (Long live Bolivia, forever with its coastline!)

Beyond the indignation at the slight to the nation, there were more tangible reasons for Bolivian outrage. If Fifa were to veto La Paz, who would be next? As the mayor of La Paz, Ronald Maclean, noted, any or all international sporting bodies might ban the Bolivian capital as a venue. Teams from Santa Cruz, Bolivia's second city, which stands a measly 400-odd metres above sea-level, could justifiably refuse to play in the capital. And why should it stop at sport? Business conventions could go elsewhere, tourism could suffer, international meetings might discreetly find reasons to avoid the city. The potential damage was incalculable.

Football has been played in the *altiplano*, the Andean plateau, for over a century. The oldest side, Oruro Royal Club, was founded in 1886 in the city of Oruro, which at 4000m above sea-level is even higher than La Paz. As elsewhere in Latin America, British influence played a key role in the early days, as football followed the railways into the country. A few clubs, such as The Strongest – one of La Paz's top teams, founded in 1908 – Blooming and Destroyers, retain their English names. The marvellously named club, Always Ready, is now sadly defunct. A league started up in La Paz in 1914 and it wasn't until the mid-1950s that teams from outside the city were admitted, eventually forming a truly national league.

Since 1950 Bolivia's national team has played some 50 times in La Paz and Oruro. Since 1960, when the Copa Libertadores was introduced, over 300 competitive international club matches have been played in Bolivia, more than 80 per cent of them in the high cities.

The Hernando Siles stadium in La Paz was built as long ago as 1930 (although not as long ago as one hundred years back). It was extensively remodelled in 1977 and, with its 50,000 capacity, stands comparison with any of the continent's major stadia. It is in a real sense the pride of the nation.

José Saavedra is clearly a man used to getting his own way. For a day-job, when not presiding over the Bolivian Football Federation, he runs a large industrial conglomerate from a suitably large office in central La Paz. A big man, he likes to turn up at the big games in his personalized silk scarf bearing his nickname, Chacho, his presence signalled by a busy knot of journalists, buzzing like worker bees eager to bear off the queen's instructions to the rest of the hive (in this case, Bolivia).

Leaning back behind his big desk, and with the slightly weary air of a man spelling out the difficult words in his address for the umpteenth time, he dismisses the medical arguments raised against playing in the city. 'It was illogical that [Fifa] should review the question of altitude when what they should have done is analyse the set of problems that different countries have, be it altitude, excessive heat, excessive cold, humidity, pollution. And when, medically, there is a study of all that, we can say what is it that does most damage to a player. Whether it's playing in a city with a lot of pollution, like Santiago de Chile, or Mexico City, or playing in a city at altitude.'

Particularly galling for him was the way in which Fifa had handled the affair. 'The Fifa executive committee left the decision in the hands of the South American countries. So it said to them: "Do you want to go and play at altitude or not?" And so eight countries said no, with the exception, of course, of Bolivia and of Ecuador, which stood by us. It's like if you ask, "Do you want to dance with the pretty one or the ugly one?" So they all said, "No, we don't want to play at altitude." But vice versa they never asked Bolivia if we want to go to play in Bahia [in Brazil] in 40-degree heat and 80 per cent humidity.' It was to become clear to me that the infernal insufferability of the Brazilian tropics had acquired mythical status in Bolivia.

Colombia, the next visitors to La Paz, had informed the Bolivian federation that they intended to stage their World Cup qualifier at midday in the heat of Medellín. It could have been worse. Colombia often likes to take visiting teams to the steamy Caribbean port of Barranquilla, which can have even the Brazilians wilting. Saavedra insists every country has the right to decide where in its territory it wants to play, especially when that city is its capital. Pedants might quibble that Bolivia in fact has two capitals, although Sucre, also in the *altiplano*, is now only the seat of the Supreme Court. Still, you can't help feeling a certain sympathy towards a country whose two capital cities translate as Peace and Sugar (OK, so Sucre was actually named after a general and it only means sugar in French, but you see what I mean).

Saavedra had led the Bolivian campaign to block the move to ban internationals in La Paz. This involved producing a glossy brochure in English and Spanish – *Bolivia: Up to the Altitude Challenge* – one of whose main purposes seemed to be to boast about the national team's poor home record. Brazil, Argentina, Uruguay, Paraguay, Peru, Colombia, it proudly declared, they've all come here and won! Since 1957 Bolivia has played in nine World Cup qualifying tournaments and has only got through once. The booklet contains reams of similar statistics demonstrating how little advantage Bolivia has gained from its geographical characteristics and how unsuccessful Bolivian teams have been. It cites articles concerning sovereignty and non-discrimination from Fifa's own regulations and from the United Nations charter. It also reproduces two pages of testimonials from international figures, led by President Jacques Chirac of France ('Morality demands that we be solidary [sic] with Bolivians. It's shameful to deprive Bolivia from the France '98 play-offs in the city of La Paz [sic]'). It also surprisingly reproduces the heartfelt support of Julio Grondona, president of the Argentinian Football Association – surprisingly, because Argentina was one of the eight South American countries which had voted against playing at altitude.

But why, after so many years of football in La Paz, had the issue been raised at all? Who had cast the first stone?

'I don't want to involve absolutely anybody,' said the Bolivian Football Federation chairman, maintaining a flawless poker face. 'I've got no reason to. All I've done is defend the sovereignty and the right of my country and I'll go on doing that.'

Sovereignty is all very well, but high altitude does have real physical effects on the body and measurably affects athletic performance. Bolivia has, of course, long since recognized this and can boast probably the leading research centre in the world, the Bolivian Institute for the Biology of Altitude (IBBA), set up to investigate precisely those effects.

Its director, Dr Enrique Vargas Pacheco, stresses that high altitude is a normal environment for millions of people in the Andean region and in Mesoamerica. Bogotá is 2600m above sea-level, Quito stands at 2800m, Cuzco is 3300m and Mexico City is 2200m above sea-level. The two greatest American civilizations at the time of the Conquest – the Incas and the Aztecs – both developed and had their capitals at high altitude. Although most of Bolivia's territory lies in the Amazon basin, about 70 per cent of its population live in the *altiplano*, the broad high plain bounded to the east and west by mountain ranges reaching over 6000m high. Potosí, at 4000m, was once the biggest city in the Americas, as immigrants poured in to excavate its silver mountain. In its sixteenth-century heyday its population equalled that of London and surpassed Paris, Rome, Madrid and Seville.

The people who have lived here for generations have developed certain physiological modifications which help them cope with the

130

thin air. The highland Aymara and Quechua peoples are typically short, with big chests. They have a greater lung capacity and more haemoglobin in their blood to transport scarce oxygen more efficiently. But most people's bodies, given a little time, will adapt well enough to the conditions at high altitude. In the short term, though, the effects can be dramatic. Some visitors arriving from low altitude feel ill the moment they step off the plane at El Alto, which, as the name implies, is even higher than central La Paz. Symptoms may include splitting headaches, nausea and tiredness, although many people feel no ill effects. *Mate de coca* (coca tea) is a traditional cure to moderate the effects of altitude sickness. It's a simple, readily available infusion, using hot water and leaves from the same plant used to produce cocaine. A few years back, a Bolivian international, Rimba, failed a dope test which detected traces of cocaine, but he managed to get his suspension rescinded by persuading the authorities that the positive result came from some coca tea he had drunk before the game, and that the minuscule quantities of the active agent could not have affected his performance.

The problem with the air at altitude is not that there's anything different about it – it has exactly the same composition as at sea-level – it's just that there's so little of it: the barometric pressure may be as little as half that at the lower level.

Because of the different ways the body generates energy during exercise, altitude affects different sports to different degrees. Aerobic sports, like long-distance running, involve the athlete consuming large quantities of oxygen to maintain his or her performance. But a sprinter may not even breathe at all during the 10 or so seconds of a 100m dash: the energy is drawn from that already stored in the muscles. These anaerobic sports – such as sprints, jumps and throws – are not significantly affected by altitude, although the thinness of the air means aerobic sports are.* According to the Bolivian

* The very thinness of the air, and consequent reduced wind resistance, may even have helped Bob Beamon to set his historic long jump record at the Mexico Olympics in 1968.

131

government's pamphlet on the subject, at the top end of the scale of oxygen consumption is cross-country skiing and at the bottom end golf, which is unfortunate, as there are many more snow-capped peaks than golf courses in the *altiplano*. Football, though, is somewhere in the middle.

'Football is a mixed sport,' explains Dr Vargas. 'A player runs for a few seconds – he never covers 100 metres at a stretch. He'll run 10 or 15 metres, then he'll release the ball or he'll make a run off the ball, but not at full speed . . . These are periods in which the body uses its own muscular energy with little oxygen. Obviously there have to be periods of rest in between, but this too depends on good training, on good tactics.'

Unfit players will quickly get found out in the rarefied atmosphere. Likewise, a team whose game is built on running hard for 90 minutes had better think again. The key lies in expending energy in short bursts and then giving the body time to recover, something that with good organization should be quite possible in a team game like football. Some players adapt physically better than others, and in the wake of Bolivia's success South America's big football nations have put considerable effort into studying this and other altitude-related problems.

Much of the controversy around the altitude issue turned on the question of acclimatization. Fifa's medical committee recommended an acclimatization period of ten days, which would make, for example, the release of players for international duty even more problematic than it currently is.

Teams visiting La Paz have dealt with the problem in a number of ways. Some have spent long periods of up to two or three weeks training at altitude beforehand. Others have arrived on the day of the game. Yet others have opted for periods in between. The average acclimatization period has been just over three days. In 1973 Argentina had to play in Bolivia in the qualifiers for the World Cup in West Germany. Known as the 'ghost' team, the squad spent several weeks training at altitude in northern Argentina and in Peru. However, only half of the 'ghosts' made the team for the game in La

Paz; the rest arrived straight from Buenos Aires on the day of the game. Argentina won 1–0.

According to Dr Vargas the most important adaptations to altitude by human body take place after 72 hours. The important thing, in terms of acclimatization, is not to do things by halves; either arrive and play the same day (before the effects of altitude fully kick in) or the following day, or else spend ten days or more adapting to the conditions. The statistics show that of twenty visiting international teams that either won or drew with Bolivia in La Paz or Oruro, two arrived the same day, nine arrived the day before, three arrived two days before and two arrived three days before. A week was the longest acclimatization period for any team which got a result (Uruguay, 1–1 in 1961).

One of the reasons the Bolivians feel put upon is that while all the countries grumble about playing up in the mountains, the change from the *altiplano* to sea-level is, they say, equally traumatic for them. Dr Vargas, born and bred in La Paz, confirms the horrors of low altitude. He used to be the team doctor for Bolivia's national football squad and travelled with them on foreign tours.

'When a person comes up to altitude one of its effects is to eliminate liquid from the person. He suffers a lot. On the other hand, when we go down, for the first few hours it doesn't affect us. After 72 hours you start to retain liquid and of course you put on weight. And a player that's too heavy is no use for anything. Indeed, in some cases – and I have worked with the national team – it has been necessary to put on a size bigger boot. We went on a tour around Brazil for a fortnight – woo! – things just got worse and worse.'

It's not just something that affects teams playing internationally. Bolivia's second largest city is Santa Cruz de la Sierra which, despite its name, is nowhere near a sierra – in fact it's as flat as yesterday's Tizer – and is more or less at sea-level (400m being as near as dammit in Bolivia). That means that players in the Bolivian league can find themselves travelling up to two miles vertically every other week. Bolivian league teams nearly always arrive on the day or the day before the game, and whatever the players may feel about it, they just get on with it and have done for decades.

'This is a phenomenon known as intermittent self-exposure. This is something we're studying at the moment – we don't have all the answers. It's clear that it could also have some influence,' says Dr Vargas.

Even commuters within the capital can be affected by these altitude changes. Central La Paz is at 3600m high, but the vast slum city of El Alto, which squats above it, is nearer 4000m high, and the Zona Sur, where well-off *paceños* live, is significantly lower.

'We're beginning to study people who live in high areas and go down to work in low-lying areas. It happens in the El Alto area and in the Zona Sur. In the high area there is a barometric pressure of approximately 452. In the Zona Sur it's 510. There's a difference in altitude and barometric pressure which is significant. In a car it would take you some 20–30 minutes depending on the traffic. They sleep up the top and spend all day working down below. And they go back to sleep in the evening. There are people who own factories who sleep down here and spend all day up there working in El Alto. The climate in El Alto is pretty harsh, pretty harsh.'

There is one further paradox about the altitude controversy. Bolivia is accused of gaining an advantage from the conditions in La Paz because its players are used to them. But in fact most of the players in the national team – as much as 80–85 per cent – are not from the *altiplano* at all, but from lowland cities such as Santa Cruz. The goalkeeper is a naturalized Argentinian, Coimbra is from Santa Cruz, and the captain, Marco Antonio Etcheverry, and Middlesbrough's first South American Jaime Moreno (both from Santa Cruz), played their club football during the qualifying campaign in the lowland environment of the US Major League. Their home ground is in Washington DC, a city built on a subtropical swamp. Even *paceño* league teams these days have a fair sprinkling of lowland players.

Still, critics of La Paz as a venue point to Bolivia's success in the last World Cup qualifying campaign, built on a flawless home record.

Bolivian football has never amounted to much, they argue, so it must be the altitude.

Dr Vargas has another answer. 'I think it's all down to the Tahuichi Academy. Because ten years ago Bolivian football didn't matter. Everybody came here and won. Sometimes we drew, maybe sometimes we won. Santos came with Pelé and gave us a thrashing. But as of at least ten years, maybe twenty years, the Tahuichi Academy began to work really seriously. And the good thing is they have developed some really good, young players.'

If you've heard anything about Bolivian football before, apart from their brief and inglorious presence in USA '94, you've probably heard about the Tahuichi Academy.

The Tahuichi Academy has been named, variously: Ambassador of the Youth of America and Pride of the Member Countries (by the Organization of American States), Messenger of Peace and Integration of the Sports Fields of the World, United Nations Goodwill Ambassador Against Drugs, and Ambassador of the Youth of Bolivia. It has been awarded Bolivia's highest honour, the Condor of the Andes, and has three times been nominated for the Nobel Peace Prize. According to a Catholic priest from New Jersey, quoted in the academy's publicity: 'The work of Tahuichi is a sign of the kingdom of God among us.'

It may therefore come as some surprise that what the Tahuichi Academy actually does is teach kids to play football.

The academy was founded in 1978 by Rolando Aguilera and named Tahuichi in honour of his father Ramón Aguilera, the doyen of Santa Cruz football in the 1940s and 1950s, whose nickname means Big Bird in the local indigenous language. Rolando Aguilera spent the years between 1971 and 1977 in the United States, having been expelled by Bolivia's military regime because he was a minister in the previous government. The school grew out of his desire that his sons, who had spent their formative years in the football desert of the States, should not miss out on the beautiful game. He hired a coach for his children but before long their friends and other local kids started coming along and, like Topsy, it grow'd and grow'd.

135

Since those homely beginnings Tahuichi has enjoyed two decades of almost unbroken success. In 1979 it won the Bolivian schoolboys championship. The following year, the team travelled to Buenos Aires for a prestigious South American schoolboy tournament. It was the first time a Bolivian team – any Bolivian team – had won anything abroad, and the victorious boys were presented to the then president, Lidia Gueiler. Since then, Tahuichi teams have played in Brazil, Argentina, Uruguay, Chile, Peru, Colombia, Cuba, the United States, China, the Soviet Union, Finland, Norway, Sweden, Denmark, Germany, Holland, England, Wales and Spain, and have won most of the competitions they have entered, including something called the Ian Rush Cup in Wales.

In 1985 Fifa specifically invited Tahuichi, as opposed to Bolivia, to participate in the World Under-16 Championship in Beijing in recognition of its achievements. The following year, the Tahuichi team, competing as Bolivia, won the South American Under-16 Championship in Lima.

The founder's eldest son, Roly, a civil engineer, helps out at the academy on a voluntary basis, as well he might since the whole enterprise was originally mounted for him. We talked in the academy's dazzling trophy room, a treasure trove the size of a bus, adorned with ranks of silverware on three sides and walls decorated with press cuttings and pictures of the likes of Maradona, Pelé and Havelange blessing Tahuichi's efforts. Many of the trophies were lifted by Roly himself as captain.

The whole idea of the academy, he says, stems from a refusal to accept that Bolivian football should be perpetually second best.

Hot, low-lying and tropical, Santa Cruz is nothing like La Paz but enjoys broadly similar geographical conditions to neighbouring Brazil, Argentina and Paraguay. Why shouldn't it, Tahuichi's founder reasoned, produce comparable footballers? Santa Cruz is a fast-developing boom town. The centre of Bolivia's oil industry, over the last two decades its population has mushroomed to around a million people, becoming the country's second city. It has also become a major transit centre for the drug trade, exporting Andean-produced cocaine via Brazil and Paraguay. Giving kids an alternative to getting into drugs is another of Tahuichi's stated aims.

At the start, says Roly Aguilera, Bolivian clubs overlooked Tahuichi's silver mine of talent. 'Nowadays the clubs like to take ex-Tahuichis, but initially there was a problem of credibility ... Etcheverry and the World Cup helped us a lot. It helped give us the credibility that our footballers could make it at international level.'

The 1994 World Cup squad contained nine Tahuichi graduates and although Etcheverry himself had a disappointing tournament – not fully fit, he came on as a sub against Germany in the first match and within minutes lashed out foolishly at a defender, was harshly sent off and missed the rest of Bolivia's matches through suspension – his and the others' heroics in qualification had not gone unnoticed.

'In Bolivia the professional teams ought to have their youth teams, but for financial and economic reasons they have dropped them because for many years Bolivian football was not solvent. We live in a very poor country. So the professional teams could barely survive.'

The Tahuichi Academy filled that gap and now the proof of the pudding is the professional success of its old boys. By 1996, 156 Tahuichi graduates had moved up to the Bolivian national league and, as the academy's reputation has grown, so its old boys have become more and more sought after.

'Our first players, like Etcheverry, Platini [nickname for Erwin Sánchez], Cristaldo, didn't benefit us much in economic terms. We practically had to give them away to the clubs. Now clubs call us asking for players, so now the Academy usually only sells half the registration to Bolivian clubs, because where the big money is is in the resale abroad. We haven't actually made any money out of this yet but the process is in train as of two years ago. With Etcheverry, with Moreno, with Juan Manuel Peña, we didn't get anything when they were sold on. All the money went to their clubs. With the new players we hope to get something to help us make ends meet.'

Some 3000 boys between 6 and 18 come to the Tahuichi Academy in six age-group bands. The youngest ones train on fields next to the city's main stadium, also called Tahuichi Aguilera, which is home to Santa Cruz's professional teams, such as Oriente Petrolero and Blooming. The Tahuichi Academy has plans to build a new centre on the edge of the city. Currently all that is to be seen is the shell of the planned administration block and the changing rooms. On three bare, rudimentary pitches, boys raise clouds of dust as they play, while grazing cattle enjoy the surrounding grass. The city of Santa Cruz provided the land – some 25 hectares – for what is to be the Villa Niño Feliz (Happy Child Town). The whole thing is set to cost about $1 million.

'Obviously we haven't got a million dollars,' says Roly Aguilera. 'So we're doing it bit by bit over the course of five to ten years. But you have to make a start somewhere.' Different non-governmental organizations have financed stages of the project while the academy waits for the next Etcheverry to be sold on.

So, is, as Dr Vargas suggested, Tahuichi ultimately responsible for the campaign to get La Paz banned as a venue?

Well, says Roly Aguilera, it was all really down to Brazil losing their unbeaten record at that game in La Paz. 'Tahuichi played a part in that defeat because two members of that team [Etcheverry and Peña] came from Tahuichi. So as for what the doctor said, I thank him, and I think we chipped in our grain of sand to achieve that victory, and to have a competitive national team which got to the World Cup.'

Of course, even Tahuichi teams are affected by altitude. 'We find that if we take eighteen players up to La Paz, maybe three won't be able to play. Some kids are affected more by altitude than others. They can't play. Others don't perform as well. And others aren't affected. It depends on each kid's metabolism.'

Etcheverry and Moreno were among several Tahuichi graduates in the team for Bolivia's World Cup clash with Colombia on 10 November 1996. But although their places in the starting line-up against the pacesetters in the group were assured, they were having great difficulty getting a game anywhere else. Both had been in at the start of the new US Major League in 1995 playing for Washington DC United. But their old clubs in Bolivia had quickly spotted an opportunity and reached an agreement with their US clubs to temporarily transfer their registration for a month during the Major League close season. This period – from 11 November to 10 December – happily coincided with the six-team play-offs which decide the Bolivian championship. It would also mean that both players would be in Bolivia and in competitive action in the build-up to the World Cup qualifier against Paraguay on 15 December.

Good for their clubs, good for the country and good for the Bolivian fans, who would have the chance to see two of the country's greatest sporting stars.

Not so good, though, for the other four teams in the play-offs. The Strongest, Real Santa Cruz, Independiente Petrolero and San José all protested that the arrangement broke the rules of the competition and should not be allowed to stand.

Mauricio González, the chairman of The Strongest, explained, more in sorrow than in anger, that it was simply a question of making sure everything was done correctly. 'We have no objection to anything or anybody as long as it's within the rules. We ask that the rules of the game and the regulations of the championship be respected, so that nobody just acts according to their own whim.' The fact that their bitterest rival, Bolívar, might be able to field the country's most prodigious footballing talent clearly had nothing to do with it.

Faced with this situation, the Bolivian Football Federation referred the matter to Fifa. The day after the Colombia match on 12 October the FBF announced the response. Although both players had been registered for the Bolivian league competition before the 30 September deadline their registration had not been transferred until the end of the US season weeks later. As Fifa does not allow a player to be registered in two countries simultaneously, Moreno and Etcheverry were out. (Jorge Campos, the flamboyant Mexican goalkeeper-cum-centre-forward, was similarly barred from turning out for his old club in Mexico.)

Bolívar's chairman, Mauro Bertero, accused the leadership of the

FBF of having acted in bad faith, of having approached Fifa with the sole aim of getting the transfers ruled illegal. 'We respect and reiterate our respect for the national football authorities. As we say, it's not the institutions who are bad but the people who run them,' he complained. Quite who he had in mind he didn't say.

Bolívar were thus obliged to struggle on without one World Cup veteran but could at least count on another World Cup finals veteran. Tommy Nkono played in goal for Cameroon in the 1982 finals in Spain, again in their heroic 1990 campaign and was also part of his country's rather sorry contribution to USA '94.

And now here he was keeping goal in La Paz of all places. He came to Bolivia, he says, accompanying a young Nigerian player. While in La Paz he turned out in a training game and the club asked him to stay. He was out of contract and said yes. As simple as that. But even so . . . Bolivia?

Outside Bolívar's stadium after a morning training session, 'Tommy' patiently signed autographs for a small knot of youngsters. In his short time in La Paz he has become a hugely popular and instantly recognizable local hero. (Bolivia's black population is small, the descendants of slaves who worked the country's mines when it was a Spanish colony, and has not preserved a distinct identity.) We took a taxi back to his apartment in one of the better parts of La Paz, which Bolívar had provided him with, where I had to wait in the corridor while he went in and pacified his wife. The somewhat lively conversation that ensued on the other side of the door seemed to turn on the theme of 'not another one of your football mates . . .'. The door opened again and I was invited in: Mrs Nkono must have relented.

A young-looking 39, Tommy Nkono was happy to talk in Spanish, French or English. He had been in La Paz nearly two years and his contract was up in a few weeks' time, after the play-offs. His children were in school in Spain, where he spent several years with Espanyol, and he was clearly keen to return to Europe.

So had he had trouble adjusting to Bolivia and to the altitude in particular?

'Well, it's always difficult, but the body, one way or another, gets used to anything. After a week or so it's fine.'

I suggested that it was probably easier for goalkeepers, as they don't have to do so much running about, but he firmly explained that goalies work just as hard as the rest of the team. 'You can say that during a game the attacks aren't constant but at the end of the day it's the same. You have to work like everyone else . . . even twice as hard as the others.' (Well, that told me.)

Nkono had played in the famous World Cup quarter-final against England in Naples, which Cameroon were leading 2–1 before eventually losing 3–2 after conceding two penalties. It was a game that had captivated a worldwide audience, with an African side tantalizingly on the brink of reaching the World Cup semi-finals for the first time ever. What had it been like to take part in such a thrilling match?

He declined to wallow in the warm glow of nostalgia, to aver that, despite the result, it had been a great match, a privilege to take part and that no, you couldn't allow Lineker half a yard in the box. In fact, his somewhat terse answer could be paraphrased as: 'It was never a penalty.' Happy-go-lucky, it wasn't.

'It's not the same thing to wear the Cameroon shirt as to wear the English one. England's has a lot more history. Referees favour the big teams. It's been the same throughout history, every championship is like that,' he said, recalling the two spot-kicks that ended Cameroon's World Cup dreams. 'The first one was much more outrageous,' he added.

The view that the big countries tend to get their way is one that will find plenty of takers in Bolivia, forced to defend its right to play home games at home. Would there have been so much fuss if Buenos Aires were up a mountain? But, backed against the wall, the Bolivians had mounted a spirited campaign in defence of their right to play football in their capital and forced Fifa to reconsider. By this time, in May 1996, Bolivia had already begun its qualifying campaign away to Argentina, so banning La Paz would mean changing the rules of the competition in midstream, the FBF pointed out. On 30

May, the night before Fifa made its final decision, a friendly match was staged in the Hernando Siles stadium – the bone of contention itself – between two Bolivian select XIs to demonstrate that football could be played safely at this altitude. Afterwards up to 10,000 people stayed on, holding a vigil in the stadium through the night until the word came from Zurich in the early hours of the morning. Fire-crackers, rockets and the La Paz city band greeted the result. There would be no ban on altitude but visiting teams were to be allowed to call up their players ten days before the match (instead of the usual five) to get them acclimatized.

'La Paz is a city for everyone, a generous city and, at 3600m, it will always be a city of peace, of sincere friendship, of hospitality, and proud capital of Indo-America,' said Mayor Maclean on the day the Fifa veto was overturned.[3] La Paz is a remarkable city. It is the most indigenous of all big cities in Latin America. Despite the buses creeping along the narrow sidestreets, the advertisements, the snack bars and all the usual clutter of a modern city, the place has a timeless air. The snow-capped peak of Illampu dominates the horizon. It's a great place for little guys to walk tall, as virtually everybody you meet will be shorter than you. Their broad Indian faces look so Asian, so alien, until you realize that it's everything else that is out of place.

The Bolivian victory was front-page news and a cause for national celebration, but for the team itself the problems were just starting. Sports diplomacy is one thing, but Bolivia now had to go out and win a few games of football, which, as their own propaganda had boasted, was something that didn't happen that often. Their World Cup qualifying campaign began with a 3–1 defeat in Argentina, followed by the expected goal-glut at home to Venezuela. A defeat in Uruguay followed a more worrying 0–0 draw with Peru in the bastion of La Paz. The team could not afford to drop home points. Bolivia parted company with Traskovic, their Montenegrin coach, and recalled Antonio López, the Spaniard who had worked alongside their most successful coach ever, Xabier Azkargorta. The next game, against the unbeaten Colombians, would be crucial.

Sunday 10 November dawned with a light drizzle and the weather flirted at the dividing line between drizzle and rain for the rest of the day and well into the night. In the Witches' Market, the stalls still offered their usual selection of herbs, potions and aborted llama foetuses, but every minibus plying the steep, wet streets seemed to have sprouted a Bolivian flag. On the main drag diminutive Indian women in bowler hats offered hats, shirts and banners in the green of the Bolivian *selección*. I bought myself a green-and-white baseball cap: *Bolivia, futbol de altura* [Bolivia: high-level football]. Even the waitresses in the restaurants wore the red, yellow and green flashes of Bolivia painted on their cheeks.

All the build-up in the Colombian media – as would be the case in all the visiting countries – stressed the altitude issue, but also repeated the new orthodoxy that altitude was just another factor and that, in any case, Bolivia had a good team which shouldn't be underestimated.

Outside the stadium young soldiers in khaki parkas sheltered under a giant football plastered with sponsors' logos. Knots of damp *paceños* trooped on to the terracing, gradually filling up the stadium which bore the legend: 'ESTADIO HERNANDO SILES SUAZO, SYMBOL OF THE DIGNITY OF THE BOLIVIAN PEOPLE' in big letters on the back wall in case the point had escaped anybody.

Minutes before the match José Saavedra and Bolivia's communications minister called an impromptu press conference to announce that the game would, after all, be broadcast in La Paz as well as the rest of the country. Evidently they had sold the last few thousand tickets. The slum city of El Alto, which rises above the stadium, was totally obscured by the dense white cloud which sat stolidly just above the level of the stands seeping rain on to the pitch below. Despite the depressing conditions the crowd were in good voice and there was no lack of atmosphere (except in the literal sense). Behind one goal they started up the '*Bo-bo-bo*', with different parts of the ground taking up the '*li-li-li*' and '*via-via-via*', but it petered out before any reference to Bolivia's late-lamented seaside.

143

Bolivia started brightly and made a couple of good chances before the defender Marco Antonio Sandy headed in a corner on 14 minutes. Etcheverry and Moreno, the two Tahuichi old boys, were linking up well and causing the Colombian defence problems. For a while Colombia looked in danger of being swept away, but it became apparent they were pacing themselves. Valderrama, the man whose haircut was largely responsible for the initial success of the US Major League, is not a box-to-box player at the best of times, but the 35-year-old's shrewd movement and pinpoint distribution were perfectly attuned to the demands of altitude. The Colombians played in short bursts and then took a breather and let someone else do the running. Asprilla was the perfect example. You could say he did almost nothing all game. The Bolivian defence seemed to have him well-shackled. He berated team-mates for not playing the ball where he wanted it or not making the run, or just for the fact that he was getting soaked to the skin by the persistent, dreary rain. Booed early on by the crowd for what they took to be a dive, he presented that figure of lank exasperation so familiar to Newcastle fans in his early days at St James's Park. After 20 minutes he was asking for a new pair of boots. But with less than 10 minutes to go to half-time, Asprilla's quick footwork took him past two defenders before he laid the ball off to his striking partner. De Avila's shot cannoned off the post but, collecting the rebound, Asprilla pushed the ball towards the goal-line before tumbling over the defender's leg left invitingly in his path. Serna converted the penalty. In the second half Asprilla wrongfooted the defence with one great turn, presenting De Avila with a clear run on goal, which he squandered. That was Asprilla's afternoon: two crucial moves and lots of standing around and getting upset.

At half-time I decided to go and mingle with the crowd but quickly got lost amid the passageways behind the stand. Someone helpfully directed me down a flight of stairs and along a tunnel. I emerged blinking in the middle of the field. This wasn't a very good position to appreciate anything except just how wet it was down on the pitch. Then I realized that if I stood where I was I could take a picture of the players as they returned for the second half. So, as the distinctive Chris Waddle circa 1989 haircut of Marco Antonio Etcheverry emerged up the steps from the subterranean changing rooms I whipped out the disposable camera I had bought at Heathrow and took a snap; likewise Asprilla, his hands characteristically hidden inside his shirtsleeves. All the other photographers down here at ground level had lenses as long as your arm, not to mention fancy fluorescent bibs, but I thought I might just blend in. I was wrong. A policeman in a green parka helpfully grabbed me by the arm and marched me to a gate near the corner flag and, as I thanked him for his kindness in directing me to the press box, threw me out of the ground. On the way I passed the FBF's head of press, who I had been chatting to a couple of hours earlier, and who had what looked uncannily like a malevolent grin all over his face.

A press pass is a wonderful thing, a licence to cheat. With a nonchalant wave of *emplasticado* accreditation I was able to walk straight back in and, eager not to miss the start of the second half, I sprinted up a few flights of stairs to the press box. At the top a Bolivian journalist I'd been talking to asked me what I thought of the first half. Instead of incisive analysis, all I could manage was a few disjointed syllables as I gulped useless lungfuls of air like a goldfish on a mat. As a lesson in the effects of altitude it was timely: I looked on the players' second-half performance with new respect. As an exercise in making me look like a complete idiot it was also pretty devastating.

Moreno had restored Bolivia's lead just before half-time and the home fans clearly felt that a little bit more history was about to be made in the stadium that had witnessed the end of Brazil's golden run. Colombia were at that point unbeaten in their 1998 campaign. But the Colombians were unflustered and knew just how much they had to do to get a result. Eight minutes after the restart Freddy Rincón, who had been a shambling giant on the left flank, getting a toe in here, laying off a short ball there, picked up the ball near the halfway line and loped forward with the defender backing off.

145

Out of the blue he wrapped his right boot around the ball and curled it sweetly, lazily around the defender in front of him and just inside the right-hand post: 2–2.

Bolivia pushed on desperately for the winner and went close with another header from a corner, but they were unable to break down the canny Colombians.

The faces of the coaches at the post-match press conference said it all. Colombia's Hernán Darío Gómez was restrained but cheerful, gracious to the Bolivians, refusing to make any pejorative reference to altitude despite several invitations. 'I think the altitude also affects some of the Bolivian players, like us when we play in Barranquilla . . . Bolivia doesn't win because of its altitude, it wins because of its team.' Except, he politely omitted to mention, Bolivia hadn't won. He left the room wearing the expression of a man who has lost a pound and found a fiver.

Antonio López took his place with a face like thunder. His captain sat alongside him. López looks like a football manager should look: short hair, starting to go bald, old enough to look like he's seen it all before, young enough to look like he could still do you in a five-a-side, and as hard as nails. By the look of him, he's the sort of man who would think you were queer for smoking filters. Whatever he happens to be talking about, his terse delivery and clipped Castilian consonants seem to be saying 'cut the crap'.

His analysis of the match was essentially that Colombia were lucky and it was never a penalty. Invited to comment on Colombia's spectacular second, he replied: 'I think Rincón's was a good goal. And Jaime Moreno's was also a good goal. So we're level there too.'

Etcheverry summed up the Bolivian view of the game. 'Colombia had two chances, not like us. The ref gave a penalty to Colombia, Jaime Moreno should have had one too – I don't know why it wasn't given. That would have made it 2–0 and really changed the match.'

One brave hack suggested that Colombia would have been more of a handful but for the altitude. López had clearly heard this one before. 'This is a game of football. Colombia ran, did their thing, we did ours, so I don't agree with that opinion.' No one brought it up again.

Another reporter dared to question his tactics. Perhaps putting a man on Valderrama would have been a good idea?

'If you were doing my job you would have got everything right. As it is we drew and they only had one corner, so, yes, we got it wrong – according to you.' López could sulk for Spain in the Olympics. Even the teenage beauties in Coca-Cola T-shirts paid to decorate these occasions were having trouble maintaining their commercially important smiles.

Finally, someone asked López what his strategy would be for the remainder of the qualifiers.

'Work and sacrifice.'

As part of the team's preparatory work Bolivia organized a friendly against Jamaica, also in contention for a World Cup place, but López must have ended up regretting sacrificing his Sunday afternoon[4] for a match that turned into a farce. The Jamaicans started off gamely enough but soon appeared flabbergasted at the effects of La Paz's rarefied air. Seeing the Bolivians easily run around them, the Jamaican players simply burst out laughing. In the second half a number of Jamaican players pretended to faint, flinging themselves spread-eagled on to the turf. When they did get the ball the Jamaicans merely whacked it anywhere as hard as they could. Apart from that they contented themselves with a series of outrageous fouls. Bolivia won 6–0 even though they more or less stopped trying. Antonio López was unimpressed. 'We had fifteen minutes of football and the rest was crap.'*

Nineteen ninety-seven held a new challenge for Bolivian football. For the first time since 1963 it was to host the South American

---

* The Jamaicans continued their tour in Mexico, where they played Toros Neza. A fight broke out after two players collided and several Jamaican players ran off the pitch only to return with pieces of wood and other makeshift weapons to carry on the fracas. At least three Toros players had to leave the field bleeding from cuts after the brawl.

147

Championship, the Copa América. For Bolivia it was a chance to demonstrate the suitability of the country – and La Paz in particular – to host international football and to consolidate its victory over the naysayers of Fifa. But no sooner had the Bolivian Football Federation designated La Paz and Santa Cruz as the principal venues than reports began to emerge that other countries were chipping away at what should have been Bolivia's sovereign decision.

Ricardo Teixeira, the president of the Brazilian Football Confederation, made it clear that Brazil had no intention of playing at altitude. 'Either we play in Santa Cruz de la Sierra until the end, or goodbye Copa América.'[5] Brazil, coming straight from a four-team tournament in France, made it clear that it could take or leave the Copa América. To nobody's surprise, when the draw was announced, Brazil were scheduled to play all their games, bar the Final, in Santa Cruz.

There were more problems. Bolivia had been awarded the tournament ten years previously, but since then South America's teams had committed themselves to an eighteen-month qualification tournament for the World Cup, with fixtures virtually every month. Most countries decided to send second-string or virtual Under-23 squads. Only Brazil, not involved in World Cup qualification, and the hosts had their best sides out. This, along with the relatively high price of tickets, meant that the people stayed away from the early games in droves. Only 13,000 watched Bolivia's opening match against Venezuela in La Paz, and crowds for the other group games were also disappointing: one match is Sucre attracted just 2000. The head of the organizing committee called it 'soul-destroying'[6] while the Bolivian vice-president urged that prices be cut. Subsequently the organizers resorted to offering two-for-one ticket deals to fill the stadia.

The tormented souls of the organizing committee were clearly feeling the pressure, for what other explanation is there for the fact that at the ceremony before their first game in Cochabamba, Chile's flag was displayed without its large white star? The Chilean foreign minister said his country would make a formal complaint. The Bolivian government blamed 'accidental human error'[7] and stressed that the Bolivian Football Federation was a completely private entity. The afternoon went from bad to worse for the Chileans. After losing 1–0 to Paraguay they discovered to their considerable dismay that there was no hot water in the dressing room. So their players were forced to take cold showers as the thermometer headed towards zero. The Bolivian organizers explained that the opening ceremony had somehow burst a pipe beneath the pitch. Curiously, the Paraguayans reported no problems, but then Paraguay is landlocked too.

For the Bolivians the altitude issue refused to go away. Bolivia held bad memories for Daniel Passarella, whose Argentinian team had lost a violent World Cup qualifier in La Paz just weeks before, and he clearly hadn't wanted to come in the first place. When he found out – from a journalist at a news conference – that depending on results the venue of his team's quarter-final match could be shifted 900 metres vertically to La Paz, he insisted, 'I'm not going, I'm not going. This is a complete disgrace.'[8] He vowed to take the next plane back to Buenos Aires. Having slept on it, Passarella reconsidered, but only somewhat. 'I've cooled down a bit since last night but the fact that I've cooled down hasn't changed my way of thinking . . . I'm not going to La Paz.'[9] His players took the same line. In the event, Bolivia won their group which meant that Argentina went, as originally planned, to Sucre, just 100 metres above Cochabamba, where they had played their group games. Argentina lost that game in disgrace with two players sent off, just like in their World Cup visit to La Paz.

The Final unsurprisingly paired the hosts with Brazil, who deigned to come to La Paz for the match. Bolivia had won their semi-final against Mexico thanks to some idiosyncratic refereeing, but went into the match with the psychological advantage of having beaten Brazil the last time they met in La Paz in their famous World Cup qualifier. (They also beat Brazil there on the way to their only Copa América title in 1963.) The game was evenly balanced but two goals in the last 15 minutes gave Brazil a 3–1 victory. But even defeat was not enough to dispel the persistent altitude controversy. The

Brazilian players' post-match interviews all dwelt on their physical distress at playing in La Paz. 'There was no air. I couldn't breathe. It was terrible. I ran and barely moved,' gasped Ronaldo, who nevertheless had managed to latch on to a Denílson pass to put his side 2–1 up. Denílson was similarly horrified at the conditions. 'I thought I would collapse,' he said. 'At the end I was playing on heart alone.'[10] Roberto Carlos said that at half-time he had thought he wouldn't be able to come back for the second period. The Brazilian press sniffed that Bolivia had only reached the Final because of the altitude and that at sea-level it was a third-rate team. And so what should have been a celebration of La Paz as a football venue merely revived the altitude controversy all over again.

In the event, Bolivia failed to qualify for France '98. Perhaps the team had not worked or sacrificed enough to make the cut. Perhaps the other teams had finally got wise to Bolivia's altitude 'trick' – Bolivia won only four of their eight home games. Or perhaps La Paz had subsided imperceptibly since the team's glorious run of victories in 1993. Sadly for the Bolivians, not even defeat and a return to South America's second division was enough to convince their critics that being allowed to play where they liked – on top of the Andes – was not an unfair advantage.

5: Godfathers of Football

NOBODY WON THE Colombian championship in 1989. And nobody came second either. The eight-team play-off series to decide the title was cancelled after a referee, Alvaro Ortega, was shot dead in the streets of Medellín.

Ortega had just run the line at a match between Deportivo Independiente de Medellín and América de Cali on 15 November 1989 when he was gunned down by persons unknown. It is believed that he was punished for failing to ensure the 'correct' result in an earlier América–Deportivo game which he had refereed. A man claiming to be one of the killers later telephoned a journalist and warned that another referee who had been 'behaving badly' would meet the same fate. 'Look,' he said, 'I'm not going to give you figures but we and our bosses lost a lot of money because the result of the Deportivo–América game was not right.'

Almost exactly a year before, on 2 November 1988, another referee, Armando Pérez, had been kidnapped and driven around Medellín for twenty hours by armed men who said they were 'representatives of six professional clubs'. 'Whoever gives the wrong decisions we'll kill,' they told him.[1]

Colombia is a violent place, and in 1989 was even more so than usual. Three presidential candidates were shot dead, airliners were blown up, car bombs exploded in busy streets and judges feared for their lives as the illegal drug trade declared war on the state. It was a time when around the world the word Colombia became synonymous with cocaine, and Pablo Escobar, the head of the Medellín drug cartel, became the most famous living Colombian. In this climate, one more death might have been easy to overlook, but the murder of Alvaro Ortega brought to a head mounting concern about the influence of *el narcotráfico* (the drug business) on the game of football.

It was all a long way from the previous occasion on which the football authorities had seen fit to suspend, temporarily, the championship. In November 1984 the Colombian league called off all its fixtures for one weekend, and again it was to take a stand on the drugs issue, although a rather different one. Their principled action was to protest at the extradition to the United States of Hernán Botero, the chairman of Atlético Nacional of Medellíin. Botero was subsequently jailed for thirty years and received a $25 million fine for laundering drug money.

The leaders of Colombian football at that stage – like the leaders of the drug trade – were much more concerned about the pernicious threat of extradition than the presence of dirty money in the game. The reason was not hard to fathom. As the justice minister, Rodrigo Lara Bonilla, had stated bluntly in October 1983: 'The mafia has taken over Colombian football.' Lara knew whereof he spoke: a few months later he was murdered by the same mafia.

Bogotá doesn't look so different from any other big Latin American city. It has tall buildings in the centre, a picturesque old colonial district and endless dreary suburbs. The 'centre' is in fact offset to the east, where the mountains curb further growth, but to the west and north the city sprawls relentlessly, unencumbered by natural barriers. Nevertheless, Colombia and its capital do have a dodgy reputation. The country has had the highest murder rate in the world for years.* It is the world leader in the use of *burundanga*, a virtually undetectable drug placed in the food or drink of the unsuspecting, whose effects include loss of will or memory and sleepiness. The effects can last for days during which time the victim is robbed

---

* The Colombian Commission of Jurists reported that 'Between 1988 and 1995, there has been an average of 76 homicides [a year] per every 100,000 inhabitants.' The national police reported that 31,525 Colombians met violent deaths in 1995, including 25,330 who were victims of murder or manslaughter.

and/or raped. The nurse giving me my travel jabs recounted, with what I felt was unnecessary relish, her friend's unfortunate experience, which began with a drink in a bar and ended in an Aids test. Of course once a place is saddled with a reputation as the new Beirut it's hard to view the place objectively. Residents will tell you to take a taxi rather than walk a few blocks at night, but there again getting mugged is part of city life in so many places. True, it's not every McDonald's that has a uniformed man with a Terminator-style shotgun standing outside, but that's probably just a sign that these people really appreciate their hamburgers. The fact is millions of *bogotanos* do get on with their lives without being machinegunned by gangsters as they walk down the street. (No, that's Medellín you're thinking of.)

On my first night in Bogotá I was returning home in a taxi. As we turned into the narrow streets of La Candelaria our way was blocked by two motorcyclists stopped in the middle of the street. Normally you might expect a taxi driver to lean on his horn and shout abuse out of the window, but mine just waited meekly. I leaned forward to see what was going on and saw each was wearing similar dark clothes and a white helmet. And on their right hip each carried a sophisticated-looking machine-pistol. 'They're not police,' said the taxi driver. So we both waited patiently until they felt like getting out of the way and roared off into the night. As brushes with danger go, it was, I concede, distant. But the fact is armed men on motorbikes do have a well-deserved reputation for murder in Colombia, as Rodrigo Lara could testify had he not been shot dead by a motorcycle-borne assassin.

But while the drug trade may not always be readily evident, it is there nonetheless. Its narco-dollars find their way into almost every aspect of Colombian life. The guys selling cheap watches from Hong Kong on the street are probably the last link in a chain aimed at disguising the origins of ill-gotten money. At the other end of the scale some £4.5 million generously donated by the Cali cartel found its way into the campaign fund of the current president when he stood for office in 1994. (It should be stressed that Colombia's

153

congress – controlled by the president's Liberal Party – exonerated President Ernesto Samper of any wrongdoing. Not everyone was convinced. The US State Department revoked Samper's visa, saying: 'People who knowingly assist narco-traffickers are not welcome in the United States.' Drug traffickers have allied themselves with the armed forces and with the leftwing guerrillas they are meant to be fighting.

The office of the state prosecutor leads the forces of justice in its uneven battle against the drug mafias. It can point to numerous successes, but even here – or maybe particularly here – some privately say that the drug war is unwinnable. They suggest that, like the Hydra, for every head you chop off, another three will grow, and that the only serious, long-term option is legalization. Rodrigo Lara, the justice minister who signalled football's malaise, was just the most high-profile of many in his field to die by an assassin's bullet. There's a roadblock at the end of the street housing the state prosecutor's offices in Bogotá and a knot of armed security men outside its fortified entrance. But, as one senior official noted, that doesn't make it particularly safe. The building faces a park and, he pointed out, anyone with a rocket launcher could take a potshot from a safe distance. Rocket launchers are worryingly thick on the ground in Colombia.

In fact it's amazing who does have their hands on military hardware. Faustino Asprilla got into trouble with the law in 1995 for carrying two pistols illegally in his hometown of Tulúa. But for a seriously tooled up footballer you have to look to Felipe Pérez Urrea, a player with Envigado FC, who was arrested in 1993 for hiding arms and military uniforms in his flat as a 'favour' for Pablo Escobar. He allegedly gave forty rifles to the Medellín cartel after Escobar's escape from his luxury prison in Envigado.

A player with his own private arsenal is not exactly run-of-the-mill, but it was only another example of the links between the drug trade and football revealed in the wake of Alvaro Ortega's murder. That killing prompted Ignacio Gómez and another journalist to research and write a book (*Los amos del juego*) about football's seamy side.

'We started to look at who were the owners of the football teams. We realized that the leaders of the drug trade were in practically all the teams. Of the eighteen teams in the league at the time there were maybe two or three who didn't have links to drug trafficking ... By 1987 there was hardly a leading drug trafficker who didn't have his fingers in football,' said Gómez.

Colombia's cocaine business grew from next to nothing in the 1970s to become one of the country's biggest moneymakers by the early 1980s. A recent study estimated that at its peak in 1984, illicit drugs accounted for 98 per cent of Colombia's export income, or $3 billion a year.[2] In the process it transformed petty criminals like Pablo Escobar – who began his career stealing gravestones, filing off the inscriptions and reselling them – into rich and powerful gangsters. Escobar revelled in his outlaw glamour: he liked to be known as The Godfather and had himself photographed in the pose of an American gangster, complete with Al Capone-style hat and machine-gun. As the billionaire head of a multinational operation, Escobar acquired an air fleet, 200 apartments in Miami, and a zoo, complete with hippos and kangaroos. Above the gateway of his estate on the Magdalena river he fixed a light aircraft, reputedly the one which flew his first cocaine shipment to the United States.

Colombia has strong regional identities, producing correspond-ingly strong rivalries. Three Andean mountain chains running north–south divide the country, with Bogotá in the east, Medellín in the centre and Cali, in the Cauca valley, dominating the south-west. Barranquilla, the traditional centre of marijuana smuggling, is the main Caribbean city, and the sparsely populated Amazon basin makes up half the national territory. Escobar's Medellín-based operation had a powerful rival in Cali in the form of the Rodríguez Orejuela brothers.

Gilberto Rodríguez Orejuela, known as The Chess Player, started out running a chemist's shop in Cali before building the empire which would eventually wrest control of the cocaine trade from Pablo Escobar and Medellín in the late 1980s. He and his brother Miguel also displayed the traditional civic pride of any self-respecting drug baron, even paying for the construction of police posts in Cali to cut down on street crime. The brothers kept a much lower profile than the flamboyant Escobar and set the businesslike tone which today's generation of drug smugglers has found profitable. Much of the Rodríguez Orejuelas' reputedly vast wealth was re-invested in legitimate businesses, including banks, car dealerships and radio stations. Appropriately enough, one of their better known investments is a nationwide chain of chemists. But the best-known mafia investments of all are football teams, although in most cases money-laundering was a secondary consideration.

Pablo Escobar's team was Alético Nacional of Medellín. The Cali cartel, in the person of Miguel Rodríguez Orejuela, controlled one of the city's two teams, América. And Millonarios, the Bogotá club with the most illustrious tradition of all Colombia's teams, belonged to another leader of the Medellín cartel, José Gonzalo Rodríguez Gacha, known as The Mexican.

In Escobar's case, his involvement with football was first and foremost because he was a fan, the familiar story of a successful businessman wanting to own a successful football club, especially his local team, except that Escobar's business was the export of huge amounts of illicit drugs. Second, Escobar was, in the 1980s, a politician, elected as an alternate member of parliament.* At that time, public disapproval of the drug trade was muted. In fact, there was a widespread acceptance of, not to say connivance with, the business. Most people did not see the ugly side of the trade and few found it convenient to ask too closely about the source of the money which was suddenly sloshing around the Colombian economy. Money-laundering financed an economic boom. Pablo Escobar nourished a Robin Hood image by building housing and other facilities in and around Medellín. It was an image enhanced by his patronage of football; he not only invested in Atlético Nacional but also created football pitches and even paid for floodlights in poor areas in and

* An alternate, or *suplente*, deputizes in the absence of the full member of parliament.

156

around Medellín, so earning the respect of a new generation of young footballers. René Higuita, the eccentric goalkeeper, and midfielder Leonel Alvarez, both internationals, were personal friends of Pablo Escobar.

Higuita's case shows how close the relationship between players and drug barons could be, and the mixed fortunes this could entail. His star rose in parallel with that of his club, Escobar's Atlético Nacional, and there were those who proclaimed him the best goalkeeper in the world, although these cheerleaders were almost exclusively Colombian. Higuita, renowned for his flamboyant forays upfield and Charles II hairstyle, visited Escobar in jail in 1991 after the head of the Medellín cartel turned himself in as part of a deal to avoid extradition to the United States – a garlic-wreathed crucifix to Colombia's cocaine kings. His popularity was such that even when his error in the 1990 World Cup led to Colombia's elimination – he was tackled on the halfway line by Roger Milla, allowing the Cameroonian to score – he was quickly forgiven. Higuita himself would ultimately spend time behind bars for his links to the drug trade. In June 1993 he was arrested for having negotiated the release of the kidnapped daughter of Luis Carlos Molina Yepes, known as one of the main money launderers for the Medellín cartel. He denied having been paid and was eventually freed after seven months, during which time the national squad publicly called for his release at a ceremony in the capital's main stadium to celebrate their qualification for the World Cup. During Higuita's enforced absence, Navarro Montoya established himself in the national team's No. 1 shirt. In November 1996, the man who gave the world the scorpion kick resigned from his club, Atlético Nacional, because of 'personal problems'. He had repeatedly missed training sessions and it was lamented that his fall mirrored that of Diego Maradona, the world's most famous cocaine addict. The plot thickened when, on 22 December, someone threw a small explosive device at his home in Medellín. Whoever was responsible, it appeared to have a powerful motivational effect: he was soon back in training at his club and reporting for international duty with the B squad.

In their 1980s heyday, the drug mafia's formal control of football was usually exercised in a semi-secret, deniable manner. Pablo Escobar did not have a seat on the board of Nacional, but the chairman acted as his frontman, a common set-up. Discretion, though, was not Escobar's strong point, and he would rather give the game away by occasionally performing the ceremonial kick-off at Nacional matches. But that was before the extradition issue led to the mafia declaring war on the state.

Miguel Rodríguez Orejuela was one of the few cartel leaders to openly run a club; in his case América de Cali. He is, at the time of writing, in jail for drug-trafficking offences. Numerous pictures exist of him at official functions with such luminaries as Juan José Bellini,* the then president of the Colombian Football Federation, who accompanied the national team to the 1994 World Cup in the United States.

A more typical approach was that of Gonzalo Rodríguez Gacha who had no official position at Millonarios. Researchers have uncovered documents detailing large loans he made to the club, but in truth The Mexican's involvement was never much of a secret. The club's players were his players. He once told a journalist: 'All I know is that if any one of those bastards tries to leave the team, he won't wake up the next day. What do I care what he's offered elsewhere? He's got to stay, at least until he's served my purposes.'[3]

Control of the players themselves was an important mechanism in the hands of the drug barons. Nowhere was this more clearly demonstrated than in Cali. There, Miguel Rodríguez Orejuela specialized in buying up the registration of top players. No one is sure just how many players' careers were in his hands in his heyday in the late 1980s – some speak of scores, others of hundreds. In addition to the players who passed through the América team, he

* Bellini is a former director of América. The most recent photo of him and other football officials alongside the Rodríguez Orejuela brothers is said by Colombian police to date from late 1993 to early 1994.

owned the *pase*, or registration, of players in Argentina, Brazil, Peru and numerous other South American countries, many of whom never set foot in Colombia. Disturbingly, he also owned the registration of professionals at many other Colombian clubs. According to Carlos Eduardo González, football writer at the Bogotá daily *El Tiempo*, eight to ten of the players at Bucaramanga were owned by América. The most notorious case was that of Santa Fe, the other main Bogotá club. América de Cali controlled some 80 per cent of the Santa Fe team, which made some question where the players' loyalties lay when the two sides met.

Surprisingly, perhaps, there is little evidence of large sums changing hands corruptly in connection with players' transfers, but this may be partly because the absolute figures involved were generally not great. The one exception is Faustino Asprilla. The Italian club Parma paid Nacional $7 million for him, but in Colombia his transfer fee is given as only $4 million.[4] Presumably the other $3 million is accounted for somewhere in the miscellaneous column.

With clubs and players owned by the narcos, it should be no surprise that many match officials were also bought up. Given the illicit nature of the activity, hard facts are not easy to come by. But events at a cup game between Tolima and Alianza Petrolera in November 1994, for example, are well documented. The chairman of Tolima and a man dressed as a policeman, who turned out to be a local referee, came into the officials' changing room before the match in clear violation of the regulations. At half-time, the 'policeman' reappeared without explanation. Then the fourth official pointed out an envelope on the table, saying to his colleagues: 'I think it's for you.'

'What's that doing there?' asked the referee, José Ruiz. 'Let's leave it until the end of the match.' Tolima won 2–1. After the game the envelope was found to contain 500,000 pesos. The referee handed the money in and reported the incident to the authorities. For their pains, the officials were rewarded with an indefinite suspension 'while the facts are cleared up'. In the manner of these things, a desultory investigation found insufficient evidence to proceed.[5]

According to the then chief of the referees' panel, in the period 1989–91, 31 referees were dropped from the list for 'strange conduct in terms of their decisions'.[6]

It wasn't just that the narcos wanted their team to win, they often had a lot of money riding on the result in the form of bets. Betting is an even shadier area than bribery – there are no betting shops in Colombia – but wagering large sums of money on football is a consuming passion for people at all levels of the drug trade.

'They don't just bet on the score, but on who gets the first corner, who gets the first throw-in . . . they bet on who's winning at half-time . . . anything,' says journalist César Mauricio Velásquez. 'They might stake $40,000 in cash. Most of the bets are done directly [face to face]. There's nothing written, it's just your word against mine. And that has to be honoured. Much of the score-settling within the mafias is because of failure to keep a verbal promise.'

In February 1990 the acting chief of police, General Carlos Arturo Casadiego Torrado, acknowledged the scale of the problem: 'The National Police did know of the existence of betting syndicates, who together with the drug cartels were manipulating several hired football teams in Colombia.'[7]

However, he urged people not to take the law into their own hands. He was speaking after a group calling itself Cleanliness in Colombian Football threatened to purge the game of its delinquent elements in the traditional Colombian manner – with bullets.

With so much money at stake, and a few powerful individuals wielding an unhealthy degree of influence, Colombian football began to smell very bad indeed.

'You would have two teams playing each other owned by the same guy, who also happened to own the betting syndicate which was taking bets on the game. Not a good idea,' said Alvaro González, head of Difutbol, which runs the non-professional game in Colombia.[8]

Meanwhile, the catalogue of football-related murders continued to grow.* In June 1992, gunmen burst into a Bogotá restaurant, pumped nine bullets into Guillermo Gómez Melgarejo, vice-president of Millonarios, and then dragged him into the street and ran over his body in their car. Mr Gómez had only just recovered from gunshot wounds received in an attack the previous December. In January 1990, the president of the same club, Germán Gómez García, was shot and wounded by motorbike-riding gunmen, a favourite tactic of the *sicarios* (the drug bosses' young hitmen) who enforce the mafia's wishes. Also in 1990, Germán Mejía Arango, a director of Cristal Caldas, was killed. In November 1992 a shareholder in Deportivo Independiente of Medellín and Envigado FC, Manuel Guillermo Zuluaga, was kidnapped and has not been seen since. The following March, Saúl Velásquez, then president of Difutbol, resigned after receiving death threats. In his resignation letter he wrote: 'It is a shame that the reign of terror once more dominates Colombian football.'[9] Francisco Santos, a journalist from the leading daily *El Tiempo*, who wrote about drug money's corrupting influence on football, was kidnapped by the Medellín cartel and held for eight months.

However, despite (or because of) the bribery, corruption, threats and murders, little was done. And one of the main reasons why not was because Colombian football was booming. It wasn't just that undreamt of millions were flowing into the game; on the field, Colombian teams, including the national side, were enjoying a period of success never before seen. For Colombian football success meant never having to say you're sorry.

Leading the way was América, the Cali cartel's representative on the football field. The traditional powers in Colombian football had been the Bogotá sides, Millonarios and Santa Fe, although Deportivo

* In February 1986 José Pablo Corea Ramos, the president of Independiente Medellín, was murdered, presumably by the drug mafia. Omar Cañas, a former Atlético Nacional player, was killed in February 1993 and Jorge Arturo Bustamante, a former director of Independiente, Cúcuta Deportivo and Envigado, was killed in September the same year.

Cali had a handful of league titles to their credit and had even reached the Final of the Libertadores Cup in 1978 before being hammered by Boca Juniors in Buenos Aires. América were determined to take their place at the top of Colombian football and go one better than their city rivals by winning the continental title.

The vast profits generated by exporting cocaine helped fund a buying spree. Miguel Rodríguez Orejuela went shopping for players around the continent, and particularly in Buenos Aires, to which Colombian football had traditionally looked for inspiration. Striker Ricardo Gareca was one star Argentinian import. The Argentinian connection extended to the management: Carlos Bilardo, the future World Cup winning manager of Argentina, was hired to coach the side. José Luis Brown, who scored in Argentina's 1986 Final victory, would also join the club at the height of his career. The investment paid dividends. In 1979 América won the league championship for the first time. Then after two third-place finishes they won five titles on the trot from 1982–86. But, despite this success, the Copa Libertadores, the South American Club Championship, which no Colombian team had ever won, eluded even the big-spending Cali club. Three times on the trot América reached the Final, in 1985, 1986 and 1987, but each time they returned with nothing.

The breakthrough for Colombian football came about only when the millions generated by the drug trade were married to the tactical nous of a coach with a distinctive, Colombian style. Pablo Escobar's Atlético Nacional of Medellín had initially followed a similar course to his rivals in Cali, throwing money at foreign players and winning the league in 1981. But frustrated at the years of América dominance, the club turned to Francisco Maturana in 1987. Maturana was not a typical football coach. He was a university graduate, a qualified and practising orthodontist.* He built a team of Colombian players playing a short-passing 4–4–2 style based on a zonal concept, with free rein given to individual talent.

* Miguel Mejía Barón, Mexico's manager at the 1994 World Cup, and Hugo Sánchez, the great Mexican goalscorer, are the other two footballing dentists.

'More than drug money, it was drug imagination,' according to Juan Carlos Pastrana of the Bogotá newspaper *La Prensa*. 'Escobar had the instinct that Maturana was a great coach. Nobody knew then.'[10]

Success was not immediate. It was Millonarios, with Gonzalo Rodríguez Gacha's millions, which ended América's long reign, taking the title in 1987 and 1988. But as runners-up in 1988 Nacional qualified for the Copa Libertadores along with the champions. After beating Millonarios in the quarter-final, Nacional faced Olympia of Paraguay in the Final. They lost 2–0 in Asunción but won by the same margin at the Campín stadium in Bogotá. The tie went to penalties in front of the intensely partisan *bogotano* crowd. Nacional won 5–4, to become the first team in Colombia's history to win the South American Club Championship.

Nacional's win capped a quite spectacular decade of success, which had transformed the status of Colombian football. But it was a victory which came only months before the murder of Alvaro Ortega, an event which brought into sharp focus the disquiet about how that success had been achieved. How much was down to the tactical mind of Maturana or the skills of the likes of Higuita and Andrés Escobar, and how much was owed to the deep pockets and malign influence of Pablo Escobar and his ilk? The fact that the Medellín leg of the semi-final had to be replayed after the referee revealed he had been threatened certainly leaves an element of doubt.

When Nacional went on to play AC Milan in the World Club Championship in Japan, the Italian papers fulminated at the immorality of having to play a team built on drug money. The Milanese tabloids claimed Nacional were 'morally unfit' to contest the title and *Gazzetta dello Sport* urged Milan to pull out, saying their withdrawal would be worth more than any trophy. Maturana responded by telling Italian reporters: 'We are athletes, we are clean. Our country has a big problem which it is fighting. We are all suffering. But if we have a mafia perhaps we inherited it from Italy.'[11]

In December that year, the Fifa president, João Havelange, dismissed claims that hot money was invested in at least four clubs in the Colombian first division as 'simply rumours'.[12]

Nacional were not to repeat their Libertadores success. The following year the South American Football Confederation banned international matches in Colombia after six men with submachine-guns impressed upon the referee their desire for Nacional to win their game with Brazil's Vasco da Gama.

Maturana's success did not go unrecognized. The Colombian football federation chose him to lead the Colombian challenge at the 1990 World Cup. He brought the same style, and many of the same players that had worked so well in Medellín to the national side, which until then had had an undistinguished history. Its previous high point had been a 4−4 draw with the Soviet Union in the 1962 World Cup in Chile, having been 4−1 down. Despite these heroics, Colombia had been eliminated, bottom of their group.

Colombia qualified for Italy via a play-off against Israel. In Italy, Colombia started brightly enough, beating the United Arab Emirates 2−0 in their opening game. But a defeat against Yugoslavia meant they had to take something from their final group game against Germany. A late goal by Freddy Rincón secured a 1−1 draw and saw them qualify in third place to face Cameroon in the second round. Colombia lost 2−1 as a result of their goalkeeper's bizarre walkabout. Despite the manner of their defeat Colombia were welcomed home as heroes, the most successful side the country had ever produced.

Maturana went on to a managerial stint in Spain, at Valladolid, but returned to guide Colombia's qualification campaign for USA '94. With broadly the same settled side from Italy they produced an impressive unbeaten sequence in a four-team group with Argentina, Paraguay and Peru. Their final game was against Argentina in Buenos Aires. They had already won the home fixture 2−1, but taking on the two-time world champions and 1990 Finalists would be a different proposition. A draw would see Colombia qualify automatically; a defeat would mean a two-leg play-off against Australia. Argentina's fate would be the obverse; only a victory would take them straight to the USA. Perhaps because of that safety net, the Colombian team arrived at Ezeiza airport in good spirits. 'The atmosphere among the

164

lads was frankly relaxed, with no big worries, a far cry from the situations you get in the days before a match with everything at stake,' Maturana recalled. They were met by a screaming crowd of Argentinian fans who jostled the players – even pulling Carlos Valderrama's famous blond afro locks – and generally let them know exactly what they thought their chances were of getting out of Buenos Aires with a result. 'I looked at my players and I was quite clear that they weren't at all cowed, and that on the contrary they responded as if rubbing their hands and saying: "Well, here we go . . ." '[13]

At the hotel, the team's booking had been inexplicably changed. During the night the familiar Latin American ploy of keeping up a cats' chorus all night in the street outside the visiting team's accommodation ensured that Maturana, at least, spent a restless night.

The scene at River Plate's Monumental stadium on Sunday 5 September 1993 was daunting. As the Colombian team came out to inspect the pitch – always a euphemism for sampling the atmosphere – they were met with the terrifying din of tens of thousands of Argentines whistling, booing and baying at the upstarts who stood between them and their rightful place in the World Cup finals. But with studied cool, Faustino Asprilla sauntered out to the centre-circle, pulled out his mobile phone and called friends and family back home in Colombia.

The game started well for Colombia, who contained the opposition's early attacks. A goal from Freddy Rincón meant that Argentina went in at half-time knowing they had to attack, but with the advantage of the fiercely partisan crowd on their side. But eight minutes into the second half history began to be made. Asprilla scored a second and the Argentinian coach, Alfio Basile, surprisingly took off the talented Redondo. For Maturana it was the turning point. Rincón added a third and then Asprilla, stealing the ball off a defender's toe, scored the goal of the game. The crowd could scarcely believe what they were seeing. At one point the referee looked as if he were about to send off one of the Argentinian players, but the Colombian midfielder Barrabás Gómez told him: 'Don't

165

send anyone off because afterwards they'll just say they only lost because they were down to ten men.'[14] As it was, there was still time for centre-forward Adolfo Valencia to get on the scoresheet: 5–0. It was Argentina's worst defeat ever on home soil. Diego Maradona, watching the game from the stands, rose to his feet with the rest of the Argentinian crowd to applaud the Colombians' display. Maturana's assistant, Hernán Darío Gómez, turned to him and said: 'Pacho, we've really screwed up. Now we're going to have to be world champions.'[15]

It was a result that was celebrated around the world by those who had been appalled by Argentina's negative tactics in the 1990 World Cup and who saw in the Colombians' play an attractive, exciting alternative that actually produced results. In Bogotá some 100 people reportedly died as the country went into two days of wild celebration.* Thrashing Argentina on their own turf is a triumph in anybody's book, but for Colombia it had a special savour. For much of Colombia's footballing history it had had a relationship with Argentina not unlike that between apprentice and master, with all the combination of admiration and resentment that implies.

Although football had arrived early in Colombia by way of ports like Barranquilla in the usual way, it was not until 1948 that a professional league was formed. The change from amateurism to professionalism is always a fraught process, but in Colombia's case it produced a unique situation. A dispute between the new professional league, the Dimayor, and the existing amateur football authority, Adefutbol, led to the latter suspending the former's Fifa affiliation. This meant that Colombian league teams were suspended from all international competitions and could not play against foreign teams. The national team was consigned to a similar limbo. Such a sanction might have stifled the new league at birth but for a fortuitous combination of circumstances.

* Other sources say 30. The figures are hard to be sure of as an element of urban myth surrounds casualty figures for Latin Americans celebrating football.

Argentinian football was at that time paralysed by a players' strike. The fact that the Dimayor was no longer internationally recognized meant that it was working outside the strictures imposed by Fifa and was therefore not obliged to pay transfer fees. Alfonso Senior, a founder of the Dimayor and chairman of Millonarios, saw the opportunity to give the fledgling league a boost by poaching a star from the Argentinian league. He sent the club's Argentinian manager, Carlos Aldabe, to Buenos Aires with instructions to come back with a big-name signing.

'About ten days later,' he recalls, fifty years later in the office of his law practice in Bogotá, 'I received a telegram saying Adolfo Pedernera was ready to come to Colombia without a transfer fee to play for Millonarios.'

Pedernera was one of the greats of Argentinian football at the time, a key part of the great River Plate forward-line of the 1940s known as La Máquina, the Machine, for the precision of their play. The other directors wondered how they could ever afford to pay for such a star and refused to back Senior's judgement. But when Pedernera was presented to the fans at the Campín stadium in Bogotá the club took $18,000 through the turnstiles, five times what they made on a normal league game. And Pedernera hadn't even played. On his debut Millonarios made $38,000, as the crowds flocked to see one of the world's best. Even taking into account his initial $5000 basic annual salary, this spelt good business.

'So the other clubs said, "Millonarios are winning on the field and making a lot of money with Pedernera, I'm going to bring in some players too,"' Senior recalls. 'So Deportivo Cali brought in players from Argentina. The people from Pereira said they would bring in Paraguayans. The Cúcuta people said they'd bring Uruguayans. Those from Medellín brought in Peruvians. And that's how El Dorado was created.'

El Dorado is the name given to the golden age between 1949 and 1954 when the best footballers in Latin America plied their trade in Colombia. And El Dorado it was for players and spectators alike. While the Spanish conquistadors had vainly scoured Colombia's mountains and forests for the mythical land,* top players who had been earning a pittance at home now found themselves making good money and playing to packed stadia.

Millonarios were in danger of getting trampled in the rush for foreign talent, so Senior sent Pedernera back to Buenos Aires on another recruiting expedition. There he signed up a whole clutch of top Argentinians, including his young replacement in the River Plate forward line, Alfredo Di Stéfano. The team, which would eventually field ten Argentinians, was known as the Blue Ballet, and it won the league championship for four out of the five years from 1949 to 1953. The club that won the 1950 title, Caldas from the coffee town Manizales, had a squad containing nine Argentinians, a Chilean and a Peruvian alongside half a dozen Colombians.

Nineteen-fifty was a sort of *annus mirabilis* for football in Colombia. Two years previously it did not exist on the football map, a country where the amateur game vied for attention with bullfighting. Suddenly it was playing host to the world's best. 'Colombia is in full football fever,' the Bogotá daily *El Tiempo* enthused[16] at the height of the excitement in October that year. It was all the more remarkable because Colombia was at that time experiencing one of the most appalling of the many periods of bloodletting in its turbulent history, known with chilling simplicity as La Violencia. In one of the bloodiest ever conflicts in the western hemisphere, some 300,000 were to die over twenty years, as a civil war between the Liberal and Conservative parties spilled out of control. Most of the killing was taking place in the countryside and the government found it convenient to encourage the prodigious growth of football as a distraction for the populace. It decided to make scarce foreign exchange available for that purpose.

'People were desperate because of the political situation,' says

* The myth grew up around Lake Guatavita near Bogotá, where Muisca Indians would throw gold offerings and into which their gold-dust-covered king would dive in a religious ritual. The Spanish mounted many largely fruitless attempts to recover treasure from the lake.

Alfonso Senior. 'So the government, President Pérez, supported our bringing in foreign players and gave us the dollars . . . because they knew we would fill stadiums. And they gave us a good rate: 1.75 to the dollar!'

The enthusiasm for Colombia's newfound role as the centre of world football expressed itself in huge crowds.

'The reception committee at the airport, although big, was nothing to the triumphant drive from the airfield into the city. We travelled by car and were accompanied by a whole procession of vehicles, all sounding their sirens and blowing their horns,' wrote Neil Franklin, describing his arrival in Bogotá from England.[17]

Eight of the Uruguayan side which had won the World Cup earlier in the year were playing in Colombia, mainly for Cúcuta. A strike in Uruguay, inspired by the Argentinians' example, had again helped create the conditions for the exodus to Colombia. Santa Fe, Millonarios' rivals in the capital, looked beyond South America and began recruiting players in Britain.

Santa Fe's chairman, Luis Robledo, a Cambridge-educated diplomat married to an English aristocrat, pulled off a coup by signing England's first-choice centre-half Neil Franklin, who had mysteriously pulled out of the squad for the 1950 World Cup in Brazil. He also picked up Franklin's Stoke team-mate George Mountford and the Manchester United winger Charlie Mitten. The anglophile Robledo even modelled Santa Fe's colours on Arsenal's.

'He thought, "If I can get this [English] sort of football here, it would take their minds off fighting each other" and all the rest of it,' Franklin recalled. Nevertheless, he wrote that 'Never a day passed without some form of political demonstration.'[18]

Millonarios responded to their neighbours' English coup by signing up Billy Higgins of Everton, and Bobby Flavell of Hearts. In England in those days of the maximum wage and the retain-and-transfer system, even when they had completed their contract players were still tied to their club and were prevented from earning a living until the club decided to play them or sell them. Mitten was on just £10 a week basic at Manchester United; Santa Fe paid him £5000 a year plus £35 win bonus. Most of the British adventurers had never heard of Colombia before and in the days before passenger jets it might as well have been the ends of the earth. To get to Bogotá, Franklin had to fly via Shannon, Goose Bay, New York, Miami, Cuba, Kingston and Barranquilla. In the event Franklin played only six games in Colombia, and of the Brits, only Mitten saw out his year-long contract. Homesickness, especially in the days when spaghetti bolognaise and chilli con carne were exotic delicacies rather than school-dinner staples, was probably the biggest problem. All were made to eat humble pie on their return – Higgins claimed he hadn't understood the contract as it was written in Spanish[19] – and were fined, suspended and generally cold-shouldered by the English game.

Throughout 1950 envoys from Fifa, the South American confederation Conmebol and various Latin American leagues descended upon Colombia in an effort to bring the bonanza to an end and restore the football world to its natural order. At one point an agreement was reached to bring in Venezuelan and Ecuadorean teams to augment the nascent South American super league.[20] But in the end, Alfonso Senior and his colleagues in the Dimayor recognized that they would do better to quit while they were ahead. A deal was struck whereby the Colombian league could continue to enjoy the services of its illicitly contracted foreign stars for four more years, until 1954, when the players would return to their original clubs. And in future Colombian clubs would have to pay transfer fees for any foreign imports, just like anywhere else in the world. Back in the fold, Senior himself went on to be a fixture in Fifa committees for years; photographs of his career as an international sporting bureaucrat adorn his office.

The situation in Argentina, which had given rise to El Dorado in the first place, was no better, and the Colombian league's Argentinians, suddenly picking up a decent pay packet, were in no hurry to get back to Buenos Aires. Adolfo Pedernera, the elder statesman among the exiles, defended their right to work wherever they liked.

'I want to express a perfectly logical human aspiration: to enjoy the same freedom as all men. You understand that it is perfectly impossible that the fact of exercising a profession – that of football – should put us in an exceptional situation in relation to the other professions, in that we are obliged to give up the freedom of labour,' he said.[21]

Di Stéfano and Rial never went back to Argentina. They found fame and fortune in the colours of Real Madrid (they were spotted on a triumphant Millonarios tour of Europe) in the great side which won the first five European Cups. Di Stéfano even took on Spanish nationality, leaving Argentina to mourn the loss of one of the world's great players.

But Di Stéfano's exit to Europe also marked the beginning of the end for El Dorado. Colombians were left to pinch themselves as their football crock of gold disappeared almost as suddenly as it had arrived.

At the height of football fever in August 1950 *El Tiempo* published a small news item. Under the headline 'MARIJUANA APPEARS IN BOGOTÁ FOR THE FIRST TIME' *El Tiempo* reported: 'For the first time marijuana has arrived in Bogotá but fortunately the police have struck a blow to nip in the bud this tremendous evil which leads people to moral and physical ruin, which degrades them horrifyingly and leads them into crime.'[22]

Drugs, crime and moral ruin . . . that was the eighties all over for Colombia. But, some would reflect, at least they got a decent football team out of it. Valderrama, Asprilla and co. went to the United States unbeaten in over two years and with many pundits, including Pelé, tipping them to win the World Cup. With Argentina still associated with the sour aftertaste of the grim 1990 Final, and Brazil's glory years an ever more distant memory, the international media seized on the dashing Colombians. Times, it seemed, had changed. Pablo Escobar was dead – gunned down on a rooftop as he tried to flee from police at the end of 1993 – and the prospect of an exciting new phenomenon sweeping up from South America was enough to banish thoughts of all that unpleasant business about drug trafficking and corruption. Well, almost. The US authorities refused a visa to one member of the Colombian federation. 'It seemed reasonably clear that the man had a long record of drug dealing,' said the head of the USA '94 organizing committee, Alan Rothenberg.[23] Nevertheless, in the feelgood atmosphere in the run-up to the tournament, the Colombians were expected to go far and to serve up a football feast for the soccer-starved American public.

But someone hadn't read the script. Instead of beating the world, Colombia lost their first game to Romania and then crashed out of the tournament losing 2–1 to the unfancied Americans after going behind to an own-goal. Before the USA game the manager had received a threat telling him to drop one of his players. The player was left out.

Worse was to follow. Andrés Escobar, the Colombian defender who had put through his own goal, was gunned down days later in Medellín. In court it was said the killer fired six shots, shouting 'Goal!' between each. Rumours spoke of big bets by the drug cartels, of threats and retribution.

Andrés Escobar Saldarriaga was not a typical Colombian footballer. He came from a middle-class family and had completed secondary school, both uncommon traits among his team-mates. Likewise, having two parents around when he was growing up was something of a novelty (his mother died in 1985 after he had already embarked on his football career). His brother was also a professional. Andrés was quiet and serious, a devout Catholic and engaged to be married to his longstanding sweetheart when he was killed. He played his first game for the national team against Armenia in February 1988 and soon established himself as a regular in central defence and in the card schools during the long *concentraciones*. Three months after his debut he scored against Peter Shilton in a 1–1 draw at Wembley, a game which in Colombia is widely seen as the team's international coming of age. As he was more articulate than most, he was often asked to appear alongside the manager at post-match press conferences. People who knew him speak of an elegant and honourable player. 'Andrés stood out for his gentlemanliness and his responsibil-

172

ity . . . He was very open and sure of what he wanted to be in the future,' said his international team-mate Alexis García.[24]

Andrés Escobar lived and played in Medellín, for Atlético Nacional. Players were not immune to the blandishments of the mafia. Indeed, for some a career in sport was all that stood between them and a life as a *sicario*. 'Andrés, like many other players, was tempted by the corrupting influence of drug-trafficking and money and to get on quickly and to be in with important people,' says César Mauricio Velásquez, a television journalist who wrote a book about Andrés Escobar's life and death.[25] 'But Andrés was also clear and strong in not giving in, not negotiating, not entering into friendship or closeness with those people.'

It was Andrés Escobar's misfortune to score an own-goal, sticking out a leg to intercept a ball across his area and diverting it past his advancing goalkeeper. It made him an obvious scapegoat, but what about the forwards who missed good chances in that match?

Andrés Escobar arrived with friends at the Salpicón restaurant/nightclub at about 10 p.m. on Friday 1 July. Almost immediately another group began to abuse him, accusing him of having taken money to score the own-goal. The group was led by two local 'businessmen', Santiago and Pedro David Gallón Henao, brothers believed to have links to the drug trade.

Andrés tried not to get involved but eventually told them: 'You don't know how I feel. Please respect me. Anyone can make a mistake.'

According to the official version, when Andrés left at 3 a.m. there was another verbal altercation with the same people in the car park. Humberto Muñoz Castro, the Gallón Henaos' driver and bodyguard, said he was asleep in his vehicle but was woken by the commotion. He said he saw his boss involved in an altercation with another man. 'I thought he was a very dangerous guy or something like that. So I panicked and fired, as I didn't know who he was.'

Andrés was sitting in his Honda Civic at the time. He had already put it into reverse, as if to leave. That much is clear, but many other questions remain. The killer may or may not have shouted 'Goal!'

173

between each shot; the evidence is not conclusive. And although Muñoz Castro was sentenced to forty-five years in jail after confessing to the crime, some doubt still surrounds who actually fired the shots.

'He says he fired the shots but there is no evidence, such as powder burns on his hands, or that someone saw him do it. It could have been the Gallón Henaos who did it,' Velásquez believes.

The Gallón Henao brothers were both fined for not reporting a crime. In fact, they had driven off with Muñoz Castro and some of their companions and helped conceal evidence, particularly the vehicle and the gun.

'Why, after the shooting, did they flee and cover it up if they weren't part of the plot? Why didn't they turn him over to the authorities? Why did no one tell him to stop – because there were six shots from a revolver. Nobody said anything. Somebody could have pushed him or done something.'

Velásquez believes that in the five hours between first seeing Andrés and his death a plot was hatched among the Gallón Henaos and their associates to kill him. 'They waited for him to leave, they waited for the other people to go home. That was the plan, to take revenge out of hatred for having lost a farm, some cars, some money . . . Part of my investigation led me to find that there were losses of property and money. The Gallón Henao brothers had lost a lot of money.'

Idle speculation? Well, somebody clearly thought it was a little too near the mark. Five days before the book was published in September 1995 the author and publishers received death threats by phone and by letter, believed to be from the drug cartels. One said: 'The bosses are very angry because the book about Andrés Escobar tells a lot of lies, so heads are going to start rolling and we're going to start shooting.'[26] The publisher's head office in Medellín received bomb threats and its offices in the capital were sprayed with machine-gun fire.

No sooner was the book published than it was hauled off the shelves after a local state prosecutor in Medellín won an injunction on the grounds that the book impugned her good name. The book claimed her daughter, one of the Gallón Henao brothers' companions, told her of the crime but she failed to act. After three court cases and many months the author won, but by this time the book had been snapped up by Colombia's thriving pirate publishing industry and had become a best-seller at the traffic lights of Medellín and elsewhere.

Meanwhile, Andrés's father, Darío Escobar, could only reflect on what might have been. 'He had two serious injuries during his career. Look at how things turn out. Nobody knows how that boy battled to recover so he could get into the national team. He had so much faith, he thought that the World Cup was going to set the seal on his career . . . It would have been better for him if he'd never recovered.'[27]

But what exactly was going on around that fateful game against the United States?

Before the match Maturana received a threatening call at his hotel warning him and his assistant Hernán Darío Gómez to drop Barrabás Gómez or they would all be dead. Surprisingly, perhaps, Maturana told the players what had happened just before the game and was too upset to give his team talk. Gómez did not play.

Although there are no betting slips to prove it, it is widely believed that the Medellín cartel was betting for Colombia to win, while the Cali cartel was betting against them. The national side was still seen in many quarters as an *antioqueño* team – one representing the Medellín region – as the ex-Nacional man Maturana had based it on current or former Nacional players. Even Asprilla, then turning heads at Parma, was an old Nacional boy. But Gómez had long been the butt of criticism which suggested he was only in the side because of his brother's influence. Although Maturana had defended Gómez in print it was reported that only his brother's threat to quit had persuaded Maturana to swallow his opposition to Barrabás. So it could be that the threat against Barrabás Gómez was not directly related to a bet on the result of the game. This, and many other points, remain mysterious.

Given the way the team's defeat upset the form book, there were immediate rumours of a fix. Some observers still suspect that winning

175

was not uppermost on everybody's mind, but there is a total lack of hard evidence and no one is keen to talk openly.

'To bet against the team you have to have influence within the team,' says Velásquez. 'With a heavy dose of corruption within the team itself . . . and I don't want to say any more.'

However, there is an alternative explanation for the Colombian débâcle in USA '94, and it goes back to that night of euphoria in Buenos Aires nine months earlier.

The 5–0 victory in the Monumental stadium had reverberated around the world and commentators soon began to talk about Colombia as one of the favourites for the World Cup. A survey found that the national team's spectacular qualification for the finals was rated the most important event of 1993 and there was a hope that success would clean up Colombia's international image, for years now synonymous with the drug trade. The Colombian media seized on any statement by international football figures – including, for example, that by Pelé – which rated Colombia's chances in USA '94. In fact, almost anyone saying Colombia was going to win was considered newsworthy, no matter how informed or uninformed the opinion of the speaker. And when Pelé later cautioned that the team might be getting too cocky and over-elaborating, some media commentators presumed to question his authority. Immediately after the famous 5–0 match the Argentinian coach, Alfio Basile, made an observation which at the time was dismissed as sour grapes. He said: 'Let's see how they deal with the pressure of a World Cup. They have thirty million people following them. It's a big responsibility.'[28]

The fact that one of the country's biggest business groups – owned by Julio Mario Santo Domingo* – was not only sponsoring the national team but also owned many of the country's most important media outlets, led to a vicious circle of self-congratulation. For Radio Caracol to talk up the team's chances was also to boost the image of Bavaria beer. The team developed the habit of celebrating goals with a raised index finger, which was also the motif of the advertising

* Personally worth $1.9 billion according to *Forbes* magazine.

campaign for Bavaria beer: 'Number one: my selection'.* Each raised finger meant a $300 bonus from the sponsor. On one occasion, against Chile in Bogotá, the team even took the field with 'Bavaria' emblazoned across their chests, in clear violation of the Fifa rule banning shirt advertising in international games. (That escapade earned Colombia a fine.) As the list of warm-up fixtures mounted endlessly, often against mediocre club opposition, some began to suggest that the purpose of the games was not to prepare the team but to promote the product and rake in more income for the national federation. And it all helped stretch the unbeaten run. Finally, in May 1994, faced with yet another match, this time against the Italian club side Cremonese in the southern town of Neiva, the players rebelled, refusing to take part in a fixture they regarded as pointless.

The players won that clash of wills, which led some to question coach Maturana's authority, but by then they were becoming used to being indulged. Amid the national mood of bullish expectancy, players' incomes swelled and, told constantly that they were world-beaters, so did their egos. Indiscipline became a problem. There were reports of women being spirited into hotel rooms during *concentra-ciones*, of excessive drinking, over-exuberant social lives. Two players are even alleged to have missed training to make a beer commercial.

'They played a match in Barranquilla and the town laid on a special ceremony for them, the president gave them awards,' recalls *El Tiempo*'s Carlos Eduardo González. 'They hardly had any time left to play. They ended up demanding money for interviews. They were bombarded with money from all sides. They thought they were big stars.'

This atmosphere was carried over to the Marriott Hotel in Fullerton, Los Angeles, where the squad based itself for the finals. Colombian journalists and fans, as well as a number of US guests, shared the hotel with them and access to the team was free and easy, with individual players holding court with their favoured coterie of reporters. The *concentración* singularly failed to concentrate the team's

---

* *Selección* in Spanish also refers to the national team.

minds on the task in hand. The squad were basking in their status as dark-horse favourites, even though the country had never won anything in its entire footballing history.

Faustino Asprilla later observed: 'I think that we were killed by emotion, we paid for the emotion and inexperience: of journalists, of the people, of the players.' His team-mate Oscar Córdoba put his finger on the precise emotion: over-confidence. 'It was as if the World Cup was just a question of turning up and playing. As if we were going to win just by walking out on to the pitch.'[29]

The night before the first game against Romania, there was a small ceremony attended by the full board of the federation and Julio Mario Santo Domingo in which the squad were given an award for their achievements. The wisdom of handing out prizes before the team had won a game seems not to have occurred to anyone. The following day the counter-attacking Romanians beat them 3–1. The recriminations didn't wait for the final whistle. The half-time interval, with Colombia 2–1 down, was 15 minutes of finger-pointing, insults and abuse, setting the tone of disunity and discord which reigned in the subsequent days. Maturana accused Valderrama of having lost his authority within the team, although some thought this was a case of the pot calling the kettle black. For the second game against the USA, Maturana dropped one of his forwards, Adolfo Valencia, because – it later emerged – of his repeated indiscipline off the field. (Inevitably, a rumour alleged the real reason was a 'suggestion' from the Cali cartel.)

And so the scene was set for the crucial encounter with the host country. Maybe the narcos did influence the result of that match. We will probably never know for sure. But the fact is there are plenty of known facts to explain the Colombians' dismal performance in USA '94 without resorting to speculation about corruption and coercion. Put bluntly, the Colombian players thought they were it, and they weren't.

A subsequent victory against Switzerland was ultimately meaningless and it was only left for Andrés Escobar's death to add horror to humiliation.

A number of things changed as a result of the whole sorry experience. In terms of the national side, initially the public stayed away from games and there was a move to drop the older players and rebuild with a younger team.

'When we got back from the World Cup,' said Faustino Asprilla, 'we all wanted to drop out of the squad: because of the murder of Andrés Escobar, which hit us hard, because of the people who no longer believed in us, who said we were no use any more, that we were too old. But we got together and said to ourselves: now is when you find out who the big names are.'[30]

A series of unimpressive results was enough to convince most people who the big names were, and that they needed to be back in the team. There was a general recognition that no ready replacements existed for the current prodigious generation of internationals and that, despite his advancing years, Valderrama, for example, more than justified his selection. The atmosphere around the national squad has essentially sobered up. Discipline and access during *concentraciones* for international games have been tightened up, although foreign-based stars such as Asprilla are still indulged to the extent of being allowed to join the squad late after first spending some time in their home town. Asprilla is popular within the squad, still seen as the baby of the team. When he arrived nine hours late – not for the first time – for the World Cup qualifier against Bolivia at home, the manager, Hernán Darío Gómez, insisted he would be dropped. He had reportedly been seen drinking with friends in the city of Manizales after attending a horse show. 'Asprilla's attitude is very bad and shows a lack of discipline. I cannot allow him to behave like this . . . This is a serious matter, so he will not play tomorrow.' But presumably the combination of a tale of 'family problems' and the rubber-legged striker's plaintive visage melted Gómez's stony heart, for within twenty-four hours Asprilla was back in the team.[31]

Most of all, the USA '94 débâcle showed that Colombia could not rely on success at international level to gloss over the questionable basis of its domestic game. The government ordered new restrictions on the ownership of clubs, forcing them to reveal the names of their shareholders and prohibiting any one individual from owning more than 20 per cent of a club or from holding shares in more than one club. How effective such measures can be against people whose *modus operandi* is based on secrecy and disguising the source of money and control is an open question.

A year after he had accompanied the national team to California, Juan José Bellini, the chairman of the Colombian football federation, was jailed for his alleged links to the drug trade. In particular, documents recovered in a raid on the house of an important narco, indicated that Bellini enjoyed a close relationship with Miguel Rodríguez Orejuela, which included the receipt of large sums of money from the jailed Cali kingpin. None of this should have been too surprising as, until 1992, Bellini had been chairman of América de Cali, the cartel's team. Bellini resigned as federation chairman on 7 July 1995, vowing to clear his name. In 1997 Bellini was jailed for six years and fined some $200,000 for drug-related illicit enrichment.

At the time of writing, Pedro Dávila, the chairman of Unión Magdalena, and César Villegas, chairman of Millonarios, are both in jail on drug-related corruption charges, which is either a damning indictment of the mafia's continuing grip on the game or a sign of the newfound determination on the part of the authorities to stamp it out. Players too have strayed from the straight and narrow. In October 1995, defender Wilson Pérez of América de Cali was arrested with 171 grammes of cocaine at Barranquilla airport on his way back from international duty against Argentina.

A bent match, as the recent revelations about European football have shown, has effects far beyond that one game. The problem with Colombia's recent history of bribery, threats and match-fixing is that no matter how a straight a game may be there will always be a small, lingering doubt at the back of the mind. A match between Millonarios and Tolima in late 1996 at the Campín stadium in Bogotá offered an example of the credibility problem Colombian football labours under. It was a perfect day for football, although those spectators on the cheaper, sunny side of the ground had the better of it, as at 2600m it can turn pretty chilly in the shade. The late afternoon sunshine picked out the blue-and-white banners of dozens of different Millonarios supporters' groups and a few from Tolima. Midway through the tedious and goalless second half the visiting goalkeeper was sent off after receiving his second yellow card, like the first, for time-wasting. It was certainly the first time I'd ever seen this happen, and was particularly surprising since the keeper had not appeared to be dawdling at all. Now, strange refereeing decisions happen all over world, but given Colombian football's recent history and Millonarios' ongoing narco links, it does make you wonder. In the event the match finished 0–0 – the referee, a certain Wilmer Barahona, turned down a Millonarios appeal for a penalty – extending the home team's run without a win to 11 games, so Mr Barahona should probably be applauded for his rigorous approach to keeping the game moving.

There are encouraging signs that things have changed. The drug-financed bonanza of the 1980s appears to be over. Colombia's top clubs are no longer studded with highly paid foreign stars. The big money is no longer there and the imports on display are generally of the journeyman variety. In 1996 the championship was won by Deportivo Cali, the club that survived the city's drug boom unsullied by the hot money it generated for its rivals, América. For many it was a sign that it was now possible for a 'clean' team to win the championship.

There is no shortage of people willing to tell you that since Andrés Escobar's murder, Colombian football has cleaned up its act. Pablo Escobar is dead; so too is Gonzalo Rodríguez Gacha, killed in a shoot-out with police at a ranch in northern Colombia in December 1989. Miguel Rodríguez Orejuela is in jail – along with his brother Gilberto – and runs a store in Bogotá's maximum security prison selling Barbie dolls, English biscuits, coffee and Pepsi, but no Coke, to other inmates. The conspicuous consumption of the 1980s has given way to a more discreet approach. It suits many people to put the past behind them, to forget. As for Andrés Escobar's murder, the supposed turning point, a senior Colombian football official privately described it as a bar-room fight, with no greater significance.

But the drug trade – cocaine, marijuana and latterly heroin – remains one of Colombia's biggest export earners.* And although every cent is illegal, somehow, sooner or later, that money finds its way back into the legitimate economy, much of it through cheap contraband products which are openly sold in shops in Bogotá. Football would need to be a very special case to be immune.

The narco-celebrities may be a thing of the past, but money still talks and nothing makes money like drugs. The drug trade has become faceless again; its influence partially hidden. 'There are many more drug barons operating than the Cali cartel and the Medellín cartel: that's why drug consumption is going up in the States,' argues César Mauricio Velásquez. 'The criminal drug trafficking industry is alive and well, and it's bigger than ever. It's less visible, but much bigger, more powerful, with more money, moving more drugs, more arms: it reaches everywhere.'

In July 1997, the Companies Superintendency, in the first systematic investigation of its kind, found that 80 per cent of the shares in the country's top five clubs were controlled by drug traffickers. América, Atlético Nacional, Millonarios and Envigado were named, as, slightly surprisingly, was Deportivo Cali. At least fifteen smaller teams are also suspected of drug links. The investigation looked at all the professional clubs, and the companies superintendent, Darío Laguardo, said 176 shareholders had either failed to explain the source of the cash they had invested or could not be fully identified, raising the suspicion that they were aliases for drug barons. Laguardo said 'between 50 and 80 people' were channelling proceeds from the drug trade into football. Envigado's manager, Javier Velásquez, called the report 'sensationalist' and added, redundantly, 'This type of investigation is damaging to the reputation of clubs and their directors.' Laguardo also said that he thought the game was much cleaner than it was fifteen years before.

* An eight-month study by Colombia's top private economic think-tank estimated that in 1995 and 1996 drugs represented 23.7 per cent of the country's exports, worth $2.5 billion a year. *Cambio 16*, 20 April 1997.

Colombian football in general is finding it hard to shake off its drug associations. In July 1997 Anthony De Avila scored the only goal in Colombia's World Cup qualifying win over Ecuador and immediately dedicated it to the jailed Rodríguez Orejuela brothers. A minute's silence was also held before the league play-off final out of respect for the Cali mobsters' mother who had recently died.

But life goes on, and so does football. In September 1995, more than a year after Andrés Escobar's murder, the manager of Nacional, Juan José Peláez, and centre-half Víctor Marulanda received telephone death threats for failing to win the Libertadores Cup. Disgruntled narco-punters were suspected. Marulanda said he was taking the threats seriously and had changed his routines, 'Although,' he noted, 'you get used to this sort of thing in Medellín.'[32]

6: The Land That Football Forgot

'I DON'T WANT to create false expectations, but Guatemala aren't going to thrash us. We've got a lot of advantages and could well go for a draw or even better.'[1] So said Livio Bendaña, a member of the Nicaraguan squad preparing for their World Cup first-round qualifying clash against their Central American neighbours.

The striker's caveat was justified. For decades, nearly all the expectations created by Nicaragua's footballers have been false. Their only previous World Cup experience, in the USA '94 qualifying competition, ended almost as soon as it had begun, with El Salvador beating them 5–0 and 5–1 over two legs. Honourable defeats have tended to be the pinnacle of the country's football aspirations. Put simply, Nicaragua has for years had the worst team in Latin America.*

In a continent where football is the ruling passion, and in a Central American region where the game has sparked a war, Nicaragua seems like the land that football forgot. Delirious fans do not dance in the streets of Managua celebrating winning the Cup Final. Football stars do not have their own range of leisurewear. (There are no football stars.) Wives do not complain about husbands spending all day in front of the television watching football. (Nicaraguan football is not on television and very few people would watch it if it were.) While in most Latin American countries, football is the national game, in Nicaragua it jostles for attention alongside motorcross and ju-jitsu, and lags some way behind cock-fighting.

* Nicaragua figured in 181st place in the August 1997 Fifa world ratings, ahead only of Cambodia, the Maldives, Vanuatu, Somalia, Andorra, Central African Republic, Djibouti, Anguilla, Chad, the Cook Islands and Guam.

Why should this be so? How did Nicaragua come to be so out of step with its continental neighbours? Nicaraguan football's problem is simple: it's called baseball.

If football is the Cinderella of Nicaraguan sport, baseball is the two ugly sisters rolled into one: Nicaragua is baseball crazy. Players, like Denis Martínez, who make the grade in the US major leagues, are the country's biggest heroes. Words like pitcher, inning and home run (or *jonrón*) have become part of the language in the same way that *gol, córner* and *time* (team) have been absorbed from English elsewhere in the continent.

When, in his ill-fated 1990 election campaign, Daniel Ortega would visit towns the length and breadth of the country, it was only natural that the candidate's gift to each proud (but ungrateful) municipality should be a set of bats, catcher's mitts and other baseball paraphernalia. And in the Sandinistas' final election rally, attended by several hundred thousand people at the lakeside in Managua, Ortega was joined by several of the country's top baseball stars, who pitched balls into the crowd in illustration of some political point long since forgotten.

It is an irony of history that from 1927 to 1933 Augusto César Sandino should have waged a tenacious guerrilla campaign to rid Nicaragua of the very people who had introduced the game that his political heirs would champion. US influence in Nicaragua has been strong since at least the nineteenth century, but from 1908 the country was occupied almost continuously by a Marine Corps garrison which had a hand in every aspect of the government administration. They may have left in 1933, unable to defeat Sandino, but their influence lingered on, and not merely in the repressive national guard they created. Tomás Borge, the Sandinista former interior minister, wrote that the Marines brought three things to Nicaragua: the phrase 'OK', chewing gum and baseball. Nicaraguans took the game to their hearts and these days it's as Nicaraguan as *gallopinto*, or dengue fever.

The baseball map of Latin America today is like a living record of the travels of yesterday's gum-chewing, wisecracking, big-hitting

185

apostles of US culture. In the same way as the sons of the British empire took football with them as they sailed the world building railways and extracting the produce of distant lands, so in the early years of this century baseball was carried in the kit bags of the US Marines, who imposed a *pax americana* on the lands to the south. The region's main baseball countries – Cuba, Puerto Rico, the Dominican Republic, Nicaragua, Panama and Venezuela – all experienced occupation by US troops, except for Venezuela, where baseball was a sporting side-effect of the oil industry which virtually ran the country for decades. The same process can be seen in Japan and South Korea, both of which have hosted large US military garrisons since the Second World War. The exception which proves the rule is Haiti, which was occupied by US troops from 1915 to 1934 but which largely failed to catch the baseball bug. Indeed, in 1974, Haiti qualified for the World Cup finals in West Germany. In fact Haiti has made a significant contribution to US football. On 29 June 1950 the United States beat an England team including Matthews, Mortenson, Wright and Milburn 1–0 in the World Cup in Brazil, a day which lives on in infamy in English football history. The winner was headed home by a Haitian, Larry Gaetjens, and although some reports said the ball hit him on the head, it was Gaetjens who was chaired off the field at Belo Horizonte.[2]

There are, apparently, other theories about how baseball came to Nicaragua. When the NBC anchorman Tom Brokaw came to Nicaragua in the mid-1980s to host his news programme from Managua he insisted that his camera crew should film some kids playing baseball by the roadside. His Sandinista minder asked why he was so keen to show such an unremarkable scene. Brokaw replied that in the official briefing he had received before leaving Washington a National Security Council official had told him the fact that Nicaraguans play baseball was proof of the extent of Cuban influence in the country. The official was a little-known Marine lieutenant-colonel called Oliver North.[3]

Wherever it came from, baseball shows no sign of going away. It gobbles up the lion's share of state support for sport which, in a poor country of little over 4 million people, is not great to start with.

The hand-to-mouth nature of football in Nicaragua is indicated by the fact that the headquarters of the national football federation doubles as a travel agent's. Julio Rocha, the federation chairman, is in the travel business. Past the front desk, flanked by posters of sun-kissed beaches and atmospheric ruins, lies his private office, its walls covered with pennants, certificates and photographs of football teams, and of himself posing proudly with João Havelange.

Despite his sport's humble circumstances, Rocha has little time for plucky underdog stereotypes. He takes a thoroughly businesslike attitude to the business of football: 'I hold the belief, which is nothing new, that the sporting development of a country is intimately related to the investment it makes in a given sport.' For him, Cuba's record in the Olympics provides all the proof necessary. Any country, with sufficient investment, can have a half-decent side, regardless of questions of innate talent. 'For me, it is an economic question; it's a question of an entrepreneurial attitude. If you want results you've got to invest.

'Of course the problem is, who is going to invest in football? The state doesn't do it. OK, the fans contribute, through gate money. For example, at the weekend [the World Cup game] we'll get a crowd of maybe 3–4000. But the receipts won't even cover the costs of getting the squad together.'

Weighed down by these most basic of practical difficulties, Rocha betrays mild exasperation that Nicaragua, which in 1979 became the centre of attention in Latin America with its popular revolution, should have remained so impervious to the attractions of that most Latin American of sports, the people's game.

'The universal sport is football. I think Nicaragua has missed that opportunity of football as a mass sport, as the mass phenomenon of the century. Unfortunately governments don't see it that way, because the political cycle is so short that they don't see any immediate benefit. So in countries like these where baseball is deeply rooted in the people, governments, especially populist and unprincipled

187

ones, seek to take advantage of what is already there for their political ends; in this case baseball.'

The chasm separating football's level of development from baseball's is apparent everywhere. Footballers in Nicaragua tend to have a much higher level of schooling than baseball players – indeed, the national team includes a number of graduates. But even this is a sign of football's weakness, not strength, because young men know that they have almost no chance of making a living out of football and so many play for fun while seeking the security of qualifications. Many give up the game once they start work.

'Playing baseball you can earn 5–6000 cordobas [£400–500] a month, which is a living wage,' says Rocha. 'Here, the most you'll get for playing football is 1000 cordobas [£80].'

Sponsorship offers little encouragement either. Sponsors, of course, want something in return for their money. It's a vicious circle. They feel they have little to gain from the level of exposure afforded by football's tiny public. But without the sponsors' money, the game has little chance of breaking out of its ghetto. Above all, sponsors want to get their name seen on television, but not even the allure of Nicaraguan football's biggest day in four years could sway the national TV stations. Sunday's World Cup qualifier would not even be shown in the home country. Rocha had sold the TV rights to the game to a New York-based company, Worldwide Business Associates, for a sum not unadjacent to $10,000, but the action was unlikely to be seen anywhere outside Guatemala.

Slightly more support is forthcoming from Fifa. The world body pays for coaching courses, for some sporting material and for a few specific development programmes. But Rocha sees their value principally as morale boosters rather than seriously raising the technical level. 'For me these programmes are about motivation, because you get a specialist who comes to the country for a week or a fortnight. But nobody becomes a coach in a fortnight.'

The Nicaraguan Football Federation (FNF) chairman does become more enthusiastic when discussing Fifa's plans for the future. 'From 2002 Fifa is going to give each association a million dollars.

It's going to give $250,000 to each country every year for four years. So I think that in that situation things are going to get better for little countries. Giving $1 million to Spanish football or to Italian football . . . fine, they'll accept it, but it's nothing. But a country like Nicaragua or Belize, having $1 million over four years means being able to pay a coach, set up a football school, buy footballs. Currently, the contribution of the state is 10,000 cordobas' – about £800.

Given his faith in investment as the route to success, it is clear that Rocha sees little prospect for improvement before 2002. Asked how he thought the team would do against Guatemala, he shrugged, as if to say 'what do you expect?' before listing some more of Nicaragua's economic limitations. You get what you pay for.

Managua is a formless, sprawling city with very few tall buildings since an earthquake levelled the whole place in 1972, so the towering floodlights of the national stadium are a distinctive landmark. That's the national baseball stadium, of course. Next to it is a small, unre- markable structure, which one could easily drive past without noti- cing, despite the words Estadio Thomas Cranshaw newly painted on the blue outer wall. Perhaps it's the lack of floodlights that makes it so anonymous, or maybe it's the fact that it has only a modest stand on one side and a blank concrete wall on the other three. (In fact, no football ground in the country has floodlights, which is why you'll never see a game in Nicaragua after 6 o'clock.) Nevertheless, this is the foremost football ground in Managua and, nominally at least, the national stadium.

Despite its humble appearance, I have a soft spot for the Cranshaw stadium because alone among the national stadia of the world it is the one in which I have actually played a game. It was in 1990 and I was playing in the Managua Recreational League with a team dominated by a bunch of voluble Italians (is there any other kind?). I can remember little about the game, not even the score, but what did stick in my mind was the suffocating afternoon sun and the remarkable state of the pitch. A choking dustbowl with barely a blade of grass on it, the surface was dotted with small, woody plants

189

which diverted the course of the ball. Six years on, the pitch still had the odd bald patch but in general was in immeasurably better shape, the tricky shrubs having given way to grass, albeit yerba india, the coarse local variety.

I was shown around by the groundsman, Salvador 'Chava' Dávila,* who pointed out the stadium's modest facilities in a tone half proud, half apologetic. On the far side of the pitch he showed off the new changing-room block, a tiny concrete shed which would disgrace many a Sunday side in England. One corner of the ground was a building site where the single, low stand was being extended to occupy the full length of one flank.

Dávila has an office of sorts beneath the stand, a windowless cubbyhole where he painstakingly repairs old balls – footballs, volley-balls, basketballs – for use by the children who attend the soccer school he runs at the stadium. Rendering the gloomy space slightly more tolerable, a collage of posters and press cuttings covers almost every inch of wall space and several portable boards. The cuttings celebrate the great moments of Nicaraguan football, but most of all they celebrate the great moments of Chava Dávila. For before he was a portly 56-year-old fretting about the state of the grass, Dávila was the greatest goalscorer in Nicaragua's football history.

'This is me,' he said enthusiastically, pointing to a yellowed picture showing a sleek young man in football kit receiving, as man of the match, a presentation pack of Old Spice. Alongside, his face gazed out of a team photograph and all around newspaper headlines shouted his achievements. His record of 54 goals in a season is likely to stand for a long time yet, and in an international career running from 1958 to 1968 he scored 21 goals. But Dávila's finest hour came on 4 January 1966 when the national side took on Estudiantes de La Plata, the Argentinian team which two years later would beat the Manchester United of Best, Law and Charlton in the World Club Championship. With the score 1–1, Nicaragua were awarded a

---

* A nickname coined in reference to Salvador 'Chava' Reyes, the then marks-man of Mexican football with Guadalajara.

penalty. Chava Dávila stepped up to take it and wrote himself a place in his country's football history. That 2–1 victory remains almost the only time that the national side's exploits have had any repercussion in the wider public consciousness. Eleven Nicaraguans had humbled the mighty Argentines and the country was prepared to overlook the fact that it was at a sport which at any other time counted for little. The thirtieth anniversary of the feat in January 1996 was celebrated in newspaper articles and radio shows. To mark the occasion, Chava Dávila was formally inducted into Nicaragua's sporting hall of fame. I couldn't help wondering if anyone in Argentina still remembered this game which loomed so large in Nicaragua's football mythology: a narrow defeat in a pre-season friendly thirty years ago.

Despite his place in the hall of fame, Chava Dávila thinks not enough people in Nicaragua remember. 'Do you think that in any other country in the world I'd be in a little cellar like this?' he asked, reminding me again of his scoring feats. 'The government has done nothing for football,' he complained. 'It all goes to baseball.'

Dávila played most of his football under the tutelage of an Englishman, Charles Hinckel. 'He was one of the most important *quijotes* we ever had. Being English, he had football in his blood.' *Quijote* is the name given in Nicaragua to someone who organizes and, more importantly, subsidizes a football team. It seems a particularly appropriate term, for there can be few more quixotic occupations than trying to nurture the seeds of football in such stony ground. Hinckel was a prime example. A coach, referee and sometime player, he managed the Triunfo club – with Chava Dávila leading the attack – to many successes. But having made his money in the carpentry business he died, his friends recall, in penury, having sunk his fortune into football. The lack of such selfless spendthrifts is regularly bemoaned as one of the biggest handicaps shackling football's development in Nicaragua.

A poorly attended children's tournament the previous weekend had been named in Hinckel's honour and his photograph hangs alongside those of half a dozen other worthies in the stadium's administration office, next to a larger photograph and text celebrating Thomas Cranshaw, another Englishman recognized as the godfather of Nicaraguan football.

Tom Cranshaw was born in Manchester on 22 September 1892, the son of a policeman and a dressmaker. Although the main stadium in Managua is called Thomas Cranshaw, in fact his birth certificate gives his name simply as Tom. He arrived in Nicaragua, probably in 1915, seeking to make his fortune as agent for the firm of Lavender and Thompson. After the long sea journey from England he would have taken the train to the city of Granada, no longer the capital, but still the elegant colonial stronghold of the Conservative families who had for generations disputed the government with the Liberals of Leon. In Granada he opened a large store selling a variety of tinned and other foods, winning a particular reputation for his English biscuits. Two years later he married a local girl, Isabel Ramírez, who bore him five children in seven years and then duly died at the age of 30.

Football was his first love. No sooner had he arrived in Granada than he had made himself the driving force in the infant local football scene, quickly making a name for himself as a goalscorer. In his letters home he was soon boasting that he was mixing with 'the best sort of people' and that he read and wrote Spanish almost better than he did English. In fact, those who remember him say that to the end of his days he spoke bad Spanish with a heavy English accent (even though he never went back to Manchester and spent the rest of his life in Central America). Nevertheless, he impressed everyone with his sociable nature and sense of humour and quickly became a popular figure, known universally as 'Mister Cranshaw'.

His businesses seemed to be perpetually on the verge of making him rich. In 1931 he moved to Managua and bought the Anglo-American Hotel there. Two days later, on 31 March, an earthquake flattened most of the capital, taking his new acquisition with it. But Cranshaw stayed in Managua, where he founded the referees' association and later became the first president of the National Sport Commission.

In his later years he would spend his days at home meticulously clipping newspapers and sports journals which he pestered his relatives in England to send to him. He still retained his prankster's sense of humour: every day as his grandchildren hurtled home from school he would stick out a leg into the narrow side corridor and send them all flying. It was a joke he seems never to have tired of, and one that the young Cranshaws seem never to have got wise to.

In the 1960s he moved briefly to Costa Rica and then finally to Los Angeles to stay with his daughter, Lillian. But two months after his arrival he died, on 4 October 1964. He was buried in Managua. Anastasio Somoza, the Nicaraguan dictator, sent a plane to Guatemala to pick up the body and a large crowd attended his funeral.

In one of his last letters to his sister in England, Cranshaw boasted that his son William, who served in the US armed forces in the Second World War, was 'well in' with the man most likely to be the next president: Somoza. Indeed he was. William Cranshaw became the minister in charge of Managua, with responsibility, among other things, for the police. Although by the time of the Sandinista revolution in 1979 he had retired, he was still reviled as one of Somoza's henchmen and was jailed until 1983 and had property confiscated. Vengeance also fell on the Cranshaw stadium – a case of the sins of the son being visited on the father. The ground was renamed Camilo Ortega Saavedra after Daniel Ortega's brother, a revolutionary martyr killed by the national guard in 1978 but not known for his footballing prowess. With the Sandinistas now in opposition and the political polarization less acute, the name of Cranshaw *père* has been restored to its place of honour.[4]

It may be the main stadium in the capital but the Cranshaw only holds some 500 people and was in no condition to stage such an important match as a World Cup qualifier. Thankfully, Nicaragua does have an alternative. There is one corner of this baseball country whose heart beats for football. Diriamba, about 30 kilometres south of Managua, on the plateau of Carazo, is the football capital of Nicaragua. For most Managuans Diriamba is a place to change buses on the way to the seaside resorts of Pochomil and Masachapa or to '*los pueblos*', the cluster of small towns in the department of Carazo, famous for pottery and witchcraft. It has its cathedral church on its main square, like many another town, and boasts a fine chocolate-and-cream-coloured clock tower which stands alone in the main street. But what makes Diriamba special is that it has the country's longest football tradition and its finest football stadium. It was here that the national team would take on Guatemala.

Football came to Diriamba in the early years of the century, although exactly when and how is not clear. Carazo was experiencing a coffee boom at the time and the department's wealthy families took to sending their sons to be educated in Europe. According to one version, it was a student or students exposed to football in Europe who brought the game back to Diriamba. Alternatively, it was the Christian orders, particularly the La Salle brethren and subsequently the Jesuits, many of whom came from Spain and France, who taught the sons of Carazo to play in the schools they established there. Others say the proximity of Costa Rica to the south provided the vector of transmission. Probably a mixture of all three factors meant that by the 1920s Diriamba and the little towns of Carazo were playing football while the rest of the country was picking up the baseball bug.

For Diriamba's many football fans, the Cacique Diriangén stadium is the centre of attraction. Appropriately, it stands next to the vast ruined shell of the Jesuit Pedagogic Institute, which did so much to inculcate the game in the town's youth before being destroyed by an earthquake. Started in 1986 and completed in 1992, the ground is the home of the oldest club – and one of the strongest – currently in the Nicaraguan league: Diriangén. The team takes its name from a local Chorotega chief who, in 1521, was the first to fight the Spanish conquistadors on Nicaraguan soil. The team are popularly known as the Caciques (Chiefs). Some of Diriamba's neighbours, such as Jinotepe and San Marcos, come close to rivalling its foot-balling enthusiasm, and little San Marcos even boasts the country's second best stadium, usually referred to as 'Olympic' because it has a running track.

The Cacique Diriangén pitch is ringed by terraces which rise up in nine steep steps all round the complete circuit. Along each flank a roof offers some shelter from the elements, particularly the fierce sun. Three days before the game Miguel Angel Urtecho, the groundsman, had three men tending the lush green pitch as sprinklers showered it with water. The Guatemalan newspaper *Siglo Veintiuno* was to compare unfavourably the poor state of the national stadium in Guatemala City with the turf of the Cacique stadium, noting that 'despite the fact that football is not Nicaragua's favourite sport, they have a stadium in magnificent condition'.

The ground holds up to 12,000 people, but Urtecho reckoned they had never had more than half that number. The average for a league game is 600–700. 'If I could see this place full, I'd die happy,' he said wistfully. Like other Nicaraguan football fans, he dreams of having been born Brazilian.

The squad turned up in dribs and drabs at about three in the afternoon, as they had every afternoon for three weeks. The FNF had suspended the league season for a month to accommodate the international preparations and the regional Cup competitions. Part of the reason was that with no floodlights in the country, it was impossible to stage evening games, and a midweek fixture in the afternoon would struggle to attract more than a few score spectators. The squad had first been assembled the previous December but the number of warm-up games had been limited by the FNF's lack of money. 'What we need is more practice,' observed Julio Rocha. 'Because we still have something of an inferiority complex. When you go out on the pitch feeling inferior it's like giving them a goal start.'

In fact, in the friendlies they did play, the team had managed some good results – although, this being Nicaragua, all of them were defeats. They lost 2–0 to the Mexican Under-20 side, 2–1 to Guanacaste of Costa Rica and, most significantly in Nicaraguan eyes, 1–0 (to a penalty) to Honduras, the strongest team in Central America at the time according to the Fifa rankings.

Economic considerations had also dictated that the squad would not be sequestered in a training camp. 'If you take them away from

195

their homes, you've got to be able to offer them better conditions than those they have at home,' Julio Rocha reasoned. 'Why take them away to eat less than in their own home, or sleep worse than at home?'

In 1990, when the FA headquarters was in the offices of the now-defunct national airline (Julio Rocha's previous business), I spoke to the then national team manager, Roberto Ríos. The Honduran team had visited recently and had stayed in one of Managua's best hotels 'eating steaks every day'. He pointed to two large sacks of rice and beans in the corner of the office: 'My boys come up from Diriamba by bus and all I can offer them is that!'

To prepare the team for their World Cup challenge this time, the Nicaraguan FA had contracted a Salvadorean, Emanuel Alfaro, who had been assistant manager of a league side in his home country. But three weeks before the first match he walked out on the squad and went back to El Salvador. 'Basically, he couldn't put up with the conditions here,' Rocha explained. 'He came with higher expectations. He demanded what he would expect in El Salvador.' Clearly a fanciful idea.

The man the Nicaraguan FA had turned to in this crisis was Mauricio Cruz, the coach of Diriangén and a former Nicaraguan international. Like Julio Rocha, he is a *diriambino*. And like many a coach in his position he was putting his faith in organization, hard work and team spirit.

'On the physical side we've prepared very well,' he said. 'We've now got a fitness coach and the lads are in optimum condition, so they can give their all for 90 minutes. In tactical terms we've tried to convince the lads that it's a team game and they should stick to the job we've given them for the match. We'll be playing 5–3–2, which is a defensive formation, but it can also be a springboard for counterattacks.'

Asked to predict how the game would go, he offered that his team would cause the Guatemalans problems and that they might just cause a surprise. On the day of the game he was quoted in *La Prensa* as saying 'only a miracle can bring us victory',[5] which made one wonder what had happened in the intervening couple of days. In truth, there's only a certain number of variations on the 'we'll-be-up-against-it-but-you-never-know . . .' theme for a coach to offer the press.

The session began with some limbering up and physical jerks. Then the three goalkeepers trained on their own while the rest practised running and passing in pairs. The sun in this part of Nicaragua comes in two strengths: blisteringly hot, and night. Even after this gentle workout the players came off soaked in sweat.

Mario Orellana, the deep-lying centre-forward, found the heat particularly hard going. Although a diriambino by birth, he moved as a young teenager with the rest of his family to California, like many other Nicaraguan families during the war years of the 1980s. He speaks fluent English, and with his accent and close-cropped hair he resembles a young Richard Gere. These days he plies his trade in the US Indoor Soccer League with the Sacramento Knights, a team managed by Keith Weller, the former Chelsea and England midfielder, of whom he is clearly in awe. Two of Mario's brothers are also in the squad: Diego and Juan, the goalkeeper, rated one of the best in the region.

Mario Orellana felt that team spirit and discipline were the squad's main strengths. 'We're really together as a team. Being underdogs inspires us. It means we've got nothing to lose and a lot to gain.'

I asked about his record in internationals. He said he had 20 caps and had scored 3 goals, adding apologetically, 'It's hard to score many playing for Nicaragua.' I wanted to tell him that Alan Shearer had at that time only managed 5 in 22 for England, but he was already off to join the rest practising set-pieces.

Sitting out the session having picked up a knock in training earlier in the week was Sergio Gastón. A black 'creole' originally from the Mines region of the Atlantic Coast, with the sort of flowing cork-screw locks Kevin Keegan in his prime would have envied, he was a regular at the heart of the Nicaraguan defence. After comparing notes about Managua's lively reggae clubs, he asked if I liked a drink. 'Tell me,' he said, 'when you really go for a drink, how many days does it last?' Clearly no refuelling problems in the Nicaraguan camp. He enthusiastically recommended Flor de Caña's new lime-flavoured rum.

A few weeks before, Juventus of Managua had taken on Sacachispas from Chiquimula in Guatemala in the first round of the Concacaf champions' cup. Sacachispas had won their home leg 3–1 but the return, which Juventus switched to Diriamba, was much more hard-fought. With 18 minutes to go the score was 2–2. Then a Guatemalan player went in over the top and was sent off. Unhappy with the decision he made a lunge for the referee. At this point, according to the Nicaraguan account, the Nicaraguan team leapt sportingly to the defence of the referee. 'It was inexperience,' said Urtecho. 'If we'd've been smart, we'd've gone and stood by the corner flag while the officials sorted it out.' Whatever the precise sequence of events, the result was a massive ruck involving the twenty-two players, the referee and several officials from off the bench. Urtecho said that some in the crowd climbed the high mesh fence which surrounds the playing area and surged on to the pitch. The players said this wasn't so, but maybe only because they were concerned at Concacaf's threat to sanction the stadium for the pitch invasion. Amid the mêlée the referee decided to abandon the match. The tie was awarded to the Guatemalan team. So, with several of the same players likely to be present in the national sides, Sunday's clash had the potential to be a needle match.

Nevertheless, given the country's meagre football pedigree, the level of public anticipation for the big match was less than intense. Most Nicaraguan friends and acquaintances had no idea that the World Cup game was taking place and were astonished at the idea that I had travelled from another country to see it. In fact, they would probably have been astonished at the thought of travelling across the street to watch it. Although the back pages of the newspapers carried news of the football team's preparations for their big match, this was dwarfed by the coverage of baseball, including lengthy reports on the US major leagues. At least the team would not be weighed down by the burden of public expectation.

But in the final days before the big match, Nicaragua's press warmed to the occasion. *La Tribuna* invoked the memory of the victory over Estudiantes[6] while *El Nuevo Diario* picked out the goalkeeper, Juan Orellana, as the key to the match.[7] *La Prensa* asked 'Have we made progress?' and answered soberly that 'In the last three years ... the defeats have been hard fought ... However, we are still light years behind the rest of the teams in the area.' It concluded: 'With this line-up Guatemala will not be trembling.'[8]

Come the day of the match, *La Prensa* had managed to whip itself up into a frenzy of enthusiasm. Extravagantly predicting a full house, it warned that: 'A defeat for the visitors would provoke a wave of suicides in that country; a draw would mean the sack for the manager; a one-goal victory would cause an earthquake in the Guatemalan FA.'[9]

The Sandinista leader and writer Omar Cabezas used to say that the first rule of politics in Nicaragua was: never arrange a meeting at the same time as the *telenovela*, the imported soap opera which is the nation's unifying rite. A measure of football's relative importance is that the FSLN party congress, at which Daniel Ortega would be nominated as candidate for the 1996 presidential election, was scheduled to coincide with the World Cup date in Diriamba. So Víctor Hugo Tinoco, the footballing former deputy foreign minister, had to forgo his place in the stands so he could be in Managua to be nominated as the party's first candidate for the national assembly.

An hour before kick-off the stadium was already filling up, with a queue to pay 20 cordobas for a seat in the roofed section. A small 'directors' box', with folding wooden seats placed on the bare concrete steps, had been rigged up for the occasion. A few brave youngsters had shinned up some of the eucalyptus trees that ringed the ground to get a distant but free view. As the teams strode out for the anthems, the crowd had swelled to a respectable 5000 or so. But it didn't sound or feel much like a football crowd. It was more like several thousand people had all decided to come for a Sunday afternoon picnic around the same patch of green grass. On this showing the existence of the Nicaraguan football chant has yet to be proved. The cheer when the teams kicked off quickly subsided into a background chatter punctuated by applause when Nicaragua won a throw-in or the like.

The signs looked ominous when in the first minute a Guatemalan through-ball sailed over the head of Gastón, languishing in no man's land. Fortunately for him, the chance was wasted. The Nicaraguan defence was looking shaky, particularly the left-back, who seemed worryingly slow, but in fact in the early stages it was Nicaragua, in dark blue, who showed more attacking enterprise, with Mario Orellana firing in a couple of shots which with more composure might have troubled the keeper. Sixteen minutes into the match, the Nicaraguan No. 3, venturing forward, was brought down and stretchered off. From the free-kick the ball found Eytel González unmarked in front of goal, but he snatched at his shot and it sailed wide. It was a golden opportunity and Nicaragua would not get a better one.

Back on the field, Nicaragua's unfortunate No. 3 pulled his winger down again but took an elbow in the face in the process. The lengthy treatment he received appeared to involve pulling one of his teeth out. To cap his unhappy afternoon he was substituted in the second half. From the free-kick Juan Orellana, in goal, had to tip a header from the Guatemala winger Mario Acevedo on to the bar.

It began to look as if the Nicaraguans' dogged chasing and closing down space, coupled with Juan Orellana's authoritative display in goal, was going to frustrate the superior technique of the visitors. Then, on 25 minutes, with the defence ball-watching, a simple flick-on from the centre-forward set up Juan Carlos Plata who duly slotted the ball past Orellana. (Two years before the same player had knocked Nicaragua out of the Central American Games in San Salvador.) You could almost hear the collective mutter of 'here we go again' rising from the crowd.

One drunken supporter began abusing the visitors' black winger,

Acevedo, declaiming that he shouldn't be playing as Guatemala wasn't a black country. It was pointed out to him that his own centre-half was equally black, but then racist logic is something of an oxymoron.

It was at this point that the Nicaraguan rainy season started. The sudden downpour sheeted in under the roof of the stand, mocking the extra we had paid to be in the shade, and continuing up to half-time.

The second half was a tight affair with few chances. Mario Orellana spent most of his time as his team's first defender rather than as a potential goalscorer. The American referee issued a cluster of yellow cards but the game never looked like degenerating into a repeat of the Juventus–Sacachispas clash. With 15 minutes left the Nicaraguans were forced to clear the ball off their line, but this was one of the few clear chances.

And then, somewhat anti-climactically, it was all over. As the crowd trooped away the realization dawned that it was a match that Nicaragua could easily have drawn, even won. At the back of the stand Chava Dávila celebrated drunkenly with some of his old football cronies. Mauricio Cruz said he was pleased with the performance but rued the wasted opportunity. 'We had three moves in the first half that could have been goals, but we lacked composure at the vital moment. That comes with more experience, to lose that fear of shooting.'[10]

The defensive midfielder Otoniel Olivas agreed. 'We have to take advantage of the other team's mistakes, and that was what we were lacking. In the first five minutes we had a chance and wasted it. They took advantage of the error we made and beat us 1–0.'[11]

Unperturbed by the seismic shock presumably rumbling through the Guatemalan FA, the *chapines'* Argentinian coach, Horacio Cordero, graciously congratulated the Nicaraguans. 'They played an excellent game against a team with greater technical and economic support. They've really achieved a lot in a short time.'[12]

Reading the Nicaraguan press on the plane to Guatemala, one might almost have believed that the Nicas had won. *Barricada* boasted:

'We weren't the Cinderellas Guatemala expected.' It quoted the goalscorer, who seemed to have got his fairytale scripts confused, as saying, 'Before [Nicaragua] were the ugly ducklings of Central America, but now we're convinced that's no longer the case.'[13]

The general verdict was unanimous: '*Nos fajamos*' (We put up a good show).[14]

The eventual winner of the tie would progress to a second-round group including the United States, Costa Rica and Trinidad and Tobago. The top two from this and two other groups would then pass to a third-phase group, from which the top three would qualify for France '98. This would be the first time that Concacaf, the regional federation representing North and Central America and the Caribbean, had been granted three qualifiers, partly because of the expansion of the finals to include 32 teams and partly in recognition of the region's respectable record in the tournament.

In the old days it used to be much simpler. Usually it would fall to Mexico to represent everything between Colombia and Alaska, and that was that. Mexico, with its huge population, relative wealth and its professional league, has more often than not proved an insurmountable obstacle to the small countries of Central America, both in the World Cup and in regional Cup competitions, when Mexican sides have deigned to take them seriously. Latterly, the emergence of the United States as a middle-sized footballing power has further cramped the region's opportunities. No Central American country appeared in the finals until 1970 in Mexico, the fact that the hosts qualified automatically having left the one Concacaf berth more open than usual.

Before this it was teams from the Caribbean, ironically the weakest by tradition of Concacaf's three areas, that had left their mark on the World Cup. In 1938 both Cuba and the Dutch East Indies played in France. Neither had any football tradition to speak of but the Cubans managed, after a replay, to beat Romania in Toulouse before taking an 8−0 hammering in the quarter-finals at the hands of Sweden. Sadly, after this brief flirtation with the game's élite, little has been heard of Cuban football.

When El Salvador eventually became the first Central American team in the finals, it was not before one of the more dramatic incidents in the history of World Cup qualification.[14] The trouble started on Sunday 8 June 1969, when El Salvador visited Tegucigalpa in the second round of qualification for Mexico '70. The players were kept awake all night by a crowd of chanting, whistling, screaming Honduran fans, who leant on their car horns and threw stones at the Salvadoreans' hotel windows. The Salvadorean press even speculated about possible poisoning of the team's food. The next day the sleepless Salvadoreans lost 1–0.

The Salvadorean media worked itself up into a fever of indignation and gave prominence to the case of Amelia Bolaños, who shot herself in response to the blow dealt by the Honduran team to national honour. Her funeral was televised nationally, the cortege accompanied by a military honour guard and the defeated football squad who had had to run the gauntlet at Tegucigalpa airport on the way home.

When the Honduran team arrived in San Salvador for the return match they found the capital bristling with the ugly tension of a lynch mob. Ryszard Kapuscinski describes it in the following way:

'This time it was the Honduran team that spent a sleepless night. The screaming crowd of fans broke all the windows in the hotel and threw rotten eggs, dead rats and stinking rags inside. The players were taken to the match in armoured cars of the First Salvadoran Mechanized Division – which saved them from revenge and bloodshed at the hands of the mob that lined the route, holding up portraits of the national heroine Amelia Bolaños.

'The army surrounded the ground. On the pitch stood a cordon of soldiers from a crack regiment of the Guardia Nacional, armed with sub-machine-guns. During the playing of the Honduran national anthem the crowd roared and whistled. Next, instead of the Honduran flag – which had been burnt before the eyes of the spectators, driving them mad with joy – the hosts ran a dirty, tattered dishrag up the flag-pole. Under such conditions the players from Tegucigalpa did not, understandably, have their minds on the game.

[Honduras lost 3–0.] They had their minds on getting out alive. "We're awfully lucky that we lost," said the visiting coach, Mario Griffin, with relief.'[15]

Visiting fans were attacked in the streets. Two died and many more were injured. Dozens of cars were damaged. Within the week the two countries had broken off diplomatic relations and El Salvador filed a charge of genocide at the Inter-American Court of Human Rights. On 14 July war broke out with the Salvadorean air force bombing four Honduran cities. The war lasted 100 hours and left between 4000 and 6000 dead and twice as many wounded. Up to 50,000 people were displaced from their homes. Such was the mutual animosity generated in this spasm of violence that fifteen years later, when Ronald Reagan was trying to fashion an anti-Sandinista alliance in Central America, there was fierce opposition in Honduras to a plan to train Salvadorean troops at the regional military school in Trujillo, northern Honduras, because the abiding hostility to their western neighbours outweighed the passing ideological distaste for the then Nicaraguan regime.

It is now a commonplace to say that the Football War wasn't really about football. El Salvador is the smallest country on the American mainland, and also the most densely populated. Honduras is about six times as large but has half as many people. Two thirds of the Salvadorean peasantry was landless, and consequently since the 1900s large numbers of Salvadoreans had settled in the relatively underpopulated lands of Honduras, many attracted by the multi-national banana companies. Most entered Honduras illegally. By the 1960s some 300,000 Salvadoreans were living in Honduras – some 20 per cent of the rural population. When agitation for land by the Honduran peasantry became intense in the 1960s, the government decided that the land occupied by the Salvadoreans was ideal for redistribution (rather than take on the US-owned fruit companies which owned large tracts of northern Honduras). In June 1969 500 Salvadorean families were evicted and thousands more returned across the border to El Salvador, many with tales of beating and harassment.

204

All of this is true and certainly formed the background to a war which was cynically exploited by the ruling élites of both countries. But the fact remains that the war did break out over a football match. And it is hard to think of any other activity which could have concentrated so much nationalistic fervour with such a mass participation. Football may have been just the catalyst, but would the people of El Salvador and Honduras have got so worked up about volleyball, or a beauty contest?

Unfortunately for the football authorities, under the competition rules scores were not aggregated, so it was necessary to stage a deciding game on neutral territory. After much hand-wringing and diplomatic discussions, the two sides faced off in Mexico City. This time the match passed off without incident, thanks in part to the presence of several thousand Mexican riot police, who the year before had distinguished themselves by massacring hundreds of student protesters just before the Olympic Games. El Salvador won 3–2 and went on to beat Haiti over three games to claim their place in the World Cup finals, where they lost every game without scoring a goal.

The Concacaf qualifiers in 1974 and 1978, Haiti* and Mexico, each suffered three defeats at the finals, and it was not until 1982, with Honduras, that Central America recorded its first World Cup points. But despite 1–1 draws against the hosts Spain in Valencia and Northern Ireland in Zaragoza, they finished bottom of their group after losing 1–0 to a late, disputed penalty to Yugoslavia. This was the first World Cup finals to feature 24 teams, and Concacaf was awarded two qualification places. Unfortunately, El Salvador's most notable contribution was to register the worst defeat in the finals' history as Hungary put 10 past them, although they had the scant consolation of registering one goal against the Hungarians before they caught the plane home.

In 1986 no Central American teams qualified (Canada took the

* The qualifying competition was held entirely in Haiti, clearly benefiting the host team.

205

only Concacaf berth, Mexico were hosts) but in Italia '90 Costa Rica became the first side from the region to progress from its first-round group. The *ticos* beat Scotland and Sweden (they only lost 1−0 to Brazil) and in the second round they were 2−1 down to Czechoslovakia with 15 minutes to go before letting in two late goals. Although Costa Rica had won the Concacaf qualifying competition with the United States qualifying in second place, they had certainly been helped by the disqualification of the Mexicans for fielding over-age players at Under-23 level. The United States joined Costa Rica in Italy after beating Trinidad 1−0 win in their final game in Port of Spain. In the 1994 finals Mexico once again took its customary place with Canada losing out in a play-off against Australia.

Concacaf was only founded in 1961 and has historically been one of the weaker Fifa affiliates. Before that, one body had notionally represented all the Americas, but this foundered because of the strength and independence of the South American federation. In recent years Concacaf has been boosted by the resurgence of football in the United States on the back of the 1994 World Cup, and in the same year the federation moved its headquarters to New York from its previous base in Guatemala City. Some of Concacaf's regional competitions had fallen into neglect, but sponsorship has helped make its Gold Cup tournament a success.

But even for the Central American countries with strong leagues and some sort of international pedigree, gaining access to top-quality coaching and testing competition remains a big problem. Costa Rica, with the oldest established league in the region, finally realized its potential in the World Cup under the tutelage of Bora Milutinovic, the Serbian coach who would also lead Mexico and the United States to international success. In 1996 Guatemala had placed their faith in an Argentinian, Honduras in a Brazilian.

International experience is a problem for all the Central American countries. Apart from Mexico and, latterly, the United States, Central American teams are relatively isolated from top-class competition. The Honduran national team had hoped to play twenty-two matches as part of its preparations for the World Cup qualifiers, but a planned tour of the Caribbean fell through, apparently the fault of the agents entrusted to arrange it, and proposed tours of Europe and South America remained on the drawing board. The Honduran football authorities were even considering waiving their $15,000 a match fee in an effort to get the team a game. 'If no one wants to hire us, we've got no choice but to offer ourselves for free,' said Daniel Bali Castillo, chairman of the Honduran FA's international committee. 'The team isn't saleable [abroad] because they haven't seen them play, and that's a worry for us.'[16]

Belize could also dispute the title of weakest team in Latin America, if anyone could agree on whether it was part of Latin America or not. English-speaking, Caribbean-oriented, Belize only joined Concacaf in 1986, which is hardly surprising since it only became independent in 1981. For many years, as British Honduras, most of the country's international games were played against visiting warships. In the France '98 qualifying competition Belize fell at the first hurdle, but did not disgrace themselves, losing to Panama over two legs. Belize's sporting history has much in common with the Anglophone Caribbean islands. In colonial times cricket was the top sport. For many years the national stadium, for football or anything else, was the MCC Grounds in Belize City. Nowadays cricket has declined and Belize City has a new football stadium, but the competition for the country's youth comes from the NBL, beamed via satellite from the USA.[17]

Guatemala is in some respects the great under-achiever of Central American football. It has the largest population of any of the regional states and a relatively strong professional league. But unlike El Salvador, Honduras and Costa Rica, it has never qualified for the World Cup. This time, fresh from victories in the Gold Cup tournament in the United States, expectation for France '98 was high.

Nicaragua's return game in Guatemala was only five days after the two teams faced off in Diriamba. The contrast between the scene then and that at the Mateo Flores stadium in Guatemala City could hardly have been more striking. Even half-full, the ground held some 20,000 chanting fans beneath its floodlights, many of them waving national flags. In a country where large concentrations of people tend to attract the unwelcome attention of the security forces, such a boisterous public gathering is something of a rarity, although this was a popular demonstration of impeccable patriotism. There was no travelling support. The press photographers were camped at the Nicaraguan end, expecting, like the rest of the crowd, that that was where the action would be.

What had been, in effect, a Guatemalan B team had just secured a morale-boosting win over Mexican club opposition and now it was expected that the first team would register a convincing victory over the *nicas* to set the team up for the next phase of the qualifying competition.

From the first whistle Nicaragua, in their red-and-white-striped change strip, were into their breathless defensive rhythm, chasing, hustling, harrying, as the Guatemalans took the game to them. But when the Guatemalan captain, Juan Manuel 'Memo' Funes, rattled the crossbar after 20 minutes, it was the first real chance they had had. Apart from a good shout for a penalty, the home team managed little else and trooped off at half-time to loud booing.

Despite their team's poor performance the crowd remained in ebullient mood. Supporters of Comunicaciones (*los Cremas*), one of the top two teams from the capital, kept up a constant tattoo on the drums, which perpetually sounded as if it was going to turn into the theme from *Stingray* ('Anything can happen in the next half-hour!'). The Municipales fans (*los Rojos*) led the singing. The chants were tuneful but a little straightforward ('Let's go, let's go, *chapines*, because we've got to win this game'). One fan chose the half-time interval to start up a powersaw he had thought to bring along (thankfully, minus the business end), presumably because it was the noisiest thing he could lay his hands on. In Diriamba the Nicaraguans' slightly more traditional equivalent had been an air-raid siren.

The second half began and within minutes Nicaragua nearly made history. A quick break down the left released Livio Bendaña, who crossed to the diminutive Sergio Gago six yards out. With only the goalkeeper to beat Gago headed over. The Guatemalans replied by forcing a fine save from Juan Orellana but then the *nicas* had three chances to force the ball into the net in 10 seconds, but squandered them all. Another good chance produced another header over the bar. Nerves and inexperience had let them down again.

Five minutes later Guatemala gave the Nicaraguans a lesson in finishing. A corner was flicked on and Juan Carlos Plata rose to head it into an empty net. The goal was greeted with a half-hearted Mexican wave. Within three minutes things went from bad to worse for the *nicas* (or as they say in these parts, *de Guatemala en Guatepeor*) as Plata – Nicaragua's nemesis – popped up to score a second, his third of the tie.

The double strike restored the crowd's good spirits, but then, with the game going into injury time, a Nicaraguan corner was met on the volley by Ezequiel Jérez on the edge of the area and his shot kept low all the way to the back of the net. For a moment there was total silence, before, as the scorer ran towards the Nicaraguan bench ecstatically kissing his shirt, respectful applause rippled around the ground.

When the final whistle went, the Guatemalan team jogged off quickly, having secured their passage but sown the seeds of doubt about their prospects in the competition. The Nicaraguans, though, savoured their moment of glory. Bearing a large national flag, they jogged around the pitch in a lap of honour: still not winners, but no longer pushovers.

7: The Football Business

A COOL EVENING at the Jalisco stadium in Guadalajara, a place that likes to call itself 'the most Mexican city in Mexico'. The not so mighty Atlas were playing their first match in front of their own fans before the start of the Winter championship. Before the game, Atlas presented their squad to the supporters. Each player was introduced individually over the Tannoy and led out to the centre-circle by a teenage girl in the club colours bearing a bunch of red and black balloons. The process continued until the entire squad, plus the coaching staff and the club chairman (who was reassuringly booed), stood in a red-and-black circle in the centre of the pitch. Two young lads dashed around them parading giant club flags. But just as the ceremony was coming to an end and the visitors took the field the Atlistas' applause was drowned out by the opposition's cheers. The yellow–and–blue flags of América seemed to occupy the whole stadium, as the glamour club from Mexico City showed its pulling power.

At the stadium no opportunity is lost to sell you something. There's a man who comes to your seat selling fizzy drinks, another selling crisps, others offering snacks, sweets, pork skins (that's unappealingly uncooked crackling), popcorn, cigarettes, fixture lists, keyrings, teddy bears, glove puppets and, outside, when the crowd walks out of the stadium and into a downpour, there are women ready and keen to sell you plastic macs. But perhaps the most civilized aspect of this rampant commercialism is the men who tour the stands offering beer at about 60p a bottle. The beer on offer is Corona, which is no surprise because Corona is Atlas's sponsor. Corona billboards surround the pitch, and the PA announcements of substitutions and the like are always 'brought to you by Corona, Mexico's best-selling beer'. A troupe of large inflatable beer bottles stands cheerily along one touchline during the pre-match formalities and takes up position again at half-time. The name on the home team's shirts is, of course, Corona. The shirts of the visitors, América, ecumenically sport Coca-Cola on the front and Sol beer on the back.

Atlas lined up with a 16, a 29 and a 58 – surely the highest number worn by any player outside a basketball court. Well, as it turns out, no. Guadalajara, known as Las Chivas, who share the Jalisco stadium with Atlas, also have a 58. Both players are paid to wear the number by a local radio station – Radio 58. And that's not the highest number worn by a Mexican player. A member of the Monterrey team recently wore the number 400 to mark the four-hundredth anniversary of the north-eastern city.

It was an open and entertaining match. Three goals, two penalties (one scored, one missed), two plausible appeals for further spot-kicks, five bookings, two punch-ups and plenty of goalmouth action. And to the victors, the spoils, in this case, inevitably, the Atlas Corona trophy.

Atlas may have given itself wholeheartedly to its sponsors, but in an important sense it remains its own master. Alone among the Mexican first division, Atlas retains its independence and is self-financing. It is not a subsidiary of a non-football company. And, so far, no company has tried to buy the club.

'The fact is that commercialization has grown so much that the people who approach us are sponsors. Our club is very different from the others, we have three social clubs in the Guadalajara metropolitan area, and for a soft drinks company or a brewery, what interests them is not only the stadium but to have contact with the 4000 families who form part of Atlas as club members,' the club chairman Francisco Ibarra told the Mexican news magazine *Proceso*.[1]

In most of Latin America, football clubs tend to be owned by their members, with elections to the top positions in the club. Club chairmen still tend to be drawn from the ranks of wealthy businessmen, but businessmen with a prior connection to their club as fans. In Mexico all the eighteen first division clubs, with the exception of Atlas, are owned by companies otherwise unconnected with football. Cruz Azul is owned by the cement company of the same name, a fact which prompted its rival in the cement business to buy a team of its own, Tigres, and take them into the first division. Grupo Modelo, which makes some of Mexico's most popular beers, including Corona, has the major stake in three first division teams, Santos, Toluca and Atlético Celaya. Las Chivas, unusually, have the name of their parent company, Mexlub, suppliers of motor oil, on their chests. Salvador Martínez Garza is chairman of both enterprises. Toros Neza are owned by a loan company, Monterrey are run by another finance company, and Puebla belongs to a hotel company.[2] And that's without mentioning the TV companies. Buying and selling clubs is a straightforward and commonplace business: as in US sports, each club is a franchise.* Back in the 1970s the deputy head of the mighty oilworkers' union took a more literal approach to putting money into his club. Salvador Barragán would turn up for Tampico–Madero's home games accompanied by an assistant carrying a bagful of cash, which he would toss into the air if Tampico scored.

Guadalajara, Mexico's second city, is a 1.6 million-strong industrial conurbation, north-west of the capital. Like Manchester in England, it is home to the country's most popular team and current champions, Las Chivas (literally, the Nanny Goats†). But if Guadalajara is Mexico's Manchester, Atlas is its Manchester City. Atlas have won the title – once – but that was in 1950–51. Since then the Atlistas have had to get by on pride, defiance and stoicism.

Atlistas like to feel that they are the authentic team of the *tapatíos*

---

* Another US-style feature of the league is the draft, in which the owners of the major clubs get together at a resort hotel before the start of the season and trade players amongst themselves, then emerge like cardinals from a conclave to tell the media (and the players affected) who is going where.
† Originally a term of derision coined by Atlas supporters.

(people from Guadalajara). On a street corner in the centre of the city a large red-and-black sign featuring the club's fox mascot trumpets the existence of the Bolería Santa Teresita, a shoeshine parlour dedicated to the slightly faded glory of Atlas. Inside is choc-full of shields, stickers, team photos, banners, flags, mascots, children's drawings and, oddly, a small penny-farthing with a nun's face in the big wheel – all bearing the Atlas colours. Pride of place goes to a poster of the victorious 1950–51 side, known then as '*La Academia*'. An asterisk next to the opening hours indicates 'except when Atlas are playing'. The shoeshine boys who work there, I reasoned, must be the most devoted fans in the city. But the young lad buffing up my trainers merely shrugged, sourly: 'You'd better ask the boss – I don't even like football.'

Jesús Castillo is the man responsible for turning his shop into 'The Foxes' Lair', as one sign proclaims. He wasn't sure whether it actually improved his business. Atlistas could come here and celebrate after a win but, frankly, that alone would never pay the rent. In fact, it's more often a really good place for Chivas fans to come and have a gloat of a Monday morning. Either way, after a match the banter tends to zing back and forth between customers on their raised seats on either side of the shop. Castillo says he began assembling the shrine when his son started playing for Atlas in their time in the second division. Jesús Castillo himself supports Chivas.

As they shoulder their burden of supporting a team which is never there or thereabouts when the prizes are being handed out, Atlistas can console themselves with the knowledge that they are not alone. Every day, one of the region's main newspapers, *Siglo Veintiuno*, publishes a cartoon strip which expresses the agony and the agony of being an Atlas fan.

The strip is drawn by Trino (José Trinidad Camacho) and its main character, Pipo, is his *alter ego*, a sufferer for the love of Atlas. If the strip has a theme it is, as the popular saying goes, 'You have to support Atlas, even if they win'.

Trino is in his thirties and has never seen his team win the title, just the odd famous victory or heroic defeat. He says the strip is

213

What's up with the
weather?

What's up with
this country?

What's up with
the stock
markets?

What's up with my
Atlas?

Ay, Pipo!
The same as always
over the last fifty
years . . . nothing

taken from life. When, in the middle of a miserable Atlas run, Pipo
wears a paper bag over his head, it's not just an artistic device. Fans
turn up at the ground with their paper bags complete with eyeholes
ready as a form of protest. 'If Atlas are on a losing streak they turn
up at the ground with their bag,' says Trino. 'If they win, they take
it off, if not, it stays.'

Although they feel they are the authentic club of Guadalajara,
Atlas's image problem is that Chivas are the people's team, which
gives Atlas class associations Trino is keen to dispel.

'Before,' he stresses, 'they used to say that it was the upper class
who supported Atlas and that Chivas were the people's team, which
is completely false. There are many, many Atlas fans who are of the
people, of modest means. And they pay very high ticket prices to
see a team that doesn't work. But they're a very faithful support.
They turn up at the stadium even if the team is losing. If you look
at attendances, a couple of years ago Chivas weren't doing so well
– they lost a few games and people stopped going to the ground.
With Atlas, no. If they're losing I want to go and support them.'

I suggest that the previous night's victory had posed a problem for him: many more results like that and he'd be out of a job.
But Trino has dealt with more persistent false dawns than this
before.

214

'What happens to the character is he gets an attack of measles, or he gets hiccups and can't speak because he gets too emotional. Once Atlas won five games on the trot and he got so sick he was almost in a coma.'

The big América presence at the game did not surprise him. Guadalajara used to divide between Chivas and Atlas, with a couple of smaller local teams attracting tiny crowds. But América are always on television and gradually they have made big inroads so that the city now splits three ways.

'That's television. People are fed up, like workers who arrive at the factory on Monday morning and Atlas have lost, and they have to put up with all the mickey taking from the Chivas fans. They can't change to supporting Chivas, because they were Atlas, so they go to América because they're a serious enemy of Chivas. And on TV they always talk up América, even if they play badly. It's because of the influence television has. It gives América a certain cachet, makes it fashionable. They've got very good players, they've got money.'

When it started, the strip was a new departure in terms of its overt partiality but, for the most part, readers find it very true and very funny, as one might expect from a cartoonist who is a big *Monty Python* fan and has all of *Fawlty Towers* on video ('"Don't mention the war" – brilliant'). It does generate a great deal of reader response, from Chivas fans fed up of all that mithering on about Atlas and from Atlistas irritated by the crown worn by the strip's other character, the Chivas-supporting Don Calvino. Another group that doesn't find Trino's strip so funny are the club's directors. Trino's name is mud to the chairman, who feels he makes Atlas a laughing stock or, as our fusty FA would say, brings the club into disrepute. That view may not be unconnected to the fact that the directors are regular targets of Trino's barbs. Nevertheless, he still has the support of a small group of dissidents on the board. While some hail Atlas as the last of the member-owned clubs, Trino thinks they might be better off taken over by a big commercial godfather like the other clubs. As it is, he claims, the rank-and-file members have little say and the wealthy businessmen who are the club's directors appear to be more concerned with seeking business advantage than returning the club to greatness. A big company would at least be able to underwrite some big-name transfers without being so concerned about balancing the books in the short term.

Chivas have certainly benefited economically from their association with Mexlub, but when they took the field at the Jalisco stadium two days after the Atlas–América game, the sponsor's name on their shirts appeared positively discreet compared to that of another company of their acquaintance. Chivas were raising the curtain on the new season with something called the Nike Cup. Of course, this was just a pre-season friendly by any other name, but one arranged by their kit sponsor. The opposition were Boca Juniors of Buenos Aires, another Nike team.* There was no possibility that anyone present could have been ignorant of Nike's role in the proceedings. Many of the spectators would have bought their tickets at the Nike shops in Guadalajara's many US-style shopping malls. The co-operative press had even offered readers advice on pronunciation (it's *nai-qui*, they explained, which must have been particularly confusing for those who had just mastered the English mysteries of 'Mike', 'like' and bike'). At the ground, double ranks of advertising hoardings around the pitch shouted 'La Copa Nike' and (in English) 'Just do it'. From the four corners of the stadium roof, two huge banners proclaiming the home team's name, above Nike's trademark 'swoosh', alternated with two Nike Just Do It banners. The centre-circle before the game was covered in a large Nike advert. At half-time two big balloons, one Chivas, one Nike, made an appearance on the pitch. The perspex roofs of the substitutes' dug-outs were adorned with the names of the seven deadly sins, each accompanied by a Nike 'swoosh' which referred to the company's current, distasteful television advertising campaign. There was worse. As they

---

* Boca were sadly without Maradona who was back in training but stayed behind in Argentina either a) to build up his fitness, or b) because Chivas could not afford his $100,000 appearance money.

entered, each spectator was handed a card – red on one side, yellow on the other, Nike Swoosh on both, bearing the instruction: 'You decide! Take part in the game! You decide if the incident deserves a sending-off and if so . . . SHOW THE CARD! Show the red card and express your point of view! You decide! [in English] JUST DO IT!' During the game (football was also played) each goal was announced over the Tannoy in the same fashion: 'Nike announces a goal for . . . another great play in the Nike Cup.' Nike also announced sundry lost children and forthcoming fixtures. The sheer intensity of the commercial assault on the senses completely dwarfed anything Corona and their dancing beer bottles could manage. The game was actually quite good, with Boca coming back to win 3–2, but it was difficult not to see the match as some sort of votive offering to the greater glory of the goddess Nike Inc.

Héctor Huerta, one of Mexico's leading sports journalists, was at the game doing radio commentary. He was horrified by the spectacle of rampant commercialization.

'What you saw on Saturday was excessive, amazing. Guadalajara has to get the role of the sponsor in proportion. OK, you're Nike, a global company, but we're Chivas. And this stadium is Chivas. The fans are receiving a series of unconscious messages. That they're not supporting Chivas but Nike. In the World Cup there's a list of sponsors who put their advertising around the ground, and that's it. Nothing compared to this excess. Not even Coca-Cola does this in the Youth World Cup, which is owned by Coca-Cola. It's the same sort of manipulation that the Nazis did and the fascists in the time of Mussolini. Probably at the 1934 World Cup you would have seen Mussolini's image everywhere, or in Germany you would have had a stadium invaded by swastikas. The other day we saw a stadium invaded by Nike.'

Unfortunately, Huerta was unable to share his thoughts with his listeners. 'Nike bought up everything. The radio station it wanted, the TV it wanted, the sound, the space. We were all Nike, willy-nilly. We had to read all the texts that Nike prepared. Total manipulation. I was amazed, because in twenty-two years in radio and newspapers I've never seen anything like it. It's a collective brain-washing. It's commercial fascism.'

The irony is that selling replica shirts – the cash cow for the top English clubs – is the one aspect of the business where Nike appear to be falling down. There is no club shop, and at the many stalls outside the ground you can pick up a pirated first-team shirt for less than a quarter of the price of the official product sold in the shopping malls. A curiously Mexican combination of North American glitz and Central American ersatz.

But Nike's dominion, of course, extends far beyond Mexico. The sports kit manufacturer put on an equally elaborate show for a match in Tokyo between Japan and Brazil about the same time.[3] Nike were evidently keen to get their money's worth, having paid Brazil $200 million[4] to wear their kit for three years. It has recruited top teams to be its mannequins in countries (or 'major markets') all over the world. Likewise, its competitor, Reebok, has wooed the Argentinian national team away from Adidas for a bargain basement $64 million (plus another $20 million in royalties) for the eight years from 1999. Boca alone cost Nike $20 million to parade the mighty Swoosh for four years.

Boca Juniors had bigger fish to fry in Mexico apart from being cheerleaders for Nike. After a lamentable season, they were in the market for a new striker and had their eye on Necaxa's Luis Hernán-dez. Mexico is more used to importing lesser footballing talents from Argentina than exporting its own stars there, but Luis Hernández had made a name for himself just weeks before by becoming the top scorer in the Copa América in Bolivia. The press had dubbed the blond-haired forward 'the mariachi Caniggia'. Boca got their man, but the chairman of Necaxa, Enrique Borja, had little say in the matter.

Boca's spokesman, Mario Lauria, explained: 'Rather than talk with Mr Borja, I believe that contacts have already taken place with the people from Televisa, which runs Necaxa, doesn't it? And it's not a question of ignoring Mr Borja as chairman, but because the boss of Luis Hernández is Televisa.'[5]

It's true. Televisa is the boss of Luis Hernández (or was, before his sale to Boca). It is the boss of Necaxa. And América. And Atlante. And it is the boss of Mexican football. It has become a commonplace recently to decry the influence of television on football, but Televisa, the biggest television company in the Spanish-speaking world, has raised the whole practice to another plane. Not content with owning the broadcasting rights, with all the influence that goes with that, it also owns clubs themselves and, through them, controls the football federation. It was not so much Mexico as Televisa which won the honour of being the first country to host the World Cup twice – a remarkable feat given Mexico's modest footballing accomplishment. Even the stadium where Pelé and Maradona celebrated their greatest triumphs is wholly owned by Televisa. And unlike Johnny-come-latelys like Rupert Murdoch's Sky TV, Televisa has been doing it for years. José Ramón Fernández, one of Mexico's top sports journalists, puts it succinctly: 'To talk of Mexican football and Televisa is the same thing.'[6]

Televisa is one of the biggest media companies in the world. The value of shares in the $1.5 billion consortium affects the whole of the Mexican stock exchange. It owns 300 television stations across the country and in Latin America, the US-based Spanish-language Univisión network, 17 radio stations, various magazines, a newspaper, three record companies, as well as being the world's biggest Spanish-language publisher. And it has not stopped growing. Televisa supplies soap operas to the whole of Latin America, including to Brazil, home of the continent's other media giant Globo. It runs a stable of performers like the old Hollywood star system. Televisa's rise and rise was presided over by two generations of one of the great dynasties of Mexican business, Emilio Azcárraga Vidaurreta, and his son, Emilio Azcárraga Milmo, who took over the reins in 1972.

Televisa (then known as Telesistema Mexicana, S.A.) bought its first club, América, in 1961. In fact, América came as part-payment of a debt owed by a soft drinks manufacturer, but the company was well aware of football's potential from the start. In the subsequent years the company would build its huge TV empire on the basis of football, variety shows and soap operas. Televisa has no Reithian mission to inform: Emilio Azcárraga Milmo responded to critics of his company's determinedly populist, lowbrow approach by insisting that 'The only thing I have sought is to entertain.' The glamorous Mexico of Televisa's soaps is far removed from the reality of most Mexican viewers, and judging by the number of blonde women presenting shows one could easily conclude that it was the Swedes, not the Spanish, who colonized Mexico.

The top team of the 1960s was Chivas, but Televisa's commentators were under instructions to forever sing América's praises. Televisa's money and its relentless, partisan coverage elevated América to the status of the Guadalajara team's main rival. Unlike Chivas' *Campeonísimo* team of the 1960s,* which used only Mexican players (a tradition still maintained), América was at the forefront of splashing money about abroad to bring in foreign talent. After América won the title for the first time in 1965–6, the rivalry between the two clubs intensified.

Televisa could, of course, have contented itself with buying up television rights for football (which it also did, for a pittance), but it had bigger ambitions. Buying a team gave it a seat in the councils of the Mexican Football Federation and consequently direct influence over the game. In the 1980s Televisa acquired another club, Necaxa, and in 1996 a third, Atlante. All three play in Mexico City in the Estadio Azteca (prop. Televisa S.A.). In England it is not permitted for one person or company to own more than one football team because of the obvious potential for a conflict of interest. In Mexico it arouses little comment. Before the 1997 Winter championship Televisa's three teams swapped several players among themselves, the effect of which was to strengthen the América squad at the expense of the other two. Nobody doubted that the idea was to restore América to what it felt was its natural pre-eminence. Necaxa, in any case, had been

* Chivas won seven years out of nine between 1957 and 1965.

doing far better than a team of its modest support had any right to expect.*

Although Televisa is a private company, its virtual monopoly has strong parallels with the position of the PRI, Mexico's main political party. The Institutional Revolutionary Party, to give it its full name, has ruled Mexico for sixty-eight years since the end of the country's period of revolutionary upheaval in the 1920s, and has enjoyed the most spectacular run of electoral good fortune ever since. The phrase elective dictatorship has been used about Mexico's party-state/state-party but it's not strictly accurate as, even if the people didn't vote for them, the PRI had a knack of winning anyway. For six decades or more opposition parties adorned the Mexican political scene but never showed any sign of upsetting the PRI's all-encompassing presence, which extended down to the village level where local *caciques* (chiefs) made sure of the votes and doled out the favours.

Televisa and the PRI have enjoyed a symbiotic relationship based on a common interest in stability (i.e., each maintaining their monopolistic position). The PRI concentrated on providing the bread, while Televisa delivered the circuses.

As late as 1993, Emilio Azcárraga stated, 'I am a soldier of the PRI.' When President Salinas asked Mexican businessmen to cough up $25 million apiece for the party, Azcárraga offered $70 million, noting that his company had done very well under the PRI.

According to José Ramón Fernández, 'Televisa has always been linked to the country's political system, it has grown within the political system on the basis of negotiations with and favours for the political system.'

When France hosts the World Cup in 1998 it will be only the second European country to do so twice. Italy, site of the World Cup in 1990, had already hosted the second-ever competition in 1934. France's previous experience was also pre-war, in 1938. But Mexico leaves both of these two trailing in its wake, having hosted

---

* Necaxa were champions in 1995. In 1997 they lost Zárate and Peláez to América, who also gained Zague from Atlante.

football's top competition twice in sixteen years. The man that brought the World Cup to Mexico was Guillermo Cañedo. Cañedo was chairman of Zacatepec, who won the league in 1958, when he was spotted by Emilio Azcárraga, who installed him to run Mexican football for Televisa. A shrewd negotiator, he represented Televisa's club, América, in the Mexican Football Federation, which he headed and which he represented in the councils of Fifa. When Guillermo Cañedo died in 1996 Televisa renamed the Estadio Azteca in his honour.

'He was very affable, very intelligent,' recalls José Ramón Fernández. 'A skilful politician, a very good negotiator. He always said that he worked for Emilio Azcárraga, that he was an employee of Emilio Azcárraga. He was Televisa's spearhead into Mexican football and particularly into Fifa, where he rose to the rank of vice-president. He didn't work for the benefit of Mexican football but for the benefit of the television company he worked for.' Rows about the distribution of World Cup profits among the clubs rumbled on long after the competing teams had gone home.*

In 1970 it was Latin America's 'turn' to host the World Cup, and the favourites were Argentina. Uruguay and Brazil, the continent's other two top football countries, had both been awarded the competition, as had the lesser footballing power of Chile, in 1962. Nevertheless, Cañedo's assiduous lobbying, and the promise of the technical expertise of Televisa,† for what was to be the first World Cup of the satellite TV era, swung the vote in Mexico's favour at a Fifa congress in Tokyo in 1964. The Argentinians were livid. Cañedo was president of the World Cup organizing committee.

Mexico '70 is remembered as possibly the best World Cup ever because of the quality of its football (and because TV was there to show it to the world), but at the time Fifa had misgivings about

---

* The organizing league usually receives 35 per cent of the overall World Cup profits. The 1970 tournament earned about $6 million in total.
† Eight years later Argentina still only had a black-and-white television system and had to install colour TV especially for its World Cup.

Televisa's approach to the project. 'I think the commercialism here is extreme,' said Fifa's then secretary-general, Helmut Kasser. 'It is specifically American and Mexican.' He said Fifa was surprised by the Mexican TV coverage. 'We were not expecting advertisements in the middle of matches,' he said, 'but apparently here it is customary even in club games. The sponsors buy the whole match and insert their adverts.' Televisa paid $1.8 million to televise the tournament and made a handsome profit. Foreign broadcasters bought rights from Televisa by paying into dollar bank accounts in the United States.

While he was lobbying for the 1970 World Cup, Cañedo struck up a good relationship with the Brazilian delegate to Fifa, João Havelange. When Havelange challenged the English incumbent, Sir Stanley Rous, for the presidency of Fifa in 1974, Cañedo started out supporting Rous but was persuaded by Havelange that he should support a fellow Latin American for the job. Havelange's victory was also good news for Cañedo and, of course, Televisa. Cañedo became a vice-president of the world football body and was involved with Havelange in setting up a company, ISL,* to market the World Cup. Cañedo himself was not a wealthy man but could count on the backing of Azcárraga's millions. In 1986 it was revealed that Televisa had done a deal to sell television programmes in Brazil with a company headed by Havelange.[7] Azcárraga also helped Havelange acquire the Record TV network in Brazil. Havelange was a man Televisa could do business with. Under his presidency, Fifa's finances were transformed as Havelange embraced the world of marketing and sponsorship – precisely the areas that Fifa had decried in the 1970 tournament. Fifa created two world youth tournaments (Under-17 and Under-20) and sold them to JVC and Coca-Cola. The number of Fifa members increased and the World Cup was expanded to allow more teams from outside Europe to reach the finals.

Mexico's second World Cup came about in unexpected circumstances. As the Italian team celebrated their victory in Madrid in

* The key figure behind ISL was Horst Dassler, the founder of Adidas.

1982, the stadium scoreboard announced that the greatest show on earth would be reconvening in Colombia four years later. It never happened.

The memory of the tournament in Spain was barely beginning to fade before the Colombian government reconsidered. The country, home to the longest-standing guerrilla insurgency in the Americas, was facing economic difficulties and, in the period since they had originally been named as hosts, the tournament had been increased in size from sixteen to twenty-four teams. The greater scale of the tournament implied investment in stadiums, training grounds, hotels, etc. The country, the government decided, could not afford it.

Colombia's misfortune was Mexico's opportunity. But it faced strong competition, particularly from the United States. Fifa had long wanted to expand into the rich, virgin territory of North America, and the US bid was fronted by the world's best player, Pelé, and no less an international dealmaker than Henry Kissinger. But Mexico had Guillermo Cañedo and Televisa. It was no contest. At the Fifa congress in Stockholm in May 1983, the US bid was not even discussed.

After the 1982 World Cup Final Havelange had flown home to Brazil in Emilio Azcárraga's private plane.[8] Neither did Havelange forget his Mexican vice-president's loyal support at each of his four-yearly re-elections. So when Mexico was named as host for the second time in sixteen years, Cañedo was again named president of the organizing committee – even though he was no longer president of the FMF, and the job normally goes to the head of the local football authorities.

But Televisa's coup was almost ruined at the last moment. On 19 September 1985, just months before the tournament was due to start, a devastating earthquake measuring 8.1 on the Richter scale struck Mexico City, killing an estimated 12,000 people. It was the worst catastrophe in the country's history. For a while it seemed that the tournament might have to be a transferred to a third country. Despite the widespread destruction in Mexico City, the infrastructure for the tournament emerged relatively unscathed. Only the stadium at Nezahualcóyotl was slightly damaged. As bodies were still being pulled out of the rubble, a relieved Havelange sent a not entirely tasteful telegram from Zurich saying, 'The earthquake respected football.'[9] Quickly Televisa dedicated itself to making sure that not too many images of damaged buildings and people crawling out of the rubble got out. The television pictures concentrated on showing a country getting back to normality. The government chipped in with a slogan: 'Mexico is on its feet.' Mystery still surrounds how many people really died in the earthquake.

After the 1986 World Cup, Televisa was riding high on the success of its football interests, unaware that it was heading for a fall. For years, international age-group competitions had witnessed widespread abuses, with over-age players turning out in youth and Under-23 tournaments with the connivance of their countries' football authorities. At the World Under-17 Youth Cup in Scotland in 1989, the full beards and manly build of the victorious Saudi teenagers drew widespread comment. African countries, where record-keeping is not always up to international standards, are believed to have specialized in this sort of deception, although many countries worldwide have come under suspicion. It fell to Mexico to be caught out.

Following an Under-19 match in Honduras in 1988, the Guatemalan football authorities formally accused Mexico of having fielded over-age players. Three players, José de la Fuente, Aurelio Rivera and Gerardo Jiménez, were named. In what became known as the *cachirules* case (after a Mexican word for cheating), the FMF denied the charges in the strongest terms, but subsequent journalistic investigations revealed that the Mexican football authorities and government had connived in falsifying players' identification documents,* and that the case might involve up to sixteen players. Finding the truth was

---

* Strong rumours to the same effect had circulated about the Mexican team at the World Under-20 Youth Cup, held in Mexico in 1983. In 1990 two more *cachirules* were detected in a Mexican national youth XI (see Gómez Anguas, Jorge, *A History of Football in Mexico* (1995), page 64.

made that much easier by the fact that the FMF had published a year-book which contained details of many of the youth-team players, including their real ages. Concacaf, the regional football authority, suspended Mexico from its competitions for two years.

The Mexicans were confident (with a confidence verging on arrogance) that they would get a better hearing at Fifa, the world governing body. But when it came to the vote, even the South Americans deserted them. Mexico's ban was extended worldwide, ruling them out of the 1990 World Cup.* One of the South American delegates accused the Mexican delegation of representing Televisa's interests rather than Mexico's.

Concacaf suspended the entire FMF national council for its role in the *cachirules* case and in the aftermath Televisa lost control of the ruling body. What followed was the biggest challenge ever to Televisa's hegemony over Mexican football – and the clearest possible warning to anyone with a notion to try doing so again.

In 1989 the FMF appointed a commission to look into the televising of football. Its main recommendation was that instead of each club selling rights to its own games, the FMF should negotiate a package for the whole league and divide up the proceeds among the clubs. Under the proposed deal, Channel 13 (later TV Azteca) would broadcast ten clubs and Televisa eight. But the key factor was that for the first time the television companies would be obliged to pay a market rate for rights that up to then had been almost given away. Televisa was outraged that its traditional *modus operandi* was being interfered with and pulled out of negotiations. The rights to screen the national team's games were awarded to a cable company, Imevisión. This was a red rag to Televisa, which already had its eyes on the qualifying competition for the 1994 World Cup, the screening

---

* The conspiracy theory of Mexico's exclusion is that Fifa wanted the United States to qualify for Italia '90 to give a boost to the Americans ahead of the tournament to be played on their own soil in 1994. The US team edged out Trinidad with a late goal in Port of Spain to qualify, but returned home from Italy having lost every game.

of which it considered its birthright. Televisa tried to get its man elected to the FMF presidency but was outmanoeuvred, despite having done a deal with state governors to pressure the clubs in their state to vote the right way. Francisco Ibarra of Atlas was the new president. He proceeded to forge an alliance with Emilio Maurer, the main shareholder of Puebla and the man behind the new TV deal.

Maurer, an abrasive, self-made millionaire, was elected president of the first division and of the international committee. By effectively taking on the might of Emilio Azcárraga, he would become the subject of a concerted campaign of denigration, which ultimately led to his ruin. Deprived of the rights to televise the national team, Televisa seized gleefully on its failures. Instead of football it screened wrestling, which led to a brief boom in the credulity-stretching pastime. The appointment of Argentina's World Cup winning manager, César Luis Menotti, to lead the national team failed to turn its fortunes around and Menotti and Maurer came under intense pressure. Then Maurer's club, Puebla, reached the league play-off final, drawing the first leg 0–0 at home against León. After the game the local authorities closed Puebla's Cuauhtémoc stadium over an alleged ticket scam, or possibly because of unpaid rent – the reason was never entirely clear. Puebla, the league runners-up after losing the second leg, were thus forced into a gypsy lifestyle, playing their home games wherever they could persuade other stadiums to take them. Inexplicably, many clubs closed their doors on Maurer's team. The peripatetic existence took a toll on the club finances and the club's sponsor, Volkswagen, pulled out. Pressure grew on Maurer to sell up. A shareholders' assembly decided the club should be sold. Maurer resisted, believing that Televisa was behind the buyout, but in the end he gave in, selling his stake for $10 million.

Maurer sold up on a Saturday. On the Monday the process to elect his successor to the FMF board was already in place on the grounds that he no longer represented a club.* Maurer accepted the

* Nevertheless, Enrique Borja had not been linked to a club when he challenged Francisco Ibarra for the presidency.

inevitable and stood down. But it didn't stop there. The new owners of Puebla accused Maurer of fraud in relation to the club's accounts. In November 1993 Emilio Maurer was jailed, albeit for just twenty-four hours, over the alleged financial irregularities. His lawyers agreed to repay $2 million to the club in exchange for the charges being dropped. Maurer was later banned from any role in football for life.

The process that had begun with Televisa losing its rights to broadcast the national team ended with their main antagonist, Emilio Maurer, displayed to the press and TV cameras behind bars. The first thing the new chiefs of Mexican football did was to break the contracts with Channel 13 and Imevisión and welcome Televisa back. Televisa reckoned that the eighteen months or so in which football had slipped from their grasp had cost them some $40 million.

These days Maurer has withdrawn with his millions to run his dairy farm and other businesses. Many feel that he was careless rather than culpable in his financial dealings, but no one seems to dispute that Televisa's knives were out for him. He certainly has no doubt what the end of his rollercoaster years at the forefront of Mexican football was all about. 'With me they wanted to make clear that anyone who opposed Televisa was going to have a bad time,' he told *Proceso* magazine. 'They didn't rest until they saw me behind bars, although it was just for a day. They wanted to demonstrate to all the other clubs that that was how they were going to be made to pay for any act of rebellion.'[10] It was a ritual sacrifice in the best Aztec tradition.

Although Televisa regained control of football, these days it faces a threat to its hegemony in the shape of TV Azteca. Formed in 1993 by the privatization of state channels, TV Azteca sees football as a crucial battlefield in its fight for the £1 billion a year television advertising market. The new company has bought up two clubs, Veracruz and Morelia, to get a seat at football's top table, even though José Ramón Fernández, now a vice-president of TV Azteca, once vowed he would give up journalism if his company owned more than one.

Each company has roughly half the teams in the league under

exclusive broadcasting contracts, although before the start of the 1997 Clausura tournament, Televisa staged a coup by stealing away the National Autonomous University of Mexico team, Pumas, for a record $3.5 million a year (Chivas were on $2 million a year). Fernández and Pumas conducted a bitter discussion of the issue in the public prints.

They say it is better to travel hopefully than to arrive. Mexicans seem to have taken this to an extreme – you can drive for hours in Mexico City without actually getting anywhere. When Cortés's men first laid eyes on the Aztec capital, Tenochtitlan, built upon a lake in the Valley of Mexico, they called it a second Venice, greater than the original. Now pleasure boats circle around the tiny vestige of the lake that remains at Xochimilco. Its waters, like the rest of the valley of Mexico, have disappeared beneath concrete and asphalt, for months of the year capped by a yellowy-brown layer of smog. Few cities can have given themselves over so completely to the interests of the motor car. Where once stood the most beautiful city on earth, they have created a car park and called it progress. But somewhere amidst the maze of busy dual carriageways in the south of the vast city, the road sweeps in a broad curve to accommodate the magnificent Estadio Azteca, undoubtedly the greatest legacy of Televisa's determination to bring Mexico its two World Cups. The road signs, I noticed, hadn't been changed to reflect its new name, the Estadio Guillermo Cañedo. It seemed perverse to change a name that was famous around the world, and for Mexicans to suddenly have to get used to seeing events advertised at a venue named after a sporting bureaucrat, however illustrious. But then, since the emergence of Televisa's bitter television rival, the name 'Azteca' had acquired different associations.

Built in 1966 and designed by Pedro Ramírez Vázquez, the Mexican architect responsible for the capital's celebrated Museum of Anthropology, it is built on four independent blocks in order to resist earthquakes. Plaques outside commemorate the 1970 semi-final between Italy and West Germany (which ended 4–3), Maradona's goal against the English in 1986 (the second one, presumably) and Manuel Negrete's goal against Bulgaria in the same tournament, a strike sadly little remembered outside his native Mexico. Another records the stadium's opening by President Gustavo Díaz Ordaz, a man so important that he got to have his name alongside that of Emilio Azcárraga.

Televisa press and public relations men give guided tours of the stadium. The slightly perfunctory ramble revealed that the car park holds over 11,000 vehicles but that the wealthy can drive their cars – or rather, have their cars driven – right up to the door of their executive boxes, bought for up to $300,000 on 99-year leases. Our little party was shown inside the comfortable, gentleman's club-style surroundings of the *palco de honor* (the dignitaries' suite) where another plaque honours the man without whom none of this might have happened, Guillermo Cañedo. A doorway from the wood-panelled bar area leads to the three rows of blue-cushioned seats which offer a perfect view of the action on the pitch. In fact, the really impressive thing about the Aztec stadium is that everywhere in the stadium gives the sense of being very close to the pitch. The guide thought for a moment and then indicated for me the end at which Carlos Alberto had got Brazil's fourth in 1970. Silly, I admit, but I just had to know.

I asked the guide what he felt about the stadium's name having been changed to 'Guillermo Cañedo'. Somehow, I suggested, it didn't have quite the same ring about it. He nodded, yes, the Estadio Azteca was known around the world. In fact, an announcement was due to be made any day that they were changing the name back.*

Guillermo Cañedo's death in January 1997 after a long illness was followed three months later by that of the big man himself, Emilio Azcárraga Milmo, who succumbed to cancer at the age of 66. His nominated successor was Guillermo Cañedo White, the elder Cañedo's son, but in a dynastic power struggle worthy of the Medicis he was edged out of the company by Azcárraga's nephew, Alejandro

* After its brief name-change, the stadium is once again the Azteca.

230

Burillo Azcárraga, who allied himself with Azcárraga's 29-year-old son, also called Emilio. Burillo emerged victorious in July 1997 and Cañedo White and his brother left Televisa to pursue other interests. It was at this time that the desirability of Televisa's flagship stadium bearing the Cañedo name came in for reconsideration, barely six months after it was renamed.

On a bright, spring morning in 1997, in the middle of a London square, a stone's throw from Victoria Station, Mexico's national football team practised unnoticed by passersby. Their most recognizable players, to British eyes, were absent. Jorge Campos, the goalkeeper-cum-striker renowned as much for his garish self-designed shirts as for his on-the-pitch achievements, and Luis García, the man who put two goals past the Republic of Ireland in Orlando, were both injured. But even they are hardly household names (although García did have the distinction of having his achievements celebrated in graffiti in loyalist areas of Belfast). John Motson, receiving a pre-match briefing on players' names from a Mexican journalist, could be forgiven for not instantly recognizing the handful of veterans of the World Cup three years earlier. The fact is, Mexico has only ever produced one truly world-class player,* Hugo Sánchez, and he, at the time, was preparing for his farewell match to be played not in Mexico but at the scene of his greatest triumphs, Real Madrid's Bernabeu stadium. Better known than his players is Velibor 'Bora' Milutinovic, the Yugoslav coach who has led three separate countries – Mexico, Costa Rica and the United States – to the World Cup finals. He comes from a family of footballing brothers, coincidentally from the same town as the coach of El Salvador, who found themselves up against Mexico in the final World Cup qualification group. Bora was tired and looked it, having not slept on the flight from Mexico, and had no prospect of an early night as he would be celebrating his wife's birthday in a West End restaurant. Unusually,

* Antonio Carbajal might beg to differ. The goalkeeper played in five consecutive World Cups from 1950 to 1966.

the game against England at Wembley was a one-off. Teams generally try to make these intercontinental trips worthwhile by playing at least two or three friendlies, but the Mexicans were to head straight back home after the game. The Mexican press wondered if the long trip across the Atlantic to face England was the best possible preparation for a World Cup qualifier two weeks later against Jamaica. The players made the right noises about welcoming a chance to play against such a good side as England, and the captain, Adolfo García Aspe, stressed the honour it would be to play in the last match at Wembley before the legendary stadium was demolished. Something appeared to have got lost in the translation, because although Wembley was due to be redeveloped, no date had been set for building work to start. In the remainder of 1997 alone, Wembley hosted two England World Cup qualifiers, the FA Cup Final, the Charity Shield, the League Cup Final, and the divisional play-offs, not to mention the likes of Rod Stewart and Jon Bon Jovi. But it was a misapprehension which everybody in the Mexican camp, right down to the travelling journalists, seemed to share. Surely the FA hadn't given the Mexicans a misleading impression of the game's 'historic' character?

On the coach back to the hotel Bora mused about the possibility of working in England, expressing his admiration for Arsenal's Arsène Wenger. He stressed that his relations with the Mexican federation were very good and that he had no problems in getting clubs to release players for internationals. It was curious then that for their earlier World Cup qualifier away to Jamaica, Mexico fielded a palpably understrength side. Although the Mexican media decried the 1–0 defeat, Mexico had already qualified for the final stage group and the result had the happy effect of knocking out Honduras, widely felt to be a more dangerous side than Jamaica, who thus took their place. In the light of these knock-on effects, I asked Bora if losing that match had been an inspired tactical move. After a pause, he replied, laconically: 'You know too much.' At the sparsely attended press conference back at the team's Kensington hotel, the manager's aside about Wembley's last match was met with baffled silence.

232

Raúl Borja, the president of the Mexican Football Federation's first division, who was travelling with the squad, shrugged off suggestions that it was long way to come for a game of football. 'No, it's very useful,' said Borja, who is also chairman of Pumas. 'And the contract they've given us is very good.' Two days later, Mexico's play, for most of the game, certainly had an air of contractual obligation about it. It was only after England had gone ahead with a rather iffy penalty and followed up with Robbie Fowler's first international goal that the Mexicans started to look dangerous, by which time it was too late. But money wasn't the only thing on Borja's mind as he watched the team train in St Vincent's Square. Reflecting on the significance of the match, he observed: 'Also, it's one of the last games at Wembley, isn't it?'

The prospect of rebuilding the old stadium had Borja reflecting on the recent disaster in neighbouring Guatemala, where 78 people were crushed to death in the overcrowded Mateo Flores stadium before a World Cup qualifier against Costa Rica.*

Borja was forthright about the responsibility of the football authorities to prevent a repeat of the tragedy: 'The obligation that we leaders of world football have is to look out for the safety of the spectator, so that we don't get things happening like what happened in Guatemala,' he said, solemnly. But it became clear that in practice he thought that responsibility was severely limited. 'We know that the spectator, having paid his money, wants to do what he likes. Sit down, stand up, chant, jump up and down. If he decides that's what he wants to do he can do it, but at his own risk. It's not the fault of football. If there's a disturbance, a crowd surge, ticket forgery, whose fault is that? Whose job is it to channel people so that they behave correctly? If there are counterfeit tickets, that's not my fault. If I decide to produce more tickets so there's overcrowding, the

* Fifa gave the families of the victims $6500 each. The Guatemala disaster was well short of the worst crowd fatality in Latin America. In 1964, 320 people were killed in crowd trouble after a match between Peru and Argentina in Lima.

people want to get in . . . there's no way out, so what do we do? Take down fences? You can't.'

In England, of course, that's exactly what happened after the Hillsborough disaster in 1989, when 96 people were crushed in scenes similar to those seen in the Mateo Flores. But fences are a fixture in Latin American stadiums and nobody is planning to get rid of them. Raúl Borja insisted that to do so would make policing costs prohibitive.

Borja said he didn't know if there had been overproduction of tickets at the Mateo Flores although he said that in Mexico the big, end-of-season play-off games are filled to overcapacity. 'But if you've got overcrowding, what are you going to do about it? If you've got guests at your house for dinner and a couple more turn up, you say, let's water it down a bit to make it go further. So you can take responsibility for the overcrowding. But when you don't know about it, you can't share the blame. But if I take responsibility for squeezing in another 10,000 in the gangways, on the stairs, I'll look after them, it's my responsibility. But if there's another 10,000, drinking, etc . . .' His voice trailed off. Borja knows whereof he speaks. In 1985 eleven people were crushed to death watching Pumas at an overcrowded league championship play-off at their Ciudad Universitario stadium.

Banning drinking at grounds is another English measure Mexico has no intention of following. Strolling beer sellers and back-of-stand bars are commonplace in Mexico and many other Latin American grounds. It's true that hooliganism has never taken on the same dimensions as in England and, perhaps more importantly, Catholic Latin America has always taken a tolerant line on the poor man's vice of boozing. Borja has a more practical reason. 'How are we going to say we're NOT going to sell beer? Most teams are sponsored by a beer company or a cigarette company. We're ruled by vice. If we don't get the money from there where are we going to get it from?'

The British were in at the birth of Mexican football at the start of the century. Expatriate mining engineers from the Compañía Real del Monte set up Pachuca Atheletic Club in 1900. They contested

234

the first championship two years later with other British-based clubs, such as Reforma, the Mexico Cricket Club and the British Club (the title was won by Orizaba, a team primarily of Scots). Football survived Mexico's decade of revolution and a truce in 1916 witnessed the formation of the Record Club, which would later become América. Most of the Brits went home during the First World War and Mexican football came under heavy Spanish influence. This increased in 1936 with the arrival of a Basque national team which had been touring Russia when the Spanish Civil War broke out. The team included several who had played in what many felt was the best team in the 1934 World Cup, in which Spain lost narrowly to the hosts, Italy. The rivalry between the Spanish-linked clubs España and Asturias – who drew their support from refugees and immigrants respectively – grew to such an intensity and led to such violence on the terraces that both clubs were wound up despite the fact that España had risen to be the country's dominant club. After the recognition of professionalism in the 1940s Mexican football developed a taste for Argentinian and Brazilian players which continues to this day. Mexico's league is one of the richest in Latin America, and consequently its clubs are full of foreigners,* with only Guadalajara still standing out for their policy of playing only Mexican nationals. Mexicans often describe their football as a mixture of Argentinian and Brazilian styles. If so, it's very much mid-table Argentinian and Brazilian fare: Mexico is not a destination for current internationals. Mexico has always suffered from a geographical problem, in that it is surrounded by weaker footballing countries in Central and North America and the Caribbean. That has made World Cup qualification relatively easy† but means that Mexico has rarely

* Teams from the capital are allowed four foreigners, those outside, five.

† Mexico has still managed to miss out on a number of occasions (see chapter 7). In 1934, a last-minute change of plan by the Italian organizers meant they were obliged to travel to Rome to play a final eliminator against the United States because Mussolini wanted to see Aldo 'Buff' Donelli, who was playing for the US team, in action. Mexico lost 4–2 and had to make the long journey back across the Atlantic without having played in the World Cup proper.

made an impression on tournaments played outside Mexico. In recent years it has benefited from being invited to take part in the South American Championship, the Copa América, where it reached the Final at the first attempt in 1993. Part of the reason for inviting Mexico, and the United States, was to increase TV revenue. The FMF is now planning a bid to stage the Copa América itself.

Mexico's league system has undergone numerous changes over the years. After the 1970 World Cup a play-off between the top eight teams was introduced to decide the title. A few years back the league season was split in two – Winter and Summer. Mexico also uses a bizarre system of dividing the first division into four groups (two of four and two of five). The top two teams in each group qualify for the play-offs, unless, that is, the second-placed team finishes below a third-placed team from another group. Even so, it is theoretically possible to have a team in 15th position qualifying for the play-offs. The league season becomes just a slightly wearisome prelude to the play-offs. Confused? Well, it gets worse. Relegation is not decided by anything so simple as finishing at the bottom of the league. Morelia, the jewel in TV Azteca's crown, got off to a good start in the 1997 Winter tournament and were expected to be among the title challengers. But because relegation is decided on the basis of average points per game over the previous three years (a criterion by which Morelia is struggling), they faced the real possibility of winning the league and getting relegated in the same season.

Another curious aspect of the league's organization is that referees are paid in cash straight from the box office by the home club. Some referees have reported being paid too much (in error, of course) but it is not known how many keep quiet and pocket the extra. Presumably there's nothing to worry about because the referees are, in any case, under the close scrutiny of the Televisa-controlled referees' committee of the FMF. Nevertheless, there have been several cases of highly questionable refereeing performances.

'The most scandalous case was in 1984–5,' says sports journalist Héctor Huerta. 'América played the third game play-off for the title against Pumas at a neutral ground. América won 3–1. The referee

236

was called Joaquín Uvea and he let América off three blatant penalties and gifted them a penalty. It was never proved that he was bought off. But it's a fact that he never refereed again.'

Huerta also recalls another case from the 1980s where a referee, Jorge Humberto Rocard, accused colleagues of selling games for half a million pesos a time. 'He called for the authorities to investigate, but nothing happened. But then suddenly about five referees were retired.'

Eyebrows were also raised in 1993 when unfancied Monterrey won a play-off semi-final with the help of a very poor performance by a Costa Rican referee who had mysteriously been drafted in. It was suggested that someone wanted to do President Salinas, who comes from Monterrey, a favour. There is, of course, no evidence to support this.

Despite all this, Mexicans in general believe that their football is clean. It's surprising, because Mexico must be the conspiracy theory capital of the world – Dallas and Roswell have nothing on it. The generations of control by the PRI mean that people suspect they are never being told the whole story, and that the omnipresent PRI, true to its nature, is arranging everything behind the scenes. In 1994 the PRI's presidential candidate Luis Donaldo Colosio was gunned down at an election rally in Tijuana. The gunman, Mario Aburto, was arrested and convicted of the murder, but few people found the official 'lone assassin' version credible. Something was afoot and it probably involved the PRI. The explanations of the assassination of another prominent PRI politician that year and the earlier death of a cardinal in a hail of bullets at Guadalajara airport (official version: mistaken for rival drug baron) met similar public scepticism. The Zapatista rising in 1994 was similarly suspected of being a put-up job, and as for the reported death in 1997 of the drug-trafficking 'Lord of the Skies', Amado Carillo Fuentes, while undergoing plastic surgery – that was just too unbelievable. How come the news broke on the eve of the first ever election for mayor of Mexico City? people asked.

'It's like [Peruvian novelist Mario] Vargas Llosa said: it's the perfect dictatorship,' says Héctor Huerta. 'In Mexico people don't believe in absolute truth because they've always doubted the truth they've been told, the official truth.

'But Mexicans want to believe that football is clean. That it's one of the few spaces in national life that is clean. They are reluctant to believe that they are being tricked, knowing that they're being tricked. That's to say, they know it's a reality that in national life cases of corruption are denounced in all areas, so how could football be immune? But people don't believe it. Fans want to believe in the result because it's one of the few things in which you can believe in this country.'

In the 1997 Summer championship play-off, Chivas surprisingly thrashed Toros Negra 6−1, having drawn the first leg 1−1. Huerta shrugs. 'How could Chivas beat Toros 6−1? But the joy of that 6−1 wipes out everything for the Chivas fans.'

8: Far Away, So Close

A SHORT, DARK-HAIRED player jinks past two defenders with a little shimmy then, taking on one too many, is upended, raising a cloud of dust as he hits the ground. Intemperate voices are raised in Spanish as the free-kick is awarded and the player dusts himself down to take it himself. At the pitchside, knots of onlookers gather near the food stalls, tucking in to fried chicken, meat-filled *empanadas* and hot, sweet coffee. Blaring horns announce another salsa track from a portable tape deck. It could be anywhere in Latin America, but in fact it's a scene that can be witnessed almost any Sunday of the year on Clapham Common in south London.

For over fifteen years, Clapham Common has been the home of London's Latin American Football League, where Chileans, Colombians, Peruvians, Bolivians, Ecuadoreans and players from the other South American countries have come to play football and be their Latin American selves. A few miles away, at Archbishop's Park in Lambeth, the scene is much the same, only here the flag strung across the chain-link fence is the yellow, blue and red of Colombia, and all the teams are Colombian.

This is the story of how London came to have two Latin American leagues when few other European cities have found a pressing case for even one.

The roots of the Clapham league go back to General Augusto Pinochet's military coup in Chile in 1973, which sent thousands of Chileans into exile. About 2000 heads of family were given political asylum by Britain's Labour government, many arriving via third countries, such as Argentina. Clearly football was not the first thing on the minds of people who had in many cases fled imprisonment and torture and were now trying to rebuild their lives in a distant country. But it wasn't that far behind. Before long, groups of Chileans were getting together to play in the towns where they had found refuge.

In Glasgow in the late 1970s a group of Chilean refugees, getting wind that a club was about to fold, took its place in the local YMCA league and competed as Burnbank FC. With pardonable nostalgia, René Meza, who played in goal for them, describes Burnbank as 'one of the best teams that the Latin Americans [in Britain] have been able to form'. Some of the players were former pros or semi-pros and had played together in exile in Argentina. 'We were quite lucky in that most of the best Chilean players ended up in Glasgow.'

It was the first all-Latin American side to play in a British league and Waldo Alvarez, another member of that team, remembers that the Chileans initially found the physical demands of the league hard to cope with. 'You had to run for ninety minutes. In Chile, it's not that all-out, physical effort.' But more than that they found that week in week out, on trips to the likes of Easterhouse and Drumchapel, their opponents were invariably fired up by the idea of putting one over on the South Americans. 'Every single Sunday was like an international for those teams,' René Meza recalls. 'They might have lost every game all season but their main thing was to beat the Chilean team.'

The matches were tough and frequently violent, as two footballing cultures clashed. Meza thinks that maybe the Scots seemed particularly aggressive to the Chileans, when in reality they were just playing their normal game. Alvarez's recollection, though, is clear. 'For the first two years, we were really kicked off the park.' Meza, on reflection, agrees. 'There was fighting almost every single bloody game. They were not used to our style of football and, whenever we had the chance – I don't know if it was done intentionally – we humiliated them: put the ball through their legs, rather than go forward to score, come back and do it again. We were not flavour of the month, or of the year, in our first year.'

The Chileans toughened up, learnt to give as good as they got, and eventually earned the respect of their Scottish opponents, who had generally viewed them as prima donnas. 'Fortunately we already had the skill,' says Meza. 'The only thing we needed was to develop the strength and the will to win of the Scottish players.' With the later addition of a handful of Scots, Burnbank played on in the league for several successful years.

As the only all-foreign team in Scottish football (apart from Berwick Rangers, perhaps), Burnbank received a good deal of media attention. Every year, the Lord Mayor of Glasgow would invite them to his office for an official send-off to a national Latin American championship, which had by then been set up in Yorkshire.

The galvanizing force behind this, and what was to become the Clapham Common league, was Gastón Avalos, an exiled Chilean communist. The labour movement had played an important role in solidarity with Chile's leftwing government and, after the coup, many Chilean refugees had settled in areas with a strong trade-union tradition. Hence Selby, in the heart of the Yorkshire coalfield, was chosen in 1979 as the venue for a mini-championship, with teams from Rotherham, Leeds, Hull, Sheffield and Swansea. Most were a mixture of Chileans and sympathetic locals. What Avalos has meticulously recorded (in one of his many photocopied bulletins) as the first national tournament proper took place two years later in Leeds and Rotherham, and this time included teams from London, Bristol and Burnbank. In 1986 the championship moved to London.

The national championship gave the Latin American community (still heavily Chilean-dominated) a taste of what it would be like to be able to play their own football with their own people. In 1980 Avalos had moved to London and wasted no time organizing a Latin American league in the capital. The league was officially founded on 6 December 1980 with eight teams, six Chilean, one mixed Chilean–Uruguayan and one Colombian. Colo-Colo, Avalos's club, fielded two teams. The league's matches were played on the all-weather pitches in Brockwell Park, near Brixton, and in June 1981 the first trophy, named for Chile's martyred president, Salvador Allende, was presented to the winning team, Colombia FC.

José Berríos, a member of the winning team, remembers: 'The trophy was donated by the Scottish miners. It was made of pure silver. At that time I was injured, so I went in goal. I let in the fewest goals in the competition, but not because I was the best but because the team was good.'

The rivalry between the Colombians and the Chileans, which was to have such a crucial effect on the development of Latin American football in London, was apparent even then, when the league moved to its permanent home on Clapham Common. According to Berríos, 'At Clapham they set up a tournament [in 1982–3] called the Camilo Torres Cup [after the radical Colombian guerrilla-priest]. It was a Cup provided by the Chileans with the intention of winning it, and then exchanging it for the Salvador Allende Cup . . . but we won that too. For many years we were the best team playing at Clapham Common.'

Colombia FC had formed in the late 1970s among young Colombians working as ancillary staff in the hospitals of Surrey. Low-paid cleaning and catering jobs were (and still are) the staple employment for many newly arrived Colombian immigrants. Twenty years ago there were relatively few Colombians in the country, but by the time the team folded in 1986 ('Many of them were illegals, I don't know what happened to them,' says Berríos) Colombians were well on their way to becoming Britain's largest non-Commonwealth immigrant group. The Colombian population in the UK is estimated by some at about 50,000,* but it's hard to be sure as many are in the country illegally. When the Latin American league first started, Colombians accounted for maybe 10 per cent of the players.

Initially ten teams turned out on three all-weather, cinder pitches at Clapham Common. Matches were played at 10, 12 and 2 o'clock. The league actually consisted of a number of separate Cups and championships contested during the course of the year, and from the start it set a pattern of playing all year round, with a short winter break for Christmas and New Year.

In the early days the league depended heavily on the commitment

* Some estimates go as high as 100,000.

in time and energy of Gastón Avalos. Pedro Montiel, who played for Colo-Colo at Clapham Common, remembers: 'Gastón ran the whole league, plus the team, plus this [national] Cup in May. It was a full-time job for the man and his whole life and energies were devoted to that. Well, it would be unfair to say that it was only Gastón; it was also his family and a whole range of people. And he used to run it in a very particular way – like in Chile, at the poor *barrios*, where the leagues are played in a very particular way around one *cacique*, who organizes everything: from who actually plays to who gets the prize, and who organizes the party and where the money goes. But nobody else would challenge that, because the actual task demanded so much time that nobody else was prepared to do it. So he would always say, "Anybody who wants to take over, fine; I'll go home and do something else." But nobody was prepared to do it. For years it was run in that fashion.'

At the outset the league consciously took on a social and political role in addition to its simple recreational function. Money raised from registrations and from the sale of refreshments went to good causes in Latin America, such as projects for human rights and political prisoners. Despite the preponderance of Chileans, support was also given to other leftwing struggles on the continent. Money was also raised for humanitarian emergencies, such as the Armenian earthquake and the families of the Hillsborough victims. The names of the trophies awarded in different tournaments catch something of the spirit of the organization: Primero de Mayo (1 May), Camilo Torres, Simón Bolívar (the liberator of much of South America from Spanish rule), Bernardo O'Higgins (liberator of Chile), Nelson Mandela, Gabriel García Márquez, Pablo Neruda, José de San Martín (liberator of Argentina), Solidaridad con Cuba . . . Solidarity with Chile was still a popular cause in Britain, but the league could boast that it regularly mobilized more people than turned up to most cultural events organized in support of the Chilean struggle. Friends and relatives would turn up to watch, and various Latin American groups would raise money or distribute propaganda. The number of teams from other South American countries steadily increased.

Pedro Montiel recalls the atmosphere of those days. 'There would be at least two or three people selling food as well the amber liquid, the stronger stuff and the wine. So you would have a whole evening out for the family, eating, drinking and heated tempers. There was bad refereeing, because the refereeing always used to be done by the community itself, so it was below standard and there were always problems. So the whole league had an atmosphere. And the other reason why it became quite successful is that there were links between the football on a Sunday and the families coming together, to share, to meet other families, to meet the community. But there was also a link in the human rights/political side of it. Most of the people were here because of the Chilean experience and the Chilean past. So most of them would be refugees or relatives of refugees. And they would have some sort of political link with Chile. This league played an important part in bringing people together. And from the proceeds of the Sunday league several groups benefited in terms of having money given to their particular projects.'

For many players, the match on Sunday was the highlight of the week. Feeling themselves on the periphery of society, lonely, perhaps, and in a crummy job, at Clapham they could be someone on the football field in a familiar Latin American environment. 'Sometimes British people feel lonely in London,' says René Meza. 'Imagine how it is for us.' Apart from the social aspect of being among their own people, many players preferred the Clapham Common league for football reasons. In English clubs they might find the very qualities which made them good players in Latin America seen as liabilities. Being greedy, trying to beat players rather than pass, letting emotions rise to the surface, coupled with not working hard and not running back to defend, could drive English team-mates to exasperation. But where was the glory in booting the ball up the pitch and chasing after it? If you couldn't scream and shout on a football field, where could you? And what was the point of playing if you couldn't show off your skills?

Colombia FC remained one of the stronger teams, but by the mid-1980s the league was dominated by Avalos's team, Colo-Colo, named after one of Chile's top professional sides. Pedro Montiel was, as Avalos puts it, 'the marshal of the defence'.

'I was introduced first to play for Colo-Colo, which was the strongest team. There used to be two or three teams that would win all the Cups, all the tournaments. I think Colo-Colo made the first move to becoming an all-around strong team. It may have been a mistake, it may not. We had a manager – you could say an owner – and he scouted for players. So it was one of the first teams that went out of its way not to put a team together for the day or the week but to put a team together for the season.'

The increased competitiveness of the league was one of the factors which caused violence to flare up on a regular basis. By the mid-1980s Clapham Common had acquired a reputation as a rough league. Fights were not uncommon. Avalos remembers the police being called on more than one occasion.

'There used to be racism in the league,' Avalos recalls. 'When Colo-Colo had three black lads, they'd say how come Colo-Colo's got black players? There are no blacks in Chile. They made fun of us. Afterwards, the black lads got fed up of this. Then all the other teams had black players. In Colombia, there are black people, in Peru there are black people. Colo-Colo was the first team to have black players. In consequence there was a period of violence, of aggression.'

One off-the-field incident illustrates the combustible nature of some of the Clapham Common encounters of that time. A Chilean team was playing a Colombian team when two robbers snatched a gold chain from the throat of one of the Colombians' watching girlfriends (had they never heard of Bobby Moore?). This was a red rag to any self-respecting Latin American macho, and suddenly the entire Colombian team, accompanied by various spectators and players from other games, gave chase. They managed to corner one of the robbers but he turned and pulled a knife. There was a second's pause and then, to the sound of flick-knives being opened, members of the Colombian team, who moments before had been playing football, produced their own blades from nowhere. Some were in the mood to castrate him on the spot but other, wiser heads prevailed and the police

245

were called. By the time they arrived, the thief was begging to be arrested. When the game resumed after this little drama, the Chilean opposition could be forgiven for pulling out of the odd tackle.

On top of this inter-nationality tension, politics and personal ambitions inevitably played a part. According to Avalos, things started to go wrong when the league won a grant from the local council. He believes at that point some people began to see the league as a potentially lucrative organization worth controlling. 'In 1985 we received the first grant from Lambeth. Once we got the grant, that's when everybody started showing their claws. That's where the discord began. After the grant the officials of the league started to get paid: the secretary, the co-ordinator, the president. The money went out and there were no accounts.'

According to René Meza, the bonanza didn't last long. 'These are rumours only – because the league has never kept proper records – but there were rumours when I took over that years before they were receiving £30,000 a year, plus equipment and all those sorts of things. When I took over as president in 1989 they didn't have anything. They didn't have a grant, nothing. We were meeting in a basement somewhere in Kennington.'

Tensions were growing between the Chileans and the Colombians. Nearly all the Chileans were political refugees. Very few among the other nationalities, notably the Colombians, had refugee status. Most, but not all, were economic migrants, seeking opportunities to make a better living for themselves and their families.

'There's a difference between political refugees and immigrants,' says Avalos. 'An immigrant comes here to make his fortune, to solve personal problems. We came here because we were condemned, and we dedicated ourselves to struggling for general solutions for other people. Not just for Chile but for other countries.'

José Berríos recognizes that there was a difference in outlook between the Chilean refugees and the Colombian migrants. 'The Chileans have a political tradition. Although the early Colombians who came may have been politically aware, they didn't come as refugees. Colombian asylum seekers started coming after 1985.' Even

246

so, most Colombians came to Britain primarily for economic, not political, reasons.

'All the Chileans here were political, and everything we did in the league was with a political orientation,' says Meza. 'Then other nationalities started coming – they were not political, they were here to earn a living – and it created a big conflict between politics and non-politics.'

Chileans were not above exploiting their privileged status as political refugees to their footballing advantage. At least on one occasion during a game the shout went up of '*la Migra*' (the immigration authorities), prompting an entire Colombian team, presumably of questionable migratory status, to abandon the pitch and flee, leaving their Chilean opponents to claim the points. It's a graphic example of how the difference in background, status and outlook between the Chileans and the Colombians spilled over on to the football field.

'In the mid-1980s there was always a fight every time a Chilean team played a Colombian team, on the pitch and off the pitch,' René Meza remembers. 'You were not going there to play football. On occasion you could see some people, rather than taking football boots they were taking knives, metal bars, and things like that. It became rough and it was about that time that I decided that I needed to find other things to do, another pastime.'

Jimmy López, later a founder of a breakaway Colombian league, confirms the atmosphere of mistrust and hostility. 'There were fights, problems, maladministration, each nationality went its own way. The different nationalities would get changed in different corners of the park, which before they didn't used to do. There were problems with administrators, because you get corrupt people, people with vested interests. There was a lot of bad feeling between Colombians and Chileans.'

Chile solidarity was one of the main internationalist causes of the British left in the 1970s and early 1980s, but as the Pinochet coup receded further, so other issues, notably support for the Sandinistas in Nicaragua, came to displace Chile from its central position. At Clapham Common too, Chileans' ascendancy was coming under threat. The Chilean population was on the decline. Many of the

247

original generation of players were getting to the age where they were hanging up their boots. The Chilean community was gradually contracting, first from the scattered regional centres towards London, and then, in many cases, back to Chile. In 1990 General Pinochet stood down as president (although he remained head of the armed forces) and was replaced by an elected civilian, Patricio Aylwin. Despite the limitations on democracy under the military-ordained transition, many refugees saw it as an opportunity to go back home. According to one estimate, the number of Chileans in London fell from a high point of around 12,000 to nearer 1000. At the same time, the Colombian population was rising sharply.

Sooner or later most of the new arrivals washed up at Clapham. It became well-known in many parts of Latin America that if you arrived alone in London, all you had to do was find your way to Clapham Common to meet people from your own country in the same boat. But as the Colombians' numbers swelled so did their frustration with the organization of the league. The politically experienced Chileans had set up the league and defined its character, but the Colombians, who made up an increasing proportion of its participants, felt that they were being marginalized.

In 1989 many of these tensions came to a head when the league split in two, with the rival organizations playing alongside each other on the same three gravel pitches at Clapham Common. 'The two leagues would play side by side,' said Berríos. 'No. 1 pitch was virtually all Chilean. Often I'd play in one league in the morning, or act as referee, and then pull on the Manuel Rodríguez shirt in the afternoon in the other league.' René Meza was president of the breakaway led by Gastón Avalos. 'After a season I decided it was ridiculous, playing side by side like that. Then we decided it was ridiculous to go on and we managed to sort out all the problems.'

So after a year of cheek-by-jowl estrangement, the league reunited, but the behind-the-scenes wrangles continued. Gastón Avalos continued his prodigious output of bulletins, with their mixture of statistical record and fiery polemic, which only increased in 1990, when a new leadership of the league was elected in what Avalos refers to as a 'coup'.

248

Amid all the in-fighting the latent breach between the Chileans and the Colombians – between a political and an apolitical approach – was widening. As Jimmy López remembers, 'There was a big activity by Chileans in this country to collect funds for those groups which were against the dictatorship in Chile. So through the football we were all involved. After a game of football, which has nothing to do with politics, we would go to the meeting of the league and find that instead of football we talked about nothing but politics. Politically, we had many differences with them. We didn't really agree. Most of the Colombians here are economic exiles.'

'The Colombians never felt it was their league,' says Meza. 'They felt it was a Chilean league. And they always felt they were being unfairly treated, that there was one rule for the Chileans and another rule for the Colombians. There was a succession of Chilean presidents of the league. And I think one day they got fed up of that and they started talking about setting up their own league.

'We started to hand out leaflets at the places our countrymen went, in the pubs, in the clubs,' says López. 'Finally we published a date when people should gather at a certain park – Deptford Park – and we were there for nearly three years. Later, we came here to Archbishop's Park, and we've been here for four years.'

'We started the Colombian league in 1990 or 1991,' says José Berríos. 'The community had grown, there were a lot of us. Sud-americano and Quintana Travel were the main teams behind it. Virtually every week it would be Quintana Travel versus Sudameri-cano, or it was a kickabout between all of us. That was in Brockwell Park initially and then in Deptford.

'The first winter was terrible. It was very cold. Not many people turned up. But it was good that the people who used to sell food came with us. It was an important factor. If they hadn't come with us it might well have failed. They provided the coffee, the *empanadas* and the *chorizos*. They were losing money because in the other place they sold more. Slowly more teams started forming and so we got to the summer of 1991. A lot of people started coming.'

London's Colombian league is now thriving, seven years on, in

Archbishop's Park next to Lambeth Palace, and just the other side of the Thames from the Houses of Parliament. All the teams are Colombian, although each is allowed to field a maximum of three non-Colombian players. At Clapham there is no such restriction and most teams, although associated with one nationality, include players from more than one. Nowadays Ecuador furnishes the largest number of teams (four). There is one Chilean team and two Colombian. The front page of the Latin American League's bulletin is ringed by the names of the countries of origin of its players which, in addition to half a dozen or so South American countries, include England, Scotland, Portugal, Egypt, Spain, Italy, Nigeria and 'Africa'. The tensions and heightened antagonisms of the 1980s seem to be largely a thing of the past, although the disciplinary report notes the case of one player banned for a year for assaulting a referee.

Gastón Avalos is no longer involved – Colo-Colo is disbanded – and he is evidently bitter about what happened. Talking of the two leagues, he refers disparagingly to 'the Clapham cartel' and 'the Lambeth cartel'. While for some the change in the league's character (its motto is still, it should be noted, 'Solidarity, Culture, Sport') is a source of regret, the struggles that went on there also reflect a wider issue about what should be the face of Latin America in London. The politicized image of the exiled Chileans, which stood for a continent in struggle, has now been replaced by the restaurants and the salsa clubs of the Colombians, which are the highest-profile representatives of Latin America in the capital. Unfortunately, Colombia is also associated in the popular imagination with cocaine, and some Chileans lament that a drug-trafficking image might unfairly attach itself to all Latin Americans in London, just as it has unfairly attached itself to Colombians.*

* Most Colombians, of course, have nothing to do with drugs. However, their hopes of escaping the national caricature of drug associations were not helped by the conviction of Leonel Sarmiento, a Colombian who played in the Clapham league, for possession of cocaine bought with £1000 innocently lent him by Newcastle United's Colombian star, Faustino Asprilla.

René Meza is one of them. 'I don't like the fact that Colombians grow cocaine, because the Colombians are so many, and on top of that Colombia's reputation is well known all over the world. So English people identify you as Latin American and think, Oh, you might be from Colombia. That is the only thing that pisses me off about Colombians. I'm from Latin America and immediately they [English people] think I'm a drug pusher or something.'

Jimmy López is also aware of an image problem. 'I'm from a small community that arrived here twenty-three years ago and I know many of these compatriots who have been here many years and are still playing here in the park. We didn't live through the scourge that Colombia has experienced in terms of violence and drugs – I never knew what cocaine was in those days. It's not that it didn't exist, but if you heard something about it, you didn't realize the power that drugs could have. Now, having lived here for so many years, we realize that our country's reputation is completely ruined around the world. There are some Colombians here who have got involved in problems, but they're a very small minority. These aren't Colombians who live by transporting drugs or live off the drug trade, rather one day they decide to get involved as a sort of adventure to get lucky and make some quick money. Most of them aren't very good at it and most of those that I know are in jail. Nowadays most of those who serve their sentence here are deported. Like I say, it's a small minority . . . we never see people around here selling drugs.' The league hopes that by showing off Colombian football, and through other activities such as salsa, they will present a different face of Colombia to the host country.

Unlike the old Clapham league, the Colombian league in Lambeth is strictly apolitical. Politically, the Colombian community, even the Colombian opposition, is fragmented, and displays of open political affiliation, it is felt, would only provoke counter-demonstrations and make the whole thing unworkable. 'In the Colombian league you'll even find rightwingers,' says Berríos. 'We respect each other. We get on OK. To me that seems fine, it's very democratic.' In the summer of 1996 teams contested a Cup named after Evert Marín, a

251

Colombian trade unionist who was kidnapped and murdered, almost certainly by an official death squad, while on a visit home from his exile in London. But Jimmy López is at pains to point out that the Cup's name is in no way political, rather it is a recognition of Marín's work setting up a union of cleaning workers in London, in organizing the community, and because he and his family played football. Another Cup is named after a travel agent's.

Human rights activists find they have their work cut out to interest the league's participants in the grim events which are all too common back in Colombia, where many more people have died in political violence than did so after Pinochet's coup in Chile. 'We've found it really difficult,' says Luis Serna, president of Colombian Committee for Human Rights. 'Many young people have been born here, others have been here for years, and they've lost the vision of the social problems of Colombia, so you find they look at the situation disparagingly. Still, we've tried to carry out some activities with them. But it's more difficult.' At the Clapham league, he says, there is a different atmosphere, 'a greater consciousness'.

But not that much greater, according to its outgoing treasurer. 'It's gone,' says Meza. 'This year I have been the treasurer of the league. And it's totally and utterly for the benefit of the people here. They've got big overheads: office, telephone, computer, fax. So even if they wanted to, I don't think they would be able to send money to support charities, etc.'

He thinks the lack of a wider role is a missed opportunity. The Clapham Common league brings together more Latin Americans than any other organization in London. 'Clapham is known all over the [South American] continent. So you could use the infrastructure of the organization and provide better services for the community: housing advice, employment advice, immigration advice and all those things.'

Unfortunately, the legacy of mistrust and disappearing funds has helped to make teams, or their representatives and sponsors on the committee, reluctant to see time and effort spent on areas other than football. Up the road at the Colombian league, López stresses that

252

the amount of money in the league is consciously kept low. 'We don't have a grant because we believe that operating on the smallest budget possible means that you avoid financial corruption. Once you get large sums of money you get corruption, and this has never existed here in seven years as far as we know. Nobody gets a wage here, it's all done by voluntary work.'*

Two pitches stand side by side with one touchline serving both, which means that spectators can encroach on two pitches at the same time. As the teams played, men, women and children (there were about 300 the day I went) watched from the sidelines, while others picnicked on the nearby grass. Two teams called Santuario were playing on one pitch. They were both composed of natives of that region of Colombia, but one was a Parisian team on an exchange visit. José Berríos, now in his mid-forties, padded about in midfield for a team filled with veterans with evident skill, but who found it hard to cope with the pace of their youthful opposition.

What is clear is that each Sunday a small English park gets turned into a little piece of Colombia for the day. 'For Colombians, the only way to express their joy is playing football,' says Berríos. 'And it's a form of communication. Sometimes my wife asks me: "What do you do all day long at the pitch?" But she understands that for me the day they take football away from me, when they take me away from the pitch, I'm dead. For me Sunday is the day I communicate with my Colombia, with my Latinness, with my family. It's years since I've seen my family, but on Sundays it's just like it used to be back in Colombia. I'd play with my father and my brothers and my mum would come along and sit in the park. It would be a day out. The Latin pitch is a place to express your culture.'

The national tournament, which in a sense started it all off, still takes place in London every spring in Battersea Park, which in some

---

* Teams pay £10 each per game for the referee and about £12 a month in subs to cover the league's running costs. Cup competitions carry their own registration fee but can involve £800 in prize money.

ways is a case of football returning to its roots. In November 1867, the Football Association staged a representative match there between Middlesex and a combined Surrey and Kent XI to demonstrate its new rules.[1] These days the tournament tends to be won by Colombian teams.

The national tournament would sometimes feature a team from Holland, but London's Latin American league has few, if any, parallels in the rest of Europe. In the United States, of course, Latin Americans and their descendants are central to soccer's rising profile. Players like Balboa and Ramos were regulars in the side which managed a respectable 1−0 defeat to Brazil in the 1994 World Cup. The clubs in the new professional Major League (launched in 1995) have tended to look to Latin America for their coaches and their star players.* As Simon Kuper has noted, Los Angeles is one of the few cities where a friendly between Denmark and El Salvador could draw a 30,000 crowd, and very few of them would be singing in Danish.[2] The *Washington Post* now publishes a soccer section in Spanish. The game in the States appears to be on the verge of taking off, but US soccer has seen false dawns before. Currently, it has two largely separate bases: as a white, middle-class, suburban game, largely for women and children; and as an urban, Latino game, part of the cultural baggage brought in in the colonization by stealth of the USA by Latin America. So far, it has made little headway among young, working-class black men, the mainstays of the country's top three sports: baseball, gridiron football and basketball.

England's Latin American community is unlikely ever to attain the size or significance of that in the United States. But maybe some day England could reap the benefit of the young Latin American talent in its midst. Jimmy López insists that the young English-born

---

* Carlos Alberto Parreira, the Brazilian who coached his country's team to World Cup success in 1994, now manages in the MLS. The stylish play and instantly recognizable hairdo of the Colombian star Carlos Alberto Valderrama is seen as one of the factors of the success of Major League Soccer in its first season.

254

Colombians feel themselves to be Colombian first and foremost, but for some, at least, loyalties are not so clearly defined. José Berríos is proud of his son, who plays in a local English league, and like many a proud father predicts a bright footballing future for him. 'When England played Colombia at Wembley, he wore his England shirt. When England scored he jumped up and cheered. And when Colombia scored he was also pleased. And when we were coming home on the train he said, "Dad, I'm glad we drew." Because he feels Colombian and English.'

Epilogue: The Road to France '98

The first kick of the 16th World Cup tournament took place on 24 March 1996 in Santo Domingo, in the Latin heart of the Caribbean. The Dominican Republic beat the Dutch-ruled island of Aruba in the first round of the labyrinthine qualifying competition in the North and Central America and Caribbean confederation (Concacaf), which would end 20 months and 97 games later with a jubilant 0–0 draw in Kingston, Jamaica. Twenty-seven teams competed for three places in the finals, the highest allocation to Concacaf in the biggest ever finals tournament, but for most of the small island states playing in the preliminary rounds, even quadrupling the number of qualifying berths to 12 would have had little impact on their chances of reaching France. The likes of Dominica (with a population a tenth that of its near-namesake, the Dominican Republic) and Antigua – who drew 3–3 in the second match of the World Cup the following day – cannot hope to compete with 100 million football-mad Mexicans or with the vast resources of the United States. But it was the largest of the English-speaking islands which was to be the surprise package.

Jamaica came in at the third-round stage, beginning their campaign with an impressive home win over Honduras. The Hondurans, though, were not the last visiting side to raise eyebrows at the uneven and unpredictable playing surface in Kingston, which would certainly never have passed muster as a Test wicket and which earned Jamaica a warning from Fifa. St Vincent presented few problems, and a 0–0 in Tegucigalpa left Jamaica needing just a draw at home to Mexico to reach the final play-off group. Mexico had already qualified for this (beating Jamaica on the way) but Honduras had shaken them with a 2−1 defeat. Mexico fielded a weakened side in Kingston, and Jamaica registered a 1−0 victory to win the group and end the World Cup hopes of the Hondurans, despite the latter's 11−4 win over St Vincent on the same day. Mexico and Jamaica next met in the final group play-offs: Mexico won 6−0.

But the two teams' final meeting was on the last day of the qualifying tournament. Once again Mexico had already booked their passage to France, and Jamaica needed a point only if El Salvador won away to the United States. The crowd were in celebratory spirits, having arrived a good four hours before kick-off to get into the mood for the Reggae Boyz' most important 90 minutes ever. Perhaps with an eye to the mighty Mexico, Jimmy Cliff sang 'The Harder They Come' on the pitch before the game. The Jamaicans' campaign, under Brazilian coach Rene Simoes, had been reinforced by English-based players of Jamaican descent, such as Derby's Deon Burton, Wimbledon's Robbie Earle and Paul Hall and Fitzroy Simpson of Portsmouth. Burton had scored in the 2−2 draw with El Salvador which set up their big day. Tension in the stadium rose as the game wore on with no score, but the news filtering through that El Salvador were losing to the USA was the cue for the party to start. El Salvador lost 4−2 and Jamaica were on their way to the World Cup finals for the first time. To do so, they had played more games than any other of the 32 competing teams.

It was one of the few fairytale stories to emerge from the qualifying tournament in the Americas. None of the Caribbean states from the preliminary rounds made it through to the final group. In the Central American section, Guatemala, the unconvincing conquerors of Nicaragua, lost to all except St Vincent in their subsequent group games. More surprisingly, Costa Rica, Honduras and El Salvador, all previous World Cup qualifiers, failed to make the cut.

The Argentinian Horacio Cordero, fresh from his failure with Guatemala, was taken on by Costa Rica, where he immediately resorted to that old standby, a sex ban on his players. 'I need all the players in full possession of their physical and mental faculties for the game against Mexico,' he stated. Not that it did them much

257

good: an uninspiring 0–0 draw was the prelude to an uninspiring campaign that never looked likely to replicate Costa Rica's 1990 success. Perhaps the players were going blind.

Of the Central American sides, El Salvador came the closest, and may have felt a little hard done by. The El Salvador–Mexico game ended in controversy after the home side were denied what appeared to be a clear penalty. Amid Salvadorean protests, the crowd hurled missiles on to the pitch, eventually forcing the referee to lead the teams off the field for several minutes before returning to play out the final two minutes. Mexico won 1–0. Fifa fined the Salvadorean federation $35,000 for the incident and coach Milovan Djoric had to pay $5000 for his part in the fracas. More controversy surrounded Jamaica's crucial 2–2 draw in San Salvador. Local police said an investigation had been launched into allegations of bribery. But within days they claimed 'no formal investigation exists' and the head of the Salvadorean FA, Juan Torres, exonerated his players from any wrongdoing, claiming, 'We are thinking of sending an apology to Jamaica to avoid misunderstandings.'

For Mexico, the strongest team in Fifa's weakest confederation (excluding Oceania, whose best team has to play off against an Asian side), qualification was one of the safer bets. Merely getting to France was not enough for Mexican supporters, though, who found coach Bora Milutinovic's defensive style hard to accept. Milutinovic must have been relieved when the fan unrest after the return match with El Salvador was for once not directed at him. Police battled with supporters – many with their faces painted in the national colours of red, green and white – angry at the murder of six men from a poor neighbourhood, allegedly, by an élite police hit squad.

On the field, though, the national team's lacklustre, if steady, accumulation of points tried the fans' patience. When Mexico secured qualification with a 0–0 draw against a United States team reduced to 10 men for most of the match, the crowd in the Aztec stadium not only called for Bora's head, but even started cheering the gringos. Within days of the last game against Jamaica, Bora's head was duly served up to the disgruntled fans. He was snapped up by Nigeria to lead his fourth different team at a World Cup finals.

For the United States, qualification cemented the national team's steady progress since 1990 and was achieved with a number of players of Latin American extraction, reflecting the demographics of the game in the USA. The national team's success was crowned by the signing of a deal – reportedly worth $120 million – to wear kit provided by Nike until 2010.

In the South American qualifying competition the early leaders were Colombia, who notched up 5 wins and 2 draws from their first 7 games (including their 2–2 in La Paz) and then didn't win a game for six months, losing to Argentina, Paraguay, Chile and Peru, and drawing with Uruguay.

Colombia's downturn coincided with a devastating loss of form by their goalkeeper, Farid Mondragón. Against Argentina in Barranquilla in February, he calmly watched a soft shot bobble by him only to sneak inside his post to give the away side a 1–0 victory. In the following game against Paraguay he was blamed for both goals in Colombia's 2–1 defeat, and his wretched run continued next time out against Peru: José Pereda fired in a spectacular shot from 25 yards, but only after Mondragón had thrown the ball straight to him.

Colombia's place at the top was taken by Paraguay, and again a goalkeeper played a crucial role. Paraguay's progress relied largely on the strength of their impressive home record. Invariably backed by an intimidating 40,000-strong crowd, they turned their Defensores del Chaco stadium into a fortress, winning seven out of eight (their only defeat in Asunción was to the eventual group winners, Argentina). But their inspirational captain and goalkeeper, José Luis Chilavert, must take great credit in a team otherwise lacking star quality.

Chilavert, who likes to describe himself as the best goalkeeper in the world, is as famous for scoring goals as stopping them. He scored six goals for his Argentinian club Vélez Sarsfield in the 1997 *Clausura* championship – all from free-kicks or penalties – but also missed two penalties in the space of four minutes to cost them an important league game. His accurate free-kicks from his own half are also a potent weapon. In Paraguay's final game, Chilavert set up their first with a monster punt from a dead-ball on the edge of his own area. In true route-one fashion, he launched the ball into the Bolivian penalty area where it was flicked on for Benítez to score from close range. The 2–1 result saw Paraguay qualify for France.

Controversy is never far from Chilavert. Chilavert's full-blooded approach to the game landed him in trouble back in Argentina, where a judge in La Plata gave him a three-month suspended prison sentence and banned him from football for 15 months for his part in an on-pitch set-to against Gimnasia La Plata. Although he was allowed to keep playing pending an appeal, Chilavert claimed it was part of a campaign to undermine Paraguay's World Cup campaign. He vowed to leave Argentina, saying he feared for his safety. 'It hurts a lot of people that a Paraguayan can be as popular as me,' he said. 'They think we should just be on building sites or cleaning houses.'

He and three other Paraguayan internationals play their club football in Argentina. Suspicious Paraguayan football officials expressed alarm after two of them, Chilavert and Independiente's Roberto Acuña, were injured in league games less than a month before the two countries were due to meet in Buenos Aires. 'We don't want to think this but it seems that they are going in very hard on our players with a view to keeping them out of the match,' said Jimmy Irala, Paraguay's national team co-ordinator. Chilavert recovered in time to score direct from a free-kick to secure a 1–1 draw against Argentina. He also scored a penalty against Argentina in the Copa América in Bolivia.

Chilavert received a four-match ban after he was sent off for fighting with Faustino Asprilla in Paraguay's game against Colombia. Asprilla was also shown the red card. On his way off, Chilavert got into a fight with Colombia's other striker, Víctor Aristizábal. The Asprilla–Chilavert clash was part of a violent Sunday in April 1997, with the Bolivia–Argentina game in La Paz producing three red cards. That bad-tempered fixture was reduced to brawling chaos when striker Julio Cruz was attacked by a player on the Bolivian bench while retrieving the ball for a throw-in. The match dissolved in a flurry of fists, threats and spittle, involving most of the players. Local police joined in enthusiastically. At one point the Argentinian goalkeeper, Ignacio González, was captured on television headbutting an opponent. The Bolivian press blamed the Argentinians for a series of incidents during the game and accused them of being bad losers: 'The Argentinians resorted to punching and hitting when they were beaten,' said *Hoy*. The worst of the trouble flared when Argentina, despite three weeks' altitude training, were 2–1 down in the second half. The Argentinian daily *Clarín* wrote: 'The cowardly attack on the physiotherapist Hernán Arsenian, the treacherous punch thrown at Julio Cruz, the paralysing gas that knocked out Roja, these attacks . . . cannot wipe out the shame caused by the unintelligent attitude of the Argentinian players.' The president of the Argentinian FA, Julio Grondona, was summoned to Congress to explain the team's behaviour. Argentina had clearly come a long way since winning the fair play award at the 1996 Olympics.

The violent Bolivia match turned out to be a blip in an otherwise triumphal second half of the qualifying campaign for Argentina. But it had all started anything but brightly. After seven games Argentina had managed only two wins, against unfancied Bolivia and Venezuela. The seventh game was the scrappy 0–0 draw in Montevideo but, in retrospect, it proved to be a turning point. In their next game, in Colombia, Argentina sneaked their 1–0 victory, partial revenge for their 5–0 humiliation in Buenos Aires four years earlier. After this game Argentina were on the up, while Colombia entered their winless run.

The draw in Montevideo with Argentina was a turning point for Uruguay too, but in the opposite direction. Afterwards they picked up only one point away from home, in another 0–0 with Argentina. Unfortunately, they needed a win, and that result in Buenos Aires knocked them out of contention for a place in France on the 80th birthday of their replacement coach, Roque Máspoli. Goalscoring

261

was their biggest problem: a quarter of their goals-for tally came in their final, meaningless match against Ecuador.

By mid-1997, Argentina, Paraguay and Colombia had established themselves as near-certain qualifiers. But five teams were still in contention for the remaining World Cup berth.

The sixth team, Venezuela, began their campaign knowing they had no chance of qualifying for France (they didn't win a game) but they were not without influence over how the other South American teams would fare. Back in April 1996 striker Daniel Fonseca picked up a ban after being sent off in Caracas in Uruguay's first match. He picked up a second yellow card for kicking the ball into the net after the referee had blown for offside. Gustavo Poyet scored one of Uruguay's goals in their 2–0 win. Venezuela did better in their next match, at home to Chile. Their 1–1 draw was followed almost immediately by the resignation of Chile's coach, Xavier Azkargorta, the man who led Bolivia to the 1994 finals. It was Chile's first game of the tournament (in fact, their first World Cup qualifier since the Rojas incident of 1989), but such is the stigma of dropping points to Venezuela. Azkargorta was replaced by Uruguayan-born Nelson Acosta, who would lead the Chileans on to France with a final-day victory over Bolivia.

Under Acosta the Chileans managed to put themselves in contention, with all their last four games at home – where their record was excellent. They won three out of four (Argentina were the exception, qualifying on the back of a 2–1 win). Chile lost their promising striker Rosenthal early in the campaign, but Inter Milan's Zamorano delivered the goals that put the Chileans into contention. But, injured and absent, he was overshadowed in the final games by the country's hottest footballing property, the 22-year-old Marcelo Salas, who at the time of writing was preparing to join Lazio from River Plate in Argentina. He scored a hat-trick against Peru and bagged one in the decisive final game against Bolivia, which also saw two Bolivians sent off. Thousands of fans in Santiago celebrated after the game by throwing rocks and bottles at police who had tried to disperse them with water cannon and tear gas. Peru, who beat

Paraguay on the final day, finished in fifth place with exactly the same playing record as Chile (won 7, drew 4, lost 5) but with a vastly inferior goal difference. Chile last appeared in the World Cup finals in 1974, just months after the military coup.

For Brazil, who qualified as holders, the problem lay in finding testing opposition during two years of friendlies. Flying the likes of Bosnia and Wales halfway round the world to receive a thrashing may be good for morale but is not necessarily good preparation for a World Cup. Even winning the South American Championship in Bolivia was devalued as an exercise by the large number of under-strength sides.

Throughout the team, but especially in the attacking positions, Zagallo is spoilt for choice. Romário and Ronaldo have developed a fruitful partnership up front. But waiting in the wings are Bebeto and Edmundo, another experienced international and the Brazilian league's top scorer. Behind them he can choose between Leonardo, Denílson, Giovanni, Rivaldo and Djalminha for at best two places – not to mention Atlético Madrid's Juninho.

Opinions in Brazil divide sharply over the qualities of the national manager. Some newspapers bemoaned the football Brazil played in the Copa América and were less than ecstatic at the team's 3–1 victory in the Final. 'WE'RE GOING TO HAVE TO TOLERATE ZAGALLO,' sighed one headline. Zagallo himself had pre-empted the line as he ran on to the pitch to congratulate his players. 'Now you're going to have to put up with me,' he shouted at television reporters.

Those looking for a more adventurous Brazilian team than that which ground out a 0–0 to win the World Cup last time are likely to be disappointed. In the Copa América, after Brazil had played a safe, cagey game to knock out Paraguay with two Ronaldo goals on the break, Zagallo had exulted: 'We were perfect. This is how we are going to play in the World Cup.'

'I'm a born winner,' Zagallo boasted. 'I was born on the right day. I was born with victory by my side.' His standard response to criticism is to point to his four world titles (two as a player, one as coach, one as assistant). 'Performances and statements are forgotten with time but what are never wiped out are the results,' he reminded journalists.

All the Latin American teams can realistically aspire to reach the second round but only Argentina and Brazil – the two historic powers – are likely to make the later stages. Colombia, on their day, are a very good side but have yet to prove that they have fully learned the lessons of their 1994 débâcle. Brazil have been top of the Fifa rankings for four years, are the bookies' favourites, and would be worthy winners. But in this European World Cup, European teams are expected to dominate. In the history of the competition only one team has ever won the Cup outside its own continent. But then that team was Brazil.

Whatever the eventual winner, in one sense at least a Latin American era will come to an end in France, where the Brazilian president of Fifa, João Havelange, will stand down after 24 years in the job. Although the World Cup draw in Marseille in December was handled by his deputy, Sepp Blatter, Havelange once again managed to stamp his influence on the event by not inviting Pelé, as he had done from the equivalent event four years earlier. His crime then, and now, was to be locked in a dispute with the head of the Brazilian Football Confederation (CBF), Ricardo Teixeira, who is also Havelange's son-in-law. This time Pelé had compounded the offence by, as sports minister, introducing a bill to reform Brazilian football which would, *inter alia*, diminish the power of the CBF. He may be on the way out but Havelange has sought to manage his succession by publicly endorsing Argentina's Julio Grondona as the new Fifa president. Whether or not a Latin American ultimately inherits the top job in world football, the continent's version of the beautiful game will certainly be one of the essential attractions of France '98.

Appendix: Qualification Results

North and Central American and Caribbean Qualifying Competition

Caribbean Zone First Round
24 March 1996
Dominican Republic 3 Aruba 2

25 March 1996
Dominica 3 Antigua 3

29 March 1996
Guyana 1 Grenada 2

31 March 1996
Aruba 1 Dominican Republic 3 (Dominican Republic qualify 6–3 on aggregate)

31 March 1996
Antigua 1 Dominica 3 (Dominica qualify 6–4 on aggregate)

7 April 1996
Grenada 6 Guyana 0 (Grenada qualify 8–1 on aggregate)

St Kitts & Nevis qualify for next round (Bahamas withdrew)

Second Round
31 March 1996
Surinam 0 Jamaica 1

21 April 1996
Jamaica 1 Surinam 0 (Jamaica qualify 2–0 on aggregate)

4 May 1996
Puerto Rico 1 St Vincent 2

5 May 1996
Dominican Republic 2 Dutch Antilles 1

11 May 1996

Dutch Antilles 0 Dominican Republic 0 (Dominican Republic qualify 2–1 on aggregate)

12 May 1996

St Vincent 7 Puerto Rico 0 (St Vincent qualify 9–1 on aggregate)

Cayman Islands 0 Cuba 1

Haiti 6 Grenada 1

14 May 1996

Cuba 5 Cayman Islands 0 (Cuba qualify 6–0 on aggregate)

Dominica 0 Barbados 1

15 May 1996

St Kitts & Nevis 5 St Lucia 1

18 May 1996

Grenada 0 Haiti 1 (Haiti qualify 7–0 on aggregate)

19 May 1996

St Lucia 0 St Kitts & Nevis 1 (St Kitts & Nevis qualify 6–1 on aggregate)

Barbados 1 Dominica 0 (Barbados qualify 2–0 on aggregate)

Trinidad & Tobago qualify for next round (Bermuda withdrew)

Caribbean play-offs

10 June 1996

Cuba 6 Haiti 1

15 June 1996

Dominican Republic 1 Trinidad & Tobago 4

23 June 1996

Trinidad & Tobago 8 Dominican Republic 0 (Trinidad & Tobago qualify 12–1 on aggregate)

Barbados 0 Jamaica 1

St Kitts & Nevis 2 St Vincent 2

30 June 1996

Jamaica 2 Barbados 0 (Jamaica qualify 3–0 on aggregate)

Haiti 1 Cuba 1 (Cuba qualify 7–2 on aggregate)

St Vincent 0 St Kitts & Nevis 0 (Aggregate 2–2: St Vincent qualify on away goals)

Central American play-offs

5 May 1996

Nicaragua 0 Guatemala 1

10 May 1996
Guatemala 2 Nicaragua 1 (Guatemala qualify 3–1 on aggregate)
2 June 1996
Belize 1 Panama 2
Panama 4 Belize 1 (Panama qualify 6–2 on aggregate)

Semi-final groups
Group 1
1 September 1996
Trinidad & Tobago 0 Costa Rica 1

6 October 1996
Trinidad & Tobago 1 Guatemala 1

3 November 1996
United States 2 Guatemala 0

9 November 1996
United States 2 Trinidad & Tobago 0

17 November 1996
Costa Rica 3 Guatemala 0

24 November 1996
Guatemala 1 Costa Rica 0
Trinidad & Tobago 0 United States 1

1 December 1996
Costa Rica 2 United States 1

8 December 1996
Guatemala 2 Trinidad & Tobago 1

14 December 1996
United States 2 Costa Rica 1

21 December 1996
Costa Rica 1 Trinidad & Tobago 1
Guatemala 2 United States 2

	P	W	D	L	F	A	Pts
United States	6	4	1	1	10	5	13
Costa Rica	6	4	0	2	9	5	12
Guatemala	6	2	2	2	6	9	8
Trinidad & Tobago	6	0	1	5	3	9	1

267

Group 2

30 August 1996
Canada 3 Panama 1

8 September 1996
Cuba 0 El Salvador 5

22 September 1996
Cuba 3 Panama 1

6 October 1996
Panama 1 El Salvador 1

10 October 1996
Canada 2 Cuba 0

13 October 1996
Cuba 0 Canada 2

27 October 1996
Panama 0 Canada 0

3 November 1996
Canada 1 El Salvador 0

10 November 1996
El Salvador 3 Panama 2

1 December 1996
El Salvador 3 Cuba 0

15 December 1996
El Salvador 0 Canada 2
Panama 3 Cuba 1

	P	W	D	L	F	A	Pts
Canada	6	5	1	0	10	1	16
El Salvador	6	3	1	2	12	6	10
Panama	6	1	2	3	8	11	5
Cuba	6	1	0	5	4	16	3

Group 3

15 September 1996
Jamaica 3 Honduras 0
St Vincent 0 Mexico 3

21 September 1996
Honduras 2 Mexico 1

22 September 1996
St Vincent 1 Jamaica 2

13 October 1996
St Vincent 1 Honduras 4

16 October 1996
Mexico 2 Jamaica 1

27 October 1996
Honduras 0 Jamaica 0

30 October 1996
Mexico 5 St Vincent 1

6 November 1996
Mexico 3 Honduras 1

10 November 1996
Jamaica 5 St Vincent 0

17 November 1996
Honduras 11 St Vincent 3
Jamaica 1 Mexico 0

	P	W	D	L	F	A	Pts
Jamaica	6	4	1	1	12	3	13
Mexico	6	4	0	2	14	6	12
Honduras	6	3	1	2	18	11	10
St Vincent	6	0	0	6	6	30	0

Final group
2 March 1997
Mexico 4 Canada 0
Jamaica 0 United States 0

16 March 1997
United States 3 Canada 0
Costa Rica 0 Mexico 0

23 March 1997
Costa Rica 3 United States 2

6 April 1997
Canada 0 El Salvador 0
13 April 1997
Mexico 6 Jamaica 0
20 April 1997
United States 2 Mexico 2
4 May 1997
Canada 0 Jamaica 0
11 May 1997
El Salvador 2 Costa Rica 1
11 May 1997
Costa Rica 3 Jamaica 1
18 May 1997
Jamaica 1 El Salvador 0
1 June 1997
Canada 1 Costa Rica 0
8 June 1997
El Salvador 0 Mexico 1
29 June 1997
El Salvador 1 United States 1
10 August 1997
Costa Rica 0 El Salvador 0
7 September 1997
United States 1 Costa Rica 0
Jamaica 1 Canada 0
14 September 1997
Jamaica 1 Costa Rica 0
El Salvador 4 Canada 1
3 October 1997
United States 1 Jamaica 1
5 October 1997
Mexico 5 El Salvador 0
12 October 1997
Canada 2 Mexico 2
2 November 1997
Mexico 0 United States 0

9 November 1997
Canada 0 United States 3
El Salvador 2 Jamaica 2
Mexico 3 Costa Rica 3
16 November 1997
Jamaica 0 Mexico 0
Costa Rica 3 Canada 0
United States 4 El Salvador 2

	P	W	D	L	F	A	Pts
Mexico★	10	4	6	0	23	7	18
United States★	10	4	5	1	17	9	17
Jamaica★	10	3	5	2	7	12	14
Costa Rica	10	3	3	4	13	12	12
El Salvador	10	2	4	4	11	16	10
Canada	10	1	3	6	5	20	6

★ Qualified for France '98

South American Qualifying Competition

24 April 1996
Colombia 1 Paraguay 0
Ecuador 4 Peru 1
Venezuela 0 Uruguay 2
Argentina 3 Bolivia 1
2 June 1996
Ecuador 2 Argentina 0
Peru 1 Colombia 1
Venezuela 1 Chile 1
Uruguay 0 Paraguay 2
6 July 1996
Chile 4 Ecuador 1
7 July 1996
Bolivia 6 Venezuela 1
Colombia 3 Uruguay 1
Peru 0 Argentina 0

1 September 1996
Bolivia 0 Peru 0
Ecuador 1 Venezuela 0
Colombia 4 Chile 1
Argentina 1 Paraguay 1
8 October 1996
Uruguay 1 Bolivia 0
9 October 1996
Venezuela 2 Argentina 5
Ecuador 0 Colombia 1
Paraguay 2 Chile 1
10 November 1996
Bolivia 2 Colombia 2
Peru 4 Venezuela 1
Paraguay 1 Ecuador 0
12 November 1996
Chile 1 Uruguay 0
15 December 1996
Venezuela 0 Colombia 2
Uruguay 2 Peru 0
Bolivia 0 Paraguay 0
Argentina 1 Chile 1
12 January 1997
Uruguay 0 Argentina 0
Peru 2 Chile 1
Venezuela 0 Paraguay 2
Bolivia 2 Ecuador 0
12 February 1997
Ecuador 4 Uruguay 0
Bolivia 1 Chile 1
Colombia 0 Argentina 1
Paraguay 2 Peru 1
2 April 1997
Bolivia 2 Argentina 1
Uruguay 3 Venezuela 1
Peru 1 Ecuador 1
Paraguay 2 Colombia 1
29 April 1997
Chile 6 Venezuela 0

30 April 1997
Colombia 0 Peru 1
Paraguay 3 Uruguay 1
Argentina 2 Ecuador 1
8 June 1997
Ecuador 1 Chile 1
Uruguay 1 Colombia 1
Venezuela 1 Bolivia 1
Argentina 2 Peru 0
5 July 1997
Chile 4 Colombia 1
6 July 1997
Peru 1 Bolivia 1
Venezuela 1 Ecuador 1
Paraguay 1 Argentina 2
20 July 1997
Bolivia 1 Uruguay 0
Chile 2 Paraguay 1
Colombia 1 Ecuador 0
Argentina 2 Venezuela 0
20 August 1997
Uruguay 1 Chile 0
Ecuador 2 Paraguay 1
Venezuela 0 Peru 3
Colombia 3 Bolivia 0
10 September 1997
Chile 1 Argentina 2
Peru 2 Uruguay 1
Colombia 1 Venezuela 0
Paraguay 2 Bolivia 1
12 October 1997
Chile 4 Peru 0
Ecuador 1 Bolivia 0
Paraguay 1 Venezuela 0
Argentina 0 Uruguay 0
16 November 1997
Uruguay 5 Ecuador 3
Peru 1 Paraguay 0

Chile 3 Bolivia 0
Argentina 1 Colombia 1

	P	W	D	L	F	A	Pts
Argentina★	16	8	6	2	23	13	30
Paraguay★	16	9	2	5	21	14	29
Colombia★	16	8	4	4	23	15	27
Chile★	16	7	4	5	32	18	25
Peru	16	7	4	5	19	20	25
Ecuador	16	6	3	7	22	21	21
Uruguay	16	6	3	7	18	21	21
Bolivia	16	4	5	7	18	21	17
Venezuela	16	0	3	13	8	41	3

★ Qualified for France '98

Notes and References

Introduction

1 David Miller. *Stanley Matthews, the Authorised Biography* (1989), page 122.

2 Rogan Taylor and Andrew Ward. *Kicking and Screaming, An Oral History of Football in England* (1995), pages 87–8.

3 Richard Adamson. *Bogota Bandit. The Outlaw Life of Charlie Mitten: Manchester United's Penalty King* (1996), pages 103–4.

4 Neil Franklin. *Soccer at Home and Abroad* (1956), page 90.

5 Ibid.

6 Jimmy Greaves. *This One's on Me* (1991), page 66. See also Bobby Moore's account of the same incident in Jeff Powell's *Bobby Moore, The Life and Times of a Sporting Hero* (1993), pages 151–2. The England players were not the only ones to witness this side of Pelé's game. The Venezuelan international Luis Mendoza approvingly recalls a World Cup qualifier in Caracas: 'In the second half Freddy Ellie showed a lack of respect to Pelé. He nutmegged him and Pelé gave him the elbow so he couldn't get past.' Edgar Broner. *Gol de Venezuela, un grito esporádico pero inolvidable* (1995), page 14.

7 Rogan Taylor and Andrew Ward (1995), page 87. According to another account, the England players watched from their hotel room in Rio as a boy kept up a piece of orange peel for 43 touches before flicking it over his head and catching it on his heel; Jackie Milburn tried to emulate him but managed only 11 touches. See Brian Glanville's *Soccer Nemesis* (1955), page 150.

1: One Hundred Years of Attitude

1 *Clarín*, 10 January 1997. Maradona was a much better player than a pundit. Argentina drew and ended up topping the South American qualifying table.

2 *Diario Popular*, 13 January 1997.

3 Different interpretations of the word 'official' mean some sources date the first international to 1902.

4 Ernesto Escobar Bavio, *Alumni, Cuna de campeones y escuela de hidalguía* (1955), page 29.

5 Ibid., page 28.

6 The same was true in Argentina, with clubs such as Ferro Carril del Oeste and Quilmes FC.

7 Eduardo Santa Cruz A., *Origen y Futuro de una pasión* (1996), page 33.

8 Mason, Tony, *Passion of the People? Football in South America* (1995), page 10. Mason includes a detailed history of the early years of football in Argentina, Uruguay and Brazil, which this chapter has drawn on.

9 Santa Cruz, page 20.

10 *Revista de Educación Física*, 30 September 1922, quoted in Escobar Bavio, pages 47–8.

11 Escobar Bavio, page 133.

12 Santa Cruz, page 34.

13 Asociación Uruguaya de Football, *Primer Campeonato Mundial de Football* (1930), pages 11–12.

14 Ibid., page 15.

15 Ibid., pages 95, 101.

16 Ibid., pages 111–12.

17 Interview with Enrique Aramburu.

18 *Reuters*, 20 July 1997.

19 Galeano, Eduardo, et al, *¿Nunca más campeón mundial?* (1991), page 110.

2: *The Sublime and the Malign*

1 Mario Benedetti, 'El Césped', in Jorge Valdano, *Cuentos de Fútbol* (1995), page 60.

2 *Reuters*, 25 April 1997. See also *Newsweek*, 14 April 1997.

3 *Sunday Times*, 1 October 1995.

4 Jimmy Burns, *Hand of God, The Life of Diego Maradona* (1996), page 162.

5 One of Maradona's nicknames is *el pibe de oro*, the golden kid. See Eduardo Archetti, '"And Give Joy to My Heart". Ideology and Emotions in the Argentinian Cult of Maradona' in Gary Armstrong and Richard Giulianotti, *Entering the Field* (1997) for a discussion of Maradona as *pibe*. Colombia's skilful playmaker Carlos Valderrama is also known as *el pibe*.

6 *True Stories – Maradona*, Carlton TV for Channel 4.

7 Quoted in Norman Barrett, *The Daily Telegraph Football Chronicle* (1993), page 218.

8 Ariel Scher, *La patria deportista* (1996), page 33.

9 Roberto Fontanarrosa and Tomás Sanz, *El Fútbol Argentino* (1994).

10 Ariel Scher, page 193.

11 Colin Malam, *World Cup Argentina* (1978), page 10.

12 For other takes on Bilardo and Menotti, see Simon Kuper, *Football Against the Enemy* (1994), pages 170–96, and Enrique Macayo Márquez, *Mi visión del fútbol* (1994), pages 205–33.

13 *El Gráfico*, No. 4023.

14 Ibid.

15 Jeff Powell, *Bobby Moore, The Life and Times of a Sporting Hero* (1993).

16 *Guardian*, 27 September 1968.

17 *Olé*, 30 October 1996.

18 Ibid.

19 Ibid.

20 Ibid.

21 *Olé*, 3 November 1996.

22 Ibid.

23 *Olé*, 30 October 1996. Alvaro Alsogaray is a conservative former Argentinian minister. Ernesto Sábato, Argentina's greatest living novelist, chaired the Truth Commission into the country's 'dirty war' of the 1970s and 1980s.

24 *Olé*, 31 October 1996.

3: The United Colours of Football

1 Mario Filho, *O Negro no Futebol Brasileiro* (1964), page 359.

2 Ibid., pages 111–16.

3 Ibid., page 113.

4 Ibid., page 95.

5 Mario Filho, *O Sapo de Arubinha* (1994), pages 87–91.

6 Mauricio Murad, *Dos pés à cabeça, Elementos Básicos de Sociologia do Futebol*, (1996), page 132.

7 César Gordon Jr, 'Eu já fui preto e sei o que é isso' in Mauricio Murad, et al, *Futebol: Síntese da Vida Brasileira* (1996), pages 71–3.

8 Ruy Castro, *Estrela solitária* (1995), pages 80–3.

9 João Máximo, *João Saldanha* (1996), page 73.

10 Armando Nogueira, Jô Soares, Roberto Muylaert, *A copa que ninguém viu e a que não queremos lembrar* (1994), page 156.

11 Ibid., page 151.

12 Quoted in Leite Lopes, José Sergio, 'Successes and Contradictions in "Multiracial" Brazilian Soccer' in Armstrong and Giulianotti, *Entering the Field* (1997), pages 83–4.

13 Ruy Castro, *Estrela Solitária* (1995), page 136.

14 Stratton Smith, *The Brazil Book of Football* (1962), pages 85–93.

15 Castro (1994), page 248.
16 *Daily Telegraph*, 5 October 1996.
17 *When Saturday Comes*, July 1996, No. 113.
18 Ibid.
19 *Jornal do Brasil*, 26 January 1997.
20 Ibid.
21 Nelson Rodrigues, *A Sombra das Chuteiras Imortais* (1993), pages 89–91.
22 Mauricio Murad, *Dos pés à cabeça, Elementos Básicos de Sociologia do Futebol*, (1996), page 132.

4: High Anxiety

1 *Reuters*, 31 May 1996.
2 *La Razón*, 10 November 1996.
3 *Reuters*, 31 May 1996.
4 23 March 1997.
5 *AP*, 21 November 1996.
6 *Reuters*, 12 June 1997.
7 Ibid.
8 *Reuters*, 17 June 1997.
9 *Reuters*, 18 June 1997.
10 *AP*, 29 June 1997.

5: Godfathers of Football

1 Fernando Araújo Vélez, *Pena Máxima* (1995), page 202.
2 *Cambio 16*, 20 April 1997.
3 Araújo Vélez (1995), page 147.
4 Interview with Carlos Eduardo González.
5 *El Tiempo*, 30 April 1995.
6 Ibid.
7 Araújo Vélez (1995), page 195.
8 *When Saturday Comes* 104, October 1995.
9 Araújo Vélez (1995), pages 195–6.
10 *When Saturday Comes* 104, October 1995.
11 *The Times*, 15 December 1989.
12 Araújo Vélez (1995), pages 194–5.
13 Francisco Maturana, *Talla Mundial* (1994), pages 127–8.
14 Ibid., page 143.
15 Ibid., page 146.
16 *El Tiempo*, 17 October 1950.

17 Neil Franklin, *Soccer at Home and Abroad* (1956), page 85.

18 Ibid., page 101.

19 *El Tiempo*, 21 August 1950.

20 *El Tiempo*, 20 November 1950.

21 *El Tiempo*, 4 November 1950.

22 *El Tiempo*, 1 August 1950.

23 *Reuters*, 2 July 1994.

24 Araújo Vélez (1995), pages 224–5.

25 César Mauricio Velásquez, *Andrés Escobar: en defensa de la vida*.

26 *El Espectador*, 16 September 1995.

27 *El Tiempo*, 2 July 1995.

28 *Sunday Times*, 12 June 1994.

29 7 July 1994. Araújo Vélez (1995).

30 *Nuevo Estadio*, 4 November 1996.

31 *AP*, 19 August 1997. Asprilla scored in Colombia's 2–0 win.

32 *El Tiempo*, 6 September 1995.

6: *The Land That Football Forgot*

1 *La Prensa*, 29 April 1996.

2 Twenty years later he was to disappear in political violence in his native Haiti. Mike Payne, *England, the Complete Post-War Record* (1993).

3 Conversation with Alejandro Bendaña, Managua, 4 May 1996.

4 The material on Tom Cranshaw is drawn principally from letters and documents held by his grandson, Patricio Cranshaw, and from conversations with Patricio Cranshaw and his sister Marta Cranshaw and also with Ing. Martin Benard, who remembered Cranshaw's Granada days, in Pochomil on 1 May 1996.

5 *La Prensa*, 5 May 1996.

6 *La Tribuna*, 28 April 1996.

7 *El Nuevo Diario*, 4 May 1996.

8 *La Prensa*, 30 April 1996.

9 *La Prensa*, 5 May 1996.

10 *Barricada*, 6 May 1996.

11 Ibid.

12 *El Nuevo Diario*, 6 May 1996.

13 *Barricada*, 6 May 1996.

14 Much of the account of the Football War is taken from *Honduras State For Sale* (1985, Latin America Bureau) and Kapuscinski, Ryszard, *The Soccer War* (1991, Granta Books). See also Galeano, Eduardo, *El fútbol a sol y sombra* (1995), pages 149–50.

15 Kapuscinski, pp. 158–59.
16 *Prensa Libre*, 11 May 1996.
17 Thanks to Pete Mason for his insights into Belizean football.

7: *The Football Business*

1 'Los nuevos dueños del futbol mexicano: grandes, grupos ecónomicos, desde televisoras y cementeras hasta vendedores de automóviles' in *Proceso* 1076, 15 June 1997.
2 Ibid.
3 *When Saturday Comes*, October 1997, No. 128.
4 AP, 6 December 1996.
5 *Siglo Veintiuno*, 18 July 1997.
6 José Ramón Fernández interview conducted jointly with Andrew Paxman.
7 *Proceso* 480, 13 January 1986.
8 Brian Glanville, *The Story of the World Cup* (1993), page 271.
9 Interview with José Ramón Fernández. See also Fernández, José Ramón, *El fútbol mexicano . . . ¿Un juego sucio?* (1994) and Gómez Anguas, Jorge, *A History of Football in Mexico* (1995), page 50.
10 *Proceso* 1068, 20 April 1997.

8: *Far Away, So Close*

1 The match ended in a 1–1 draw and attracted many new clubs to the new FA. Graham Williams, *The Code War* (1994), page 29.
2 Kuper, *Football Against the Enemy* (1994), page 157.

Bibliography

This book is indebted to the work of many journalists, whose 'first draft of history' has informed my researches. In addition to the many newspapers and magazines cited in the text, I have found *World Soccer* a consistently thoughtful and reliable guide. Of the books listed below I am particularly grateful to Guy Oliver's invaluable *Guinness Book of World Soccer*.

Adamson, Richard, *Bogota Bandit, The Outlaw Life of Charlie Mitten: Manchester United's Penalty King* (1996), Mainstream, London.

Araújo Vélez, Fernando, *Pena Máxima, Juicio al Fútbol Colombiano* (1995), Planeta, Bogotá.

Archetti, Eduardo P., and Romero, Amílcar G., 'Death and violence in Argentinian football' in Giulanotti, Richard, Bonney, Norman, and Hepworth, Mike, *Football, Violence and Social Identity* (1994), Routledge, London.

Armstrong, Gary, and Giulianotti, Richard, *Entering the Field, New Perspectives on World Football* (1997), Berg, Oxford.

Barret, Norman, *The Daily Telegraph Football Chronicle* (1993), Carlton, London.

Broner, Edgardo, *Gol de Venezuela, Un grito esporádico pero inolvidable* (1995), Cárdenas Lares, Caracas.

Burns, Jimmy, *Hand of God, the life of Diego Maradona* (1996), Bloomsbury, London.

Carías, Marco Virgilio, con Daniel Slutzky, *La guerra inútil, Análisis socio-económico del conflicto entre Honduras y El Salvador* (1971), EDUCA, San José.

Castro, Ruy, *Estrela solitária, Um brasileiro chamado Garrincha* (1995), Companhia Das Letras, São Paulo.

Delaney, Terence, *A Century of Soccer* (1963), Heinemann/FA, London.

Escobar Bavio, Ernesto, *Alumni, Cuna de campeones y escuela de hidalguía* (1955), Difusión, Buenos Aires.

Fernández, José Ramón, *El fútbol mexicano ¿Un juego sucio?* (1994), Grijalbo, Mexico City.

Filho, Mario, *O Negro no Futebol Brasileiro* (2nd ed., 1964), Civilizacão Brasileira, Rio de Janeiro.

Filho, Mario, *O Sapo de Arubinha: os anos de sonho do futebol brasileiro* (1994), Companhia Das Letras, São Paulo.

Fontanarrosa, Roberto, & Sanz, Tomás, *El Fútbol Argentino, Pequeño Diccionario Ilustrado* (1994), Clarín Aguilar, Buenos Aires.

Franklin, Neil, *Soccer at Home and Abroad* (1956), Stanley Paul, London.

Galeano, Eduardo, *Open Veins of Latin America, Five Centuries of the Pillage of a Continent* (1973), MR, New York.

Galeano, E., Tabárez, O., Batalla, H., Bayce, R., Reisch, M., y otros, *¿Nunca más campeón mundial? Uruguay: fútbol, deporte . . . alternativas* (1991), Logos, Montevideo.

Galeano, Eduardo, *El Fútbol a Sol y Sombra* (1994), TM, Bogotá.

García Candau, Julián, *Epica y Lírica del Fútbol* (1994), Alianza Editorial, Madrid.

Glanville, Brian, *Soccer Nemesis* (1955), Secker & Warburg, London.

Glanville, Brian, *The Story of the World Cup* (1993), Faber, London.

Gómez Anguas, Jorge, *A History of Football in Mexico* (1995), Heart Books, Rijmenam, Belgium.

Gordon Jr., Cesar, 'História Social dos Negros no Futebol Brasileiro, Primeiro Tempo: "Essa Maravilhosa Obra de Arte da Mistura"' in *Pesquisa de Campo No. 2* (1995), Rio de Janeiro, and 'Segundo Tempo: "Eu já fui preto e sei o que é isso"' in Murad, Mauricio, et al, *Futebol: Síntese da Vida Brasileira* (1996), UERJ, Rio de Janeiro.

Greaves, Jimmy, *This One's on Me* (1991), New English Library, London.

Gugliotta, Guy, & Leen, Jeff, *Kings of Cocaine* (1989), Simon & Schuster, New York.

Kelly, Stephen F., *Back Page Football: A Century of Newspaper Coverage* (1988), Macdonald/Queen Anne Press, London.